THE
SUMMER SOLDIERS

The 1798 Rebellion
in Antrim *and* Down

.

A.T.Q. STEWART

THE
BLACKSTAFF
PRESS

BELFAST

First published in 1995 by
The Blackstaff Press Limited
3 Galway Park, Dundonald, Belfast BT16 0AN, Northern Ireland
with the assistance of the
Cultural Traditions Programme which aims to encourage
acceptance and understanding of cultural diversity

Typeset by Paragon Typesetters, Queensferry, Clwyd

Printed in Ireland by ColourBooks Limited

A CIP catalogue record for this book
is available from the British Library

ISBN 0-85640-558-2

These are the times that try men's souls. The summer
soldier and the sunshine patriot will, in this crisis, shrink
from the service of their country; but he that stands it
now, deserves the love and thanks of man and woman.

TOM PAINE
ON THE EVE OF THE BATTLE OF TRENTON, 1776

These are the times that try men's souls. You will no doubt
hear a great number of stories respecting the situation of
this country, its present unfortunate state is entirely owing
to *treachery*, the rich always betray the poor.

HENRY JOY McCRACKEN
AFTER THE BATTLE OF ANTRIM, 1798

for
Chris and Peter

CONTENTS

ACKNOWLEDGEMENTS

The materials for this book have been collected in many places and over many years since the idea of attempting to write a continuous narrative of the 1798 Rising in Antrim and Down first occurred to me. My sincere thanks are expressed to the former and present staffs of all the depositories of archives where I have worked, for their courtesy and assistance, and for permission to consult and quote from documents in their care. I owe particular gratitude to the Public Record Office of Northern Ireland, and the Deputy Keeper of the Records of Northern Ireland, Dr A.P.W. Malcomson; to the Linen Hall Library, Belfast, and the Librarian, John Gray; to the National Archives and the Library of Trinity College in Dublin; and in Edinburgh to the Scottish Record Office, the New Register House, the National Library of Scotland and the Library of Edinburgh University.

John Killen, the Deputy Librarian and historian of the Linen Hall Library, and Gerry Healey, the Irish and Reference Librarian, have been indefatigably kind in helping me to trace rare or obscure publications. I am grateful to Mrs M. Kelly and the Wesley Historical Society (Irish Branch); Mrs M. Montgomery of Eglinton, Co. Derry; and Mrs Rosalie White, for permission to quote from papers in their possession.

For assistance of various kinds in my research I am indebted to the following: Jonathan Bardon, Robert Bell, Dr Betty Crawford, Dr W.H. Crawford, Dr Nancy Curtin, Tony Canavan, Arthur Davidson, Richard Doherty, Michael Duffin, Eull Dunlop, Professor Marianne Elliott, Rory Fitzpatrick, Peter Francis, Sir Peter Froggatt, John Gamble, the Very Reverend Professor Finlay Holmes, Sheila Hutchings, Professor Edith Mary Johnston, Dr Ian McBride, John McCabe, the late Aiken McClelland, Dr W.A. Maguire, Dr Ian Maxwell, Professor David W. Miller, Kathleen Neill, Graham Quincey, Dr H.E. Shields, Dr J.G. Slater, Dr P.D.H. Smyth, Professor Helen Mary Thuente, Dr Brian Walker, Professor David Wilson and Ian Wilson.

I owe a considerable debt of gratitude to Louis Lord who read the manuscript with his customary vigilance, and saved me from many errors and infelicities. Neither he, nor anyone else mentioned here, bears responsibility for such as may remain. No words would be adequate to acknowledge the support and encouragement I have received from everyone at Blackstaff Press from the moment the project was first discussed. As ever, my deepest debt is to my wife, Anna, for her willing help, advice, and inexhaustible patience.

A.T.Q. STEWART
BELFAST, 1995

PROLOGUE

Sometimes in the north of Ireland, between the chill of spring and the oppressive days of midsummer, there comes a spell of remarkably fine weather, lasting perhaps a week or ten days. At dawn there is a white mist in the hollows, the air is warm and still, and as the sun climbs higher, a blue haze settles on the hills of Antrim and Down, that is the remembered bliss of childhood and a perpetual ache in the heart of the exile. 'Clay of the pit whence we were wrought yearns to its fellow clay.'[1]

Just such a spell of warm dry weather began on 6 June 1798, and lasted until 19 June, when the temperature fell and there was some rain. The register of weather observations kept at the Library of the Belfast Society for Promoting Knowledge (now better known as the Linen Hall Library) recorded that on Wednesday 6 June the temperature was already 64 degrees Fahrenheit before noon, and the barometric pressure 30.44 inches of mercury. Over the next four days the temperature fell back a point, but the barometer rose. Then for three days there are no entries, and in the blank space an anonymous hand has written: 'The town shut up and no liberty to pass to and fro.'[2] This is the story of those seven days.

I

THE
MURMURING
SURGE

The murmuring surge,
That on th' unnumb'red idle pebbles chafes
Cannot be heard so high.

KING LEAR, ACT 4, SCENE 6

A GREEN UMBRELLA

Jacques Louis de Bougrenet was very attached to his green umbrella. It had been the Frenchman's constant companion on his extended ramble through Ireland in the summer of 1796, and was by far the most useful item of his meagre baggage. In reality it was a swordstick, which the twenty-two-year-old ex-cavalry officer had brought with him as a deterrent to footpads, but he soon discovered that in Ireland the climate was a greater menace than highwaymen. As a Breton, he was not unaccustomed to rain, but the Irish variety astonished him – its persistence, copiousness and ability to penetrate the traveller's clothing and chill him to the bone. For all he knew, it might be even worse in winter. At Cork, therefore, he had his swordstick adapted as an umbrella.[1]

When he opened the umbrella, six or seven inches of the stick still projected beyond it, making him an object of curiosity and amusement in the towns and villages he passed through, but it served him well in the autumn and winter as he made the circuit of the island, sometimes walking up to thirty miles in a day. It was not until he reached Armagh that anyone drew his attention to its colour. As he passed through splendidly scenic country near Tandragee he fell in with a company of 'Orangemen' wearing orange-coloured cockades and cravats, and though they paid no particular heed to him, he noticed that some of the country people seemed afraid of them. He began to sense an unfamiliar constraint when he stopped at wayside cabins for refreshment, and at length a woman said to him, 'You have come from afar, my dear sir. I hope that your umbrella, or the string of it, will not bring you into trouble.'[2] De Bougrenet laughed at her fears, but he took the hint and reluctantly cut off the bright green string of his umbrella.

He knew well enough what she meant. Only a day or two earlier he had watched soldiers moving through the fair at Banbridge, County Down, ordering women who were wearing anything green – ribbon or otherwise – to take it off. He was not unaware of the tensions building up in Irish society, and on his travels he had taken a particular interest in the semi-secret organisations like the Whiteboys, Peep o' Day Boys, Defenders and United Irishmen. He was only too familiar with the bitter manifestations of faction, for they had ruined his own career. He preferred the title of the Chevalier de Latocnaye, and was one of the hundreds of French émigrés driven from his native Brittany by the convulsions of the French Revolution.[3] De Latocnaye had been living in London in 1793, at the time of the disastrous royalist attempt to invade Brittany with English help and assist the revolt of the Chouans. The two émigré commanders had quarrelled with each other and with the Chouans, and had been routed by the republican armies led by the young General Lazare Hoche. Scores of prisoners who surrendered on parole were marched through the night to the town of Vannes, with only a few guards and every opportunity to escape in the darkness if they broke their word. Then, to the horror of all Bretons, they were summarily executed on orders from Paris.

These events, which are still remembered in Brittany, set Breton against Frenchman, aristocrat against peasant, and émigré against émigré. There was hardly a French family in London which had not to mourn the loss of a father, a husband or a brother. People shunned one another, de Latocnaye recalled, and all the bonds of society seemed to be broken. A sullen grief alienated the few friends who remained, for the exiles had divided into two camps, with mutual recrimination. It was partly to withdraw for a while from these painful pressures that de Latocnaye began his travels in Scotland and Ireland, of which he subsequently wrote entertaining accounts in books he published at his own expense. Whether he was merely an eccentric with a taste for travel, or an agent in some particular interest, is not easy to determine. One can only admire his stamina and courage, for he was always likely to be suspect while Great Britain was at war with France, and he admitted that he began to feel more nervous when he reached the north of Ireland, where the warm sympathies evoked by the French Revolution had led to the formation of the radical United Irish movement five years earlier.

In 1791 a handful of public-spirited merchants and tradesmen had formed the first Society of United Irishmen in Belfast. The structure of Irish politics had been transformed by the revolt of the American colonies in 1775. For most of the eighteenth century political power in Ireland had been exercised by the lord lieutenant and his executive with the consent of a parliament which represented only the Episcopalian landowning class. The steady operation of the Penal Laws, though they were much modified as the century progressed, had deprived most of the Catholic aristocracy of their land, but, irrespective of what property they might own, Catholics, Presbyterians, and all other Nonconformists, were automatically excluded from representation in the Irish parliament. History had cast the Catholics and Presbyterians as enemies, mistrustful of each other's political aims, but the socio-economic changes of these years had created a Catholic middle class in towns in the south and west of Ireland, and a Presbyterian one in the rapidly developing port of Belfast. In time these two groups began to discern an identity of economic and political interest.

The northern Presbyterians had warmly, and disloyally, espoused the cause of the rebelling American colonists, partly because of the massive emigration of Ulster Presbyterians to colonial America between 1718 and 1775. They felt themselves to be subject to the same injustices as the Americans, and they admired their example. The American War also created a problem of military security in Ireland: the troops sent across the Atlantic had to be replaced by some force capable of defending Ireland's shores from foreign invaders, which generally meant the French. Very reluctantly, the government of the day agreed to the creation of a citizen volunteer army, independent in theory and organised locally in companies and battalions. The Presbyterians were quick to realise the political potential of the Volunteer movement. When it became a national pressure group for the reform of parliamentary representation, they were in the forefront of the campaign.

The leadership of the Volunteer movement, however, remained in the hands of a group of members of parliament, who had long pleaded Ireland's cause with unsurpassed powers of oratory, and who had become known collectively as the Patriot Party. The most eloquent of them, men such as Henry Grattan and Henry Flood, appeared in uniform as officers of Volunteer companies and regiments, until the movement became almost an extension of parliament with a much greater element of popular representation.

The Volunteers' greatest achievement came in 1782, when they appeared to force the British government to concede the independence of the Irish parliament, though this was as much the result of the humiliating loss of the American colonies. A campaign for the reform of the legislature itself began to falter in 1784, and finally foundered on the rock of Catholic emancipation. Even the Presbyterians became bitterly divided over the question of whether the admission of Catholics to equal rights of representation should be immediate or gradual. The Volunteers lost their political strength, but the continued existence of local Volunteer companies kept alive a martial fervour, which could be volatile when mixed with local politics. The French Revolution, breaking out so suddenly and unexpectedly in 1789, fanned the dying embers of Irish radicalism into flame, and this time it threatened a wider conflagration, for the ranks of the dissidents had now been swelled with hitherto inarticulate artisans and rural workers.

In the spring of 1791 one group of radicals within the Volunteers in Belfast formed a secret committee to plan a more effective strategy, and out of this was born their society, which at first they called the Irish Brotherhood. Believing that the ordinary people of France had taken matters into their own hands and established Utopia on the ruins of a corrupt government, the society drew up a programme which included the reform of parliament, the restoration of all rights to Catholics and the independence of Ireland on a republican model. If France provided the example, the working manual was Tom Paine's *The Rights of Man*, published in the year of the society's formation.

The course of events in both America and France had suggested that the ideal democracy should take the form of a republic, a doctrine reinforced by a century of Protestant republican ideology since the English Civil War. However, eighteenth-century republicanism was cosmopolitan rather than local: French revolutionaries thanked the 'democrats' of Cracow and Belfast for their support. Its application to Ireland, with its savage history of religious war, meant that, in the long run, universal tenets were fatally confused with narrow tribal hatreds, a confusion which has persisted to the present day.

The Belfast radicals were all Presbyterian. Two at least were sons of the manse, and so was their ideologue, Dr William Drennan, who was the son of a former minister of the First Belfast congregation. The elder Drennan had been a close friend of the philosopher Francis Hutcheson. Dr Drennan had practised medicine in Dublin since 1790, but his sister Martha was married to Samuel McTier, a veteran Belfast radical who was one of the society's founders, and who died in 1795. The Drennans were outstanding examples of that independent Nonconformist spirit in politics which characterised much of the thought behind the revolt of the American colonies, and which initially greeted the French Revolution as yet another giant step for mankind. The correspondence between the sister in Belfast and the brother in Dublin is a valuable source for the rise and fall of the United Irish ideal.

A month after the foundation of the new political club a second one was formed in Dublin, of a more representative composition, since it embraced Catholics and Episcopalians as well as Presbyterians. The Belfast society had taken into its counsels one outsider, a half-pay officer called Thomas Russell, stationed in Belfast with his regiment, and through him it made contact with his friend Theobald Wolfe Tone, a young Dublin barrister who had just published *An Argument on Behalf of the Catholics of Ireland*. This pamphlet had greatly impressed the Belfast men, and though Tone and Drennan were jealous of each other, and Tone complained that he had little influence in the society's affairs, it was he who gave the movement its name (replacing Drennan's Irish Brotherhood) and he who is forever associated with it in the popular mind.

The society was initially open and constitutional, agitating for a reform of the Irish parliament and the removal of the Penal Laws against Catholics, though many of its members felt, like Drennan, that this could be achieved only if Ireland was entirely separated from England.

Even before they founded their political club, the Belfast radicals had been planning to launch a newspaper to disseminate their views. In September 1791 a committee of Belfast business-men met to outline the preliminary steps. Robert Caldwell, Samuel Neilson and Robert Simms were deputed to write to prominent liberals in various parts of Ulster, asking them to recruit subscribers, and twelve partners raised the initial capital of £2,000. Again, all of them were Presbyterians, and their vocations indicated the level at which the Society of United Irishmen then found support – William Tennent, John Boyle, and the brothers Robert and William Simms were merchants, William Magee was a printer and bookseller, Samuel Neilson and John Haslett were woollen drapers, Henry Haslett was a shipbroker, William McCleery, a tanner, Robert Caldwell, a banker, Thomas McCabe, a watchmaker, and John Robb, a clerk.

The first edition of the *Northern Star* appeared on 1 January 1792. Well printed and produced, it was an instant success, thanks largely to an excellent system of distribution. It had agents in every part of Ulster, and also in Dublin, London, Liverpool and Edinburgh.[4] At a time when the columns of the

Belfast News-Letter and most contemporary newspapers were filled up with dispatches from Great Britain and abroad, the *Northern Star* was able to provide a larger content of local news and political comment, making it as critical and close to the bone as it dared. Political satire came to be its stock in trade, attracting the talents of able polemicists like the rising lawyer William Sampson who was Episocopalian, and a clutch of Presbyterian ministers, notably the Reverend James Porter of Greyabbey, the Reverend Sinclair Kelburn of Third Congregation, Belfast, and the Reverend William Steel Dickson, then minister of Ballyhalbert in the Ards Peninsula.

The moving spirit in the enterprise was Samuel Neilson. Born at Ballyroney near Rathfriland in County Down in 1761, he was the third son of the Presbyterian minister there. He became a very prosperous wholesale woollen merchant in Belfast and an active man in local politics. An ardent Volunteer and patriot, he took a leading part in the last of the Volunteer reform conventions, which was largely inspired by the United Irishmen, at Dungannon, County Tyrone, in 1793. He was the editor, and eventually the sole proprietor, of the *Northern Star*, which swallowed up his fortune.

In 1796 the French traveller de Latocnaye observed at first hand, and tried to analyse, the nature of the vicious sectarian warfare which had been simmering in County Armagh for almost twenty years. Its origins were complicated and obscure. To begin with, it had not been sectarian at all, but was merely the traditional and ritualised faction fighting familiar at Irish fairs. The sectarian form it later took reflected powerful economic and social pressures, and by the time of de Latocnaye's visit it had led to the emergence of mutually hostile groups of Protestant Peep o' Day Boys and Catholic Defenders.[5]

It used to be thought that the basic economic cause was the competition for land in the overpopulated county of Armagh, but more recently historians have turned their attention to conditions in the domestic weaving industry, by which the small tenants augmented their income. Competition for land to rent was sharpened by the rapid recovery of the linen trade in the 1780s, when there was a marked increase in the numbers of Catholic weavers, regarded as a threat by the Protestants. Historical research has also thrown more light on the Defender movement, once seen as just another agrarian secret society, but now revealed as a more sophisticated and well-organised movement with a political programme which had a significant element of nationalism. For most of the eighteenth century, Irish nationalism had been expressed through Protestant channels, both Episcopalian and Presbyterian, and had found its most extreme form (paradoxically as it now seems) in the United Irish Society, cradled in Belfast.

De Latocnaye discerned, with more perceptiveness than many later commentators, that when the Defenders became politicised, their quarrel with the constituted authorities was of a different character from that of the United Irishmen. For that very reason, there were also territorial divisions. The troubles in Armagh belonged to an old religious war, while the potential troubles of Antrim, Down and Derry had more to do with the reform of parliament, and the United Irish leaders 'affected to speak with indifference of all religions'.[6] The fashionable spirit of Enlightenment radicalism was embarrassed by the Armagh disturbances and regarded them with contempt. For the moment the government considered the United Irishmen, because of their connection with France, to pose the greater threat.

Despite the fact that he was a royalist, de Latocnaye found his sympathy veering towards the honest country folk he met with on his travels, for in his opinion their heads had been filled with the propaganda of the French Revolution by the educated middle-class radicals of Belfast. He rather admired the firmness with which the British government had reacted to the first signs of sedition. If only the same resolution had been shown in France in 1789! He foresaw all too clearly the fate impending over these sturdy, hospitable country people. His view was that 'the poor peasant on this occasion, as on so many others, was the dupe of rogues, who put him in the front, and were very careful themselves to stay behind the curtain'.[7] He tried as far as possible to avoid being drawn into political discussion, and sometimes in an inn parlour he found it prudent to feign sleep, or pretend that he was a Scotsman, for he could mimic the accent.

It was less easy to sidestep political discussion when he was a guest in one or other of the great houses. Often, when benighted on the road, de Latocnaye was obliged to shelter in the most primitive cabins, sharing his couch with the livestock and even less congenial forms of life, but he had come to Ireland well armed with letters of introduction from influential people. These he presented when he could, with all the aplomb of a visiting aristocrat, and generally he was hospitably received, only once being refused a bed for the night, by the Marquess of Waterford. He carried his belongings slung on his back, or stowed in six capacious pockets. He made sure that they always included a clean shirt, silk stockings and court shoes, so that he could appear decently dressed at dinner, often to the astonishment of his hosts.

In the autumn of 1796 he came to Mount Stewart in County Down and was warmly received by Lord and Lady Londonderry. It pleased him to see that Lady Londonderry, though she was the sister of Lord Camden, the lord lieutenant of Ireland, led a very retired life, devoting herself to the education of her family. There was some excitement on the estate, for the earl and his eldest son were engaged in raising a corps of yeomanry among the tenants, a process which involved administering the oath of allegiance to them. The initial response was disappointing. 'Man is a sheep everywhere,' de Latocnaye observed. 'They had much trouble in getting the first ten or twelve to join, and in the days following seven or eight hundred came forward.'[8]

Relations between landlord and tenant at Mount Stewart were more complicated than de Latocnaye could have known. The Stewarts were a family of relatively modest planter origins who came to great power and wealth by a succession of fortunate marriages. The earl's father, Alexander Stewart, had been a Presbyterian merchant of strongly Whiggish politics who married the heiress to the fortune of a governor of Bengal. The Stewarts' first foothold in Ireland had been in Donegal, but this wealth was used to purchase an estate in County Down, along the shores of Strangford Lough, and to build the original house at Mount Stewart. From this base Alexander's son Robert had entered the politics of County Down. This was inevitably re-garded as a challenge by the local aristocracy, and in particular by the 'leviathan of the county', the Marquess of Downshire, the governor of County Down. In subsequent elections the Stewarts were able to draw on the enthusiastic support of the Dissenters of Belfast and north-east Down, where they were strongest, but in time a coolness developed between these adherents and their patron, who had meanwhile deserted Presbyterianism for the Established Church. The Dissenters reluctantly came to the conclusion that he was a cold and cal-culating man who put his own interests before theirs and was prepared to enter into political arrangements with the Tories to advance his family's standing in the world.

When de Latocnaye came to Mount Stewart, its owner had just been granted an earldom, an advance in the peerage which allowed his eldest son and namesake to assume the courtesy title of Lord Castlereagh. He was to be known by that title for the rest of his life, though when he died he was the Marquess of Londonderry. Castlereagh was the son of his father's first marriage, to Lady Frances Seymour Conway, the sister of the second Marquess of Hertford, who controlled the important borough of Lisburn. Endowed with good looks, intelligence and polished manners, Castlereagh was in his youth the idol of the local Presbyterian radicals. In the days of the raising of the Volunteers, they saw him as their future champion in the Irish parliament, but the experience of being educated at Cambridge, rather than one of the Scottish universities, freed him from some of the bonds of local sentiment, and Castlereagh early began to think of a political career in even more ambitious terms.

Lord Camden encouraged him to take the first steps along the road which would one day lead him to the highest reaches of British politics, but also to a horrifying suicide as he fell victim to unpopularity and chronic overwork. Britain honours him as one of the greatest of her foreign secretaries; the Irish continue to revile him as the chief architect of the Act of Union. All this lay in the future. When de Latocnaye came to Mount Stewart, Castlereagh was just twenty-seven, already a member of both parliaments, and married to Emily Hobart, daughter of a previous lord lieutenant. He was also the youthful colonel of the Londonderry Militia. His visit to Mount Stewart in the autumn of 1796 was a brief respite from the ever-increasing demands of a busy public life. He wrote to tell his young wife in Dublin how the tenants had been won over at a dinner in the market house in Newtownards at which both Lord Londonderry and the local Presbyterian minister had become rather drunk.

> Between three and four hundred took the oath of allegiance yesterday. They did it with every mark of sincerity after the ice had been broken and their panic a little removed . . . We had a very jolly dinner. Cleland quite drunk, Sinclair considerably so, my father not a little, others lying heads and points, the whole very happy.[9]

Before his departure, Castlereagh had the satisfaction of enrolling the more prosperous farmers in the nucleus of a troop of yeoman cavalry. He could have raised any number of infantry, too, but thought it risky to presume on so miraculous a conversion. Its completeness had alarmed Lord Londonderry, and it dismayed the residue of middle-class radical opinion in Belfast. Mrs Martha McTier, also writing to Dublin, reported these events to her brother, William Drennan, but in rather different terms.

> Lord Londonderry for 50 years was an honest private and public man. When the King let *Mr Stewart* know that he intended to godfather his son, the Dissenter was not flattered out of his principles, but returned for answer that he christened without

sponsors. He then pledged himself by a fine of £1,500 to his country friends that he would ever be the same Mr Stewart; yet as a lord, he threatens a poor country parson with the loss of six guineas stipend and his fields if he did not take the oath. He disapproved of Mr Sinclair not choosing to do this . . . The Old Light congregation, before so very bigoted as to have no connection with the other, have come forward and pledged themselves to make up to Mr S. whatever loss he may sustain by His Lordship's present system of Christianity.[10]

The Reverend William Sinclair had perhaps sorrows to drown, and time would indeed show that his conversion was less than sincere.

'A SORT OF TRAITORS'

It was inevitable that the character of the United Irish movement should change when Britain went to war with France in 1793. The radicals came to be regarded, like communists in the twentieth century, as dangerous potential traitors and enemy agents, liable to have their new-fashioned ideas of reform exploited by an enemy country for thoroughly old-fashioned purposes of aggrandisement. On that assumption, William Pitt's government at once initiated measures to suppress the societies, further fuelling radical grievance. Edmund Burke used all his powers of argument to persuade the Whigs that sweeping away the Penal Laws against Catholics in Ireland would create the surest bulwark against Jacobinism and render Protestant radicalism negligible, but that option was finally closed in 1795 when a Whig lord lieutentant, Earl Fitzwilliam, who had committed himself to support emancipation, was abruptly recalled, and even moderate middle-class reformers felt a sense of total frustration. In many ways it was the culmination of the criticism, which had been growing throughout the century, of the metropolitan government's handling of Ireland, which the Irish always proudly insisted was not a colony but a sister kingdom. Nevertheless, the Irish had the same grievances as the colonists in America had when they resorted to arms, and the Ulster Presbyterians, in those days before the great Irish Catholic diaspora, had the closest family links with the American rebels.

With the first prosecutions of the United Irishmen, the movement began to go underground. Drennan, who in 1794 was tried for seditious libel and acquitted, afterwards took little part in the society's activities, and there were many less prominent who did likewise. Others, like Neilson, became even more determined, and began to reconstruct the organisation on revolutionary and military lines. Wolfe Tone, compromised by his contacts with a French agent, escaped imprisonment by agreeing to emigrate to America. After taking leave of the United Irish leaders in Belfast, he sailed with his family to Wilmington in North Carolina, but within a short time he had returned to Europe and was in Paris, working hard to persuade the French government to assist the United Irishmen by an invasion of Ireland.

The suppression of the Dublin society in 1794 stimulated its Belfast counterpart to pre-emptive measures. Meanwhile the personnel of radicalism was changing. New societies were being formed in Ulster by 'mechanics, petty shopkeepers and farmers', who wanted 'a practical engine by which the power and exertions of men like themselves might be most effectively combined and employed'. Delegates meeting in Belfast in May 1795 approved a constitution for the 'New System', as it was called.[11] Each society was to have between seven and thirty-five members, dividing to form a new society when the upper limit was reached. When there were three societies in a barony, they were to form a baronial committee. When such a committee represented eight societies, a new committee would be formed. When a county had three baronial committees, a county committee would be formed. County committees would send representatives to a provincial committee, and a provincial committee to a national committee, which would appoint some of its members as the executive of the whole revolutionary movement. This pyramidal structure betrayed its Presbyterian origins: it was a reflection of their method of church government.[12]

In 1796 the New System transformed itself into a secret army – three societies would form a company, and several companies a battalion. The various vaguely defined military units would elect their own colonels, captains and lieutenants. This military system proved very popular and developed swiftly in areas not reached by the first United Irish movement. The chief reason for this was that it managed to recruit large bodies of Catholic Defenders. It was not entirely a coincidence that the New System and the Orange Society were born in the same year. The origins of the latter were to be traced in the sectarian war in County Armagh between Peep o' Day Boys and Defenders. In the engagement in September 1795 that became known as the Battle of the Diamond, and led to the formation of the Orange Order, the Protestants claimed that they were not the aggressors.[13] However this might be, in the five months which followed, five thousand Catholics were driven from their homes in the county. When Orangeism spread to other counties, it drove more Catholics into the United Irish ranks. 'Wherever the Orange system was introduced, particularly in Catholic counties, it was uniformly observed that numbers of the United Irishmen increased most astonishingly.'[14]

The advantages in this situation for the leadership of the New System were obvious and immediate. A secret agrarian army was being recruited that was already accustomed to conspiratorial procedure and ready to take up arms at short notice in the event of a French landing. But there were disadvantages, too. Whatever the objectives of the Defenders were, they did not entirely coincide with those of the United Irishmen.

So disturbed had the state of Ireland become that in 1796 an Indemnity Act was passed to exempt magistrates from proceedings taken against them when 'in order to check insurrection and maintain the peace' they had committed acts 'not justifiable by law'. It was accompanied by an Insurrection Act, one of the severest and most comprehensive pieces of legislation ever enacted in Ireland, which extended the powers of justices of the peace and made the administering of an unlawful oath a felony punishable by death.

The recruiting drive at Mount Stewart in the autumn of 1796 had its origins in a quiet rectory in County Tyrone during the previous June, when the rector of Clonfeacle, the Reverend

William Richardson, and Thomas Knox, the local landowner, sat down to discuss what might be done to halt the slide into anarchy in their neighbourhood. Richardson suggested that tenants of proven loyalty might be formed into armed associations to assist the army and the militia to keep the peace. The idea was instantly popular with landed proprietors and was taken up in various parts of Ireland, reinforcing the well-established pattern of self-defence.[15]

This demand for the raising of local corps of yeomanry was one which the government found very hard to resist. It was strenuously urged on the lord lieutenant, Lord Camden, by his unofficial cabinet of advisers and by General Robert Cunninghame, the commander-in-chief of the army in Ireland. From the outset, however, it was controversial. For one thing, members of the new Orange association were eager to flock into its ranks. In Ireland citizen armies had a way of rapidly becoming political. Camden did not want to be swept off his feet by the landlords, nor to be accused of arming Protestants against Catholics. He admitted frankly that he did not want to resort to yeoman cavalry if he could help it; in the end he could see no alternative.[16]

All the evidence flowing in to the government agreed that an insurrection was planned for after the harvest, and that it would be assisted by a French invasion. There would have been no hesitation in rounding up the ringleaders if the authorities had had enough information to bring them to trial. Early in August, Castlereagh obtained some evidence from Belfast, including a sworn deposition which he thought would be sufficient to convict six men, two of them United Irish leaders. He took the information to Dublin and was asked to carry out the arrests.

His first move on going north was to take into his confidence the Stewarts' old rival, Lord Downshire. Downshire had just arrived from England and had convened a meeting of the local gentry at Newtownards, in Stewart territory, in order to enlist support for raising a corps of yeomanry by subscription. The gentry were not all of one mind, and there were flickers of the old flame of independence. Gawen Hamilton, once president of the Northern Whig Club, opposed the plan as 'a reflection on the county that was wholly unmerited', but after some heated debate it was adopted.[17]

When he got back to Hillsborough, Downshire found Castlereagh waiting for him along with Major-General George Nugent, who was on the Irish staff, and John Pollock, one of the Crown lawyers, and the news that the leading United Irishmen in Ulster were to be arrested immediately. They were joined almost at once by the Earl of Westmeath with a considerable body of troops. There was a snag, however, which caused a few more days' delay. The warrants had to be returned to the undersecretary's office for alteration, so that the more important prisoners could be lodged in Dublin jails instead of the county jails at Carrickfergus and Downpatrick. The coup was eventually planned for 16 September. On the eve Castlereagh slept at Lisburn Castle, the substantial stone mansion in Lisburn's main street which was the residence of his uncle, Lord Hertford. Early next morning Castlereagh set out to execute the warrants with the Reverend Philip Johnson, a magistrate from Derriaghy, and they had gone only a short distance when they encountered the man whose name was first on the list.

Charles Teeling was eighteen on that autumn morning when he met Lord Castlereagh in the street, and he could not have been more astonished, for Castlereagh had been for years on friendly terms with his father, who was riding alongside Charles. The Teelings were Catholics in comfortable circumstances, and active liberals who had ardently supported the Volunteers, and worked for the Stewart interest in the 1790 election. The elder Teeling admired Castlereagh as a youthful advocate of civil and religious liberty, and brought up his sons to regard him as a model of patriotism. Castlereagh greeted them 'with his usual courtesy and politeness' and rode back with them as far as the gates of the Hertford mansion. Then, as they were about to take their leave, he said to the father, 'I regret that your son cannot accompany you', and conducted Charles Teeling through the outer gate, which was immediately shut behind him by the military guard. Young Teeling indignantly protested, demanding that the gate should be opened and his father allowed in. This Castlereagh agreed to, after some deliberation, and Luke Teeling at once asked why his son had been arrested. 'High treason,' Castlereagh told him. Teeling was a proud man. He pressed his son's hand and said nothing, but as he departed his eyes flashed defiance and contempt. Unruffled, Castlereagh went on to conduct the search of the Teeling home, seizing some unimportant papers and a brace of pistols.[18]

It was still only a few minutes after nine o'clock when Castlereagh joined Downshire, Pollock and Westmeath on the road to Belfast, and by ten the party, now augmented by a large squadron of cavalry, was cantering past the tollgate on the outskirts of the town. The garrison had been turned out and troops were stationed at all the key points. All the shops and businesses were closed and bodies of troops and artillery were kept moving through the streets. Later that day Mrs McTier described the scene in a letter to her brother, and reported the arrests.

> Since ten o'clock this morning Belfast has been under military government. A troop of horse is before my door. A guard on Haslett's, which is near us. One at Church Lane, the Long Bridge and every avenue to the town. Haslett is taken; Neilson and Russell have been walking the streets till about an hour ago, when the Library being broken open and a search made for them they delivered themselves up, with one Osborne, Kennedy, printer at the *Star* office, one Shannon, young Teeling, taken, I am told, by Lord Castlereagh, with several more in Lisburn.[19]

In the evening Castlereagh returned to Lisburn, desperately tired, and shared a meal with Teeling in the room in which the latter was confined. Castlereagh was, as always, the soul of courtesy, and Teeling's account of the conversation presents a man racked with guilt, and particularly uncomfortable when Neilson's name was mentioned, since Neilson had been an active supporter of Castlereagh in the 1790 election, but it is probable that Castlereagh was merely hoping to glean a little further information. As he handed his guest over to the waiting escort of dragoons he gave instructions that Teeling was to receive every indulgence consistent with his safekeeping.

Outside in the street Teeling was astonished to see that a dense silent crowd had gathered. The cavalry was ordered to clear the way, and at this the people began to cheer and wave their hats in the air in support of the prisoner. Teeling had been put into a coach, and when it reached the town square he could see nine other coaches drawn up, all of them closely guarded. As soon as his escort reached the rear the whole cavalcade moved off on the road south. People turned out in all the villages they passed through and it was nearly midnight when they reached Newry.[20] One arrest had not been made in Belfast because the suspect was not at home, and his where-abouts were unknown. His name was Henry Joy McCracken.

For the next few weeks Castlereagh was preoccupied with regimental duties and attendance in the Irish parliament, but by mid-October he was recalled to his father's estates by the critical situation there. In consequence he felt obliged to write to William Pitt, whose confidence he was steadily gaining, and explain his absence from the autumn session at Westminster. Like de Latocnaye, he believed that the vigorous action taken by the government would be sufficient to carry the country through its present difficulties.

> Indeed I have no apprehension that the mischief existent within can ever be productive of any serious calamity, unless the enemy should pay us a visit. The associations in the North are certainly as formidable in their extent as in the purpose they have in view. Like yours, they have artfully availed themselves of the various descriptions of Reformers, and have bound together in one solemn covenant agst. the State. Nothing is committed in writing by their leaders – everything is managed by emissaries. The printed Constitution alone appears, which is in itself no evidence agst. the person in whose possession it is found. Their

Oath enjoins the strictest Secrecy, and the whole is promoted by a system of intimidation, and guarded agst. discovery by the Assassination which inevitably awaits those who are suspected even of a design of proving unfaithful. I trust we shall be more successful than you were, in bringing to justice those offenders now in confinement. If by examples we can alarm the inferior Conspirators, I have the greatest confidence that the spirit of loyalty, which has so extensively shown itself in other parts of the Kingdom, in taking up arms under the King's Commission, will not only discourage the leaders in their hopes of throwing the Country into confusion and of separating it from Gt. Britain; but that a great portion of the Lower Orders [who] must have as yet escaped the infection, will gain a degree of confidence, which their Landlords cannot at present inspire them with, and be prevailed on to show themselves in support of the Constitution.[21]

Castlereagh's reference to planned assassination was not alarmist rhetoric; the threat of it was one reason for the reluctance of some of his father's tenants to take the oath of allegiance. At least one tenant was murdered, and there was an attempt on the life of Londonderry's agent, the Reverend John Cleland, vicar of Newtownards and sub-sheriff. But in the second week of November, Castlereagh surprised a meeting of the United Irish Ulster provincial executive in Portaferry. 'We apprehended six men in about an hour,' he told his wife, 'which I hope will bring the people to their senses.' From Portaferry he went to Belfast, where he met by arrangement Lord Carhampton, now commander-in-chief of the army in Ireland, and almost at once they arrested several more leading United Irishmen, including four members of the cell which actually called itself the Assassination Committee. These men had 'pulled off their green coats' and pretended to be a meeting of Freemasons.[22]

DIGGING POTATOES

A strange and novel custom now appeared in some parts of the Ulster countryside. When United men were taken up and held in custody, bodies of their neighbours gathered to reap their corn and lift their potatoes, to demonstrate respect for the people concerned and attachment to their principles.[23] These assemblies consisted of five hundred to two thousand country people, some of whom would be women, conspicuously wearing green ribbons or kerchiefs. De Latocnaye was intrigued to see these parties, and enquired after their purpose. He was much impressed by the order and efficiency with which they were conducted.

> A man, with nothing special to distinguish him, exacted obedience and directed affairs by signs with the hand or by certain calls. The whole time the work went on men, women and children sang, accompanied by one or other kind of instrument. No-one is allowed at such gatherings to drink any strong liquor, and this certainly requires a great effort in this part of the country. I can say with truth that the regulation is observed most literally, for I have never seen a single person under the influence of drink near these potato gatherings. I do not say there were not a few in the neighbouring villages, it would have been a miracle had it been otherwise. For the occasion the peasantry had put on their best clothes; the air of gaiety and good-humour which showed itself among them would have made any spectator believe that he had arrived on a *fête* day. The road was covered with horses belonging to the farmers who assisted in the gathering.[24]

At Swatragh, in County Derry, at the raising of the potatoes of Mrs Clark, whose son was in prison, the Reverend John

Smith, the Presbyterian minister of Kilrea, was seen among the workers 'in his new castor hat'. When they finished their labours, these bodies proceeded home in regular military order, four or six men deep, through the neighbouring towns and villages, each man carrying his spade on his shoulder, and accompanied by the sounding of horns, conch shells and long glass tubes called trumpets.[25]

On 26 October 1796 Edward McNaghten, a magistrate in north Antrim, informed the authorities in Dublin that in his district 'people assemble in bands of hundreds, and sometimes even of thousands, for the ostensible purpose of cutting corn and digging potatoes, but in my opinion, for the real purpose of settling their plans and accustoming themselves to rise in great bodies at the shortest notice. It is easy enough to foresee that this practice will not end without something very dreadful happening.' A graphic account of a potato-digging on a large scale came from Derry, where it had been witnessed by the landowner Sir George Hill. Not less than six thousand men took part, some of whom had marched over the mountains during the night in order to be there.

> They were clean, well-appointed men, from many quarters, acting systematically together. They carried their spades like muskets, and marched with an erect and defiant mien; but when ordered by the soldiers to disperse, they at once obeyed, saying with an affected humility that it was hard to be impeded in their charitable purpose 'of digging a forlorn woman's potatoes', and asking if they were allowed to dig their own.

What frightened the magistrates most was the calm dignity and discipline of these men, who seemed to be 'under the control of an invisible guidance'. Sir George asked some of them if they would resist the French in case of an invasion, and they replied that they could not resist the French; as good Christians they were resigned to their fate. 'The system of rebellion,' Sir George concluded, 'is planned deeply, and all that is wanting to give it opportunity of breaking forth, is the landing of a few

Frenchmen...' It was assumed that the purpose of the potato-digging was to enable the leaders to judge how their men would act at the word of command.[26]

One November day Castlereagh fell in with a potato-digging party on his way to Comber. He was investigating an audacious theft of arms from a party of dragoons by some local United men who he was fairly sure were his father's tenants, but he was utterly charmed by the sight of the potato-diggers, as he reported in a letter to his wife.

> I had the opportunity of seeing this morning a large body of potato-diggers – it was a pretty sight; a great number of young men marching along with smart girls on their arms – they were going towards Comber to dig Maxwell's potatoes. I rode some distance with them and had a good deal of funny conversation; you may easily conceive I neither scolded, nor attempted to argue them out of their intentions. We had a great number of jokes and nothing could be more good-humoured than they were to me.[27]

On the previous day, however, the lord lieutenant and Privy Council had issued a proclamation expressly forbidding the assembling of people under the pretence of reaping corn or digging potatoes. It was ignored in the North. On the following Saturday a large body of people met at Stoneyford in County Down, and accompanied by martial music and a green flag, began to dig the potatoes of Jeremy Galway, against whom a warrant had been issued for treasonable practices. The Reverend Philip Johnson went with six dragoons and other armed men to disperse them. Forty-four of the potato-diggers were arrested, but soon afterwards released on their taking the oath of allegiance. On the same day Lord O'Neill, the governor of County Antrim, and seventeen magistrates assembled in Antrim town to deliberate on the disturbed state of the country.[28]

As the winter set in, with early sharp frosts, de Latocnaye decided that it might be prudent to return to Scotland for the time being. A day or two before Christmas he crossed from

Donaghadee to Portpatrick, with four hundred head of horned cattle for company.[29] And while he was away, what Castlereagh had dreaded came to pass. The enemy paid Ireland a visit.

The French expedition sailed from Brest on 16 December, seventeen ships of the line, thirteen frigates, and numerous corvettes and transports carrying fifteen thousand troops and a huge supply of arms and ammunition.[30] The fleet was commanded by Admiral Justin Bonaventure Morard de Galles and the soldiers by General Hoche. Aboard the *Indomptable* were the chief of staff and 'Adjutant-General Smith', who was better known to his Irish friends as Wolfe Tone. Even before they left the port, the *Fraternité* collided with other vessels, and thereafter disaster stalked the expedition. The *Séduisant*, a capital ship of 74 guns, perished on the terrible Pointe du Raz with almost all her complement of 1,300 men. Other ships lost their way and were separated from the main force as the admiral's orders became confused with the distress signals of the *Séduisant*. Then for two days they were all totally becalmed in a dense fog. But at last, on 22 December, fifteen of the French vessels came to anchor off Bere Island, in the shelter of Bantry Bay.

That night the weather changed. A strong easterly breeze sprang up, and with it came snow. Simultaneously General William Dalrymple, commanding the English forces at Cork, received the first intelligence of impending danger. Meanwhile, with all communications interrupted by a howling blizzard, Richard White of Seafield Park, the landed proprietor nearest to Bantry, steeled himself to the duty of holding back the French until the regular troops could arrive. He assembled and took command of the local yeomanry, arranged for all the cattle to be driven inland and set up a system of communication through the mountains. On Christmas Eve he managed to get a message through to General Eyre Coote, the English commander at Bandon. 'I will stand with my faithful fellows to the last, certain of your support. All ranks nobly support me. They cannot land for some hours – the wind is against them.'[31]

Apart from one ship's boat, with an officer and a handful of men, driven ashore on Bere Island, the French did not land at all. Tone endured agonies of frustration, and vented his anger on every French officer in sight. 'I have a merry Christmas of it today,' he confided to his diary.[32] The expedition was now prey to the kind of nemesis which so often waits even the most meticulously planned military operation, a shambles of adverse weather, broken communications, misunderstood orders and sheer bad luck. As the storm worsened, the *Immortalité*, with both commanders on board, was forced to make for the open sea and was blown far out into the Atlantic. By 27 December most of the other French ships had cut their cables and sailed for France.

By some kind of osmosis the news of the French arrival at Bantry was known in Belfast with amazing speed, and the town was thrown into excitement and confusion. On Christmas Day the Highland regiment of Reay Fencibles, then in garrison, mounted an extra picquet, reinforced with a subaltern, two NCOs and sixteen gunners, manning two six-pounders. The regiment was put on stand-by to march at a moment's warning. The broken ammunition was taken in, and fresh ammunition, with four flints, was issued to every man on orders from Lieutenant-General Gerard Lake, commander in the North. Next day each soldier was furnished with twenty rounds of good ball cartridges.[33]

It had been a close call, but England survives on close calls. For the moment the Royal Navy appeared to have lost control of the seas – the French had not encountered a single British warship from Brest to Bantry Bay. As a new year dawned, the establishment, breathing relief at every pore, gave public thanks for a merciful deliverance. Lieutenant Proteau, who had jumped ashore on Bere Island and been arrested by the people he came to deliver, surrendered his sword to the viceroy, and Mr White was made a peer as Lord Bantry. 'England,' said

Tone, 'has not had such an escape since the Spanish Armada.' Though he would go on working for French intervention, he knew in his heart that such an opportunity would not come again.[34]

'If the expedition had started but a few days earlier, when the weather was still propitious,' so the historian W.E.H. Lecky was to write almost a century later, 'if it had not encountered a storm of extraordinary violence and duration, at a time when success had almost been attained, or if the naval part of the expedition had been conducted with common skill, it is certain that an army of fifteen thousand French soldiers would have been landed without difficulty within forty-five miles of Cork before there was any considerable force to oppose them, and it is scarcely less certain that the second city in Ireland must have fallen into their hands. It is only too probable that such a success would have been followed by a rebellion in Ulster, if not in the other provinces.'[35]

I I

A
SILENCE
in the
HEAVENS

But as we often see, against some storm,
A silence in the heavens, the rack stand still...

HAMLET, ACT TWO, SCENE TWO

BLARIS MOOR

The black year of 1797 began with more snow and keen frost. De Latocnaye, making his way up to Glasgow, was dismayed to find that his riding breeches had split, and though he insulated himself as well as he could with hay and handkerchiefs, he thought he would die of the cold.[1] In Ireland, whither he was soon to return, the harsh weather was accompanied by an upsurge in agrarian violence. Such violence was not new. Since 1792 bands of Defenders had been raiding houses for arms, and administering a Defender oath in the counties of Louth and Meath. Their grievances were often local, but they identified themselves in a vague way with a more general Catholic nationalist cause, the cause of all those dispossessed in the Restoration and Williamite land settlements of the previous century.

At the same time the United Irish system was spreading very rapidly among the rural population in the North. It reached its greatest numbers and potential about the summer of 1797, when once more there were rumours of a French invasion. The United Irish leaders worked hard to bring about a junction of the two revolutionary forces. The people were ready, the arms were stored, and there were hopes of a national uprising on 1 May. The militia, partly conscripted through a ballot, contained a large proportion of Catholics and some regiments were believed to be disaffected because of Defender influence.

'The great Irish Rebellion of the eighteenth century is always called the Rebellion of 1798,' wrote Lecky, 'but the letters from Ulster in the spring and summer of 1797 habitually speak of the province as in a state of real, though smothered, rebellion.'[2] All the evidence bears out the justice of his claim, and there is no doubt that this was the opinion of people at the time. The summer of 1797 was the moment fate had chosen for the over-throw of government in Ireland, and only the notorious wilfulness of history makes 1798 seem more important. And until that moment the main threat was always perceived as northern and Presbyterian.

Far from disheartening the radicals of the North, the Bantry Bay expedition filled them with renewed hope. In the spring Chief Secretary Thomas Pelham wrote to General Lake that the insurrectionary spirit which had manifested itself in certain parts of Ulster had obliged the lord lieutenant to draw up a procla-mation. Issued at Belfast on 13 March, it placed a large area of the North under regulations tantamount to martial law, order-ing the surrender of all arms, except those held by persons holding His Majesty's commission, and promising inviolable secrecy to informers.

Since the dramatic events of the previous September, Belfast had grown accustomed to the daily arrests of suspects. Men were taken from their families and sent to county jails, or the artillery barracks, or put on board the prison tender in Belfast Lough, and kept there for months without trial. The regulations for the disarming of the province came as a surprise, however, as the obvious so often does. The whole ethos of the Volunteer movement over the previous twenty years had been that it was noble and patriotic for the citizenry to arm themselves to repel foreign invaders and defend the rights of Ireland. Both Henry Grattan in the Irish House of Commons, and Charles Fox in the British, reacted to the slur cast on these Ulstermen 'of the old leaven', who had rescued the country from the tyranny of Charles I and James II: they were 'the leaven which had kneaded the British Constitution'.[3]

The intention was certainly to disarm what was left of the Volunteers. The government had succeeded in disbanding them in 1793, after they had tried to reconstitute themselves as a national guard in imitation of the French, but many of the com-panies had maintained a sporadic existence. The concealing of

Volunteer arms now became rapid and general. Under cover of night, they were spirited away to hiding places on farms, in caves and turf mosses, and even in the Presbyterian meeting houses. The six cannon which had been the proud possession of the Blue Battalion of Belfast mysteriously disappeared, and defied all the military efforts to discover their whereabouts until the eve of the Rebellion.

The mythology of the Rebellion represents the disarming of Ulster as an operation carried out with the utmost brutality by an army acting outside the law, and often out of control. The reality was more complicated. It is true that little sympathy was extended to those thought to be guilty of concealing arms. Suspects were sometimes flogged for information, or had their homes burned, and there were undoubtedly lapses of discipline encouraged, or at least condoned, by overzealous commanders. One notorious example occurred in south Down. The Ancient Britons, a Welsh regiment of fencible cavalry commanded by Sir William Watkins-Wynne, reduced the country around Newry into submission by a series of atrocities. The often-quoted eyewitness account of John Gifford, an officer of the Dublin Militia, speaks of the wholesale burning of houses and the slaughter of defenceless old men and boys.[4]

Episodes like these, which were certainly equalled at the time in other parts of Ireland, were not characteristic of the dis-arming of Ulster as a whole. For the most part it was success-fully conducted within the law, and was a severe setback to the plans of those who were contemplating insurrection. General Lake was indeed exasperated by the political and legal restraints placed on him. A seasoned and respected soldier, but a ferocious martinet when it came to military discipline, he had not the temperament for the demands of policy or the law's delays, and he was infuriated when writs of habeas corpus, or the refusal of informers to take the witness stand, prevented him from bringing prisoners to trial. He despised the merchant class of Belfast, most of whom he held to be culpable, at a time when a more perceptive man might have noticed that quite a few of the most substantial of them were swinging over to loyalism.[5]

On 17 March 1797, Saint Patrick's Day, Martha McTier had reported to her brother the steady deterioration of affairs in Belfast. Murders and assassinations had become commonplace, the natural consequence when men were 'torn from their friends and country and put aboard the tender without trial'. The army continued its searches, but the officers were well liked and did not seem to relish the searching business. The country people treated them well, asked them to breakfast, and gave them the old rusty guns. 'They shall never get Sam McTier's gun,' she added grimly. Lord Londonderry had been guarded by soldiers all winter at Mount Stewart, though his father had seldom bolted his windows. Not a penny of rent was paid to him. The bank was closed. Dr William Bruce and Dr Patrick Vance (two prominent Presbyterian ministers) were on bad terms over the yeomanry oath, and the latter was just as like to become a United Irishman. Nevertheless, life went on and humanity continued to concentrate on the important matters, like feminine fashions. A girl 'in the present rage for a slim person' had caught a cold through going to a ball with one thin petticoat.[6]

The arrests continued – of the Reverend Sinclair Kelburn, of two young apothecaries, of Dr Alexander Crawford, an eminent physician at Lisburn, and of Henry Joy McCracken's brother William. Crawford and Kelburn were sent to Kilmainham to join Neilson and Haslett.[7] In all, a batch of twenty or so Ulstermen were sent to the Dublin prisons in March. Many of the suspects had been arrested on the evidence of an informer called Edward John Newell, a miniature-painter. Newell's brother published a statement in the *Northern Star* that his family had disowned him, as he was 'in the practice of going through the town of Belfast disguised in the dress of a light horseman, with his face blackened and accompanied by a guard of soldiers, pointing out certain individuals who have in consequence been immediately apprehended and put in prison...'

Newell claimed to have been given unlimited powers – '*take up all you know*, no matter about warrants, you can get them afterwards when we know their names. General Lake and Colonel Barber will assist you in *anything*.' He later expressed regret for having denounced Dr Crawford, 'the friend of the poor, the comforter of the afflicted and a man of respectability'; and the Reverend Sinclair Kelburn, who had spoken to him once in the street.[8]

The attempt to subvert soldiers of the militia had been an important part of United Irish strategy since 1796. Either as Defenders or as United Irishmen, and preferably as both, they could be expected to switch sides once the insurrection began. According to Edward Cooke, one of the undersecretaries at Dublin Castle, some of the principal Belfast radicals had made it their business to visit the soldiers regularly in their barracks in Belfast, or at Blaris, near Lisburn, where the accommodation had just been extended by the construction of a large hutted camp, and to bring them money and presents. Thus in July 1796 there was a report of Daniel Shanahan and Joseph Cuthbert, 'notorious leaders' in Belfast, driving out to Blaris on a Sunday in July, with their wives, 'in a coach and four with loud liveries', and distributing five guineas among the soldiers. These fellows boasted that the 'citizens' of the camp had erected a room for their meetings, to which no one was admitted who was not '*up and up*' (that is, both a Defender and a United Irishman). More than 650 of the soldiers were both, and as many as 1,600 were simply United. 'The whole camp is at the disposal of Belfast,' complained Cooke, 'but they intend to keep still until the harvest is in.'[9]

In May 1797 Colonel Charles Leslie uncovered a conspiracy in his regiment, the Monaghan Militia. A great many of the soldiers had been persuaded, apparently by people in Belfast, to take the United Irish oath, and the plan had gone so far forward that they had secretly chosen their own officers. Leslie assembled the regiment and told them that their only hope lay in confession, so that he could apply to the lord lieutenant for pardon, through General Lake. More than seventy of the militiamen came forward and admitted that they had taken the United oath. Lake at once wrote to Pelham: 'Let me know his Lordship's decision while their minds are in a state of repentance and fear, and before the designing villains of the town can cause any change in their sentiments.' Lake's view was that every regiment of militia in Ireland had been infiltrated, and that a very strict watch should be kept on them.

Once the soldiers confessed, it was not difficult to pick out the ringleaders, who allegedly had sworn in the others. They were identified as Daniel Gillan, Peter Carron, and the two brothers Owen and William McKenna. Lake fully endorsed Leslie's opinion that they should be tried by court martial, and if condemned, executed. For the moment, however, he thought it would be unwise to embark on any further investigation into the militia regiments until this was done – he might find so many guilty that he would not know how to deal with them. Ominously, he ended his letter by asking if anything could be done about the *Northern Star*. 'It is worse tonight than ever, and causes much mischief. May it not be suppressed?'[10]

A court martial was duly held, with Colonel Henry Gore Sankey of the Dublin Militia presiding, and all four were found guilty on three counts, of 'exciting, causing, and joining in, a Mutiny and Sedition in the said regiment', of not using their utmost endeavours to suppress it, and of not informing their commanding officer as soon as they became aware of it. They were sentenced to be shot at Blaris on 17 May. Lake lamented that the people of Belfast, who were the cause of the mischief, were 'too guarded to be laid hold of'. He was certain that men of property and good circumstance were deeply involved. He knew who some of them were, but could not get the necessary evidence against them. In particular, he was very suspicious of the two merchants, Jordan and Greg, who seemed 'very busy about something now'. Lake recognised, too, that the verdict gave rise to some familiar Irish problems. While it pleased him that no lawyer had been bold enough to come forward in the men's defence, he wondered what was to be done about the witnesses for the prosecution – 'they must be taken care of and protected, as their lives if releas'd are not worth an hour's purchase'.[11]

Lake expressed some superficial regret for the hard decisions which duty obliged him to make, but he gave every sign of looking forward to the sentence being carried out. He promised Pelham that he would make the executions 'as awful as possible', using the utmost ceremony to impress not only the other soldiers, but the disaffected citizens of Belfast. 'The prisoners will be acquainted with their fate tomorrow, and know that they are to be shot on Tuesday at Blaris. By this means they will have sufficient time to prepare themselves for eternity, which I believe is right and according to the usual methods on these occasions...'[12]

Part of the Monaghan Militia was quartered in the Old Barracks in Belfast, and the remainder were sharing the New Barrack with the Reay Fencibles. News of the sentence caused great excitement among the men's comrades and there was fear of a mutiny. On the night before the execution a rumour spread that the militia regiment, which was over one thousand strong, intended to break out of their barracks at midnight, overpower and murder the guard at the New Barrack and set the condemned men free. Guard duty that night fell upon the Reays, and they determined, without the knowledge of their officers, to make sure that no outbreak would occur. As soon as it was dark a party of the Highlanders, who were all Gaelic-speakers, slipped out of their quarters, with weapons under their plaids, and sat up with the guard, while those still in the Barrack extinguished all lights and continued in arms on the watch, waiting for the slightest alarm.

General David Stewart in the second volume of his *Sketches of the Highlanders* has a vivid picture of that night in the guardhouse:

Slowly the hours crept on, no sign of life appearing from the barracks, whose gaunt outlines showed dim against the darkened sky. Within the guard-house, where lights still burned cheerily, all was quiet save for a subdued though animated conversation carried on in the mountain tongue. The guard clustered round the fire – for it was a chill night – the rough weather-beaten faces of the men almost matching the brick-red hue of their lapelled coats; while the tanned and muscular knees exposed by the dark folds of the belted plaid, the high-plumed bonnets, and the glint of firelight on polished accoutrement and shoe-buckle, all combined to make up a scene at once picturesque and not easily forgotten. Without, the alert steps of the sentinels rang sharp on the rough cobble-stones: an occasional flash of steel showing as the bayonet reflected the shafts of rosy light that pierced the darkness.

In a room adjoining the guard-house sat the officers of the guard. They too had heard the threatened rumour, but could not give it credence. Still, they awaited with some anxiety the coming of the sergeant with his hourly reports.

Midnight chimed from a neighbouring church, to be taken up and re-echoed in other parts of the town. Within the barracks, silent as the grave, the excitement was tense. Hundreds of straining eyes and ears awaited anxiously the smallest glimpse or slightest sound that would betray the approach of the intending murderers. Hour after hour passed, until the flush of early dawn crept across the eastern sky – the world had awakened to a new day and the danger was passed.[13]

There was no one on hand to chronicle how the night passed for the four soldiers in the black hole, from which, two days before, they had addressed a pathetic petition for mercy to Lake, humbly acknowledging that drunkenness and bad advice had been their downfall, and expressing willingness, if they were pardoned, to serve George III in any regiment of the line. They added that they would 'pray for the prosperity of your Honour's self and family'.[14] Lake was unmoved. He arranged for a slow march of the regiment and accompanying units, all the way from Belfast to Blaris, escorting the two carts which carried the prisoners, their priests and their coffins.

Detachments of the 22nd Dragoons, the Royal Artillery, the 64th Regiment of Foot, the 3rd Battalion of Light Infantry, the Monaghan and Carlow Militia, and the Breadalbane and Argyle Fencibles, were drawn up on Blaris moor, and at 1 p.m. precisely the four men, kneeling on their coffins, were shot to death by firing squad. Then the troops were marched in division past the bodies as they lay on the ground. At three o'clock Lake wrote to assure Pelham that everything had been carried out with great solemnity, and that the example appeared to have had the desired effect. There had been no disturbance, 'nor any improper word made use of', throughout the whole occurrence, despite the fact that 'the procession from Belfast to the place of execution was as public as possible'.[15]

There was no doubt about the shock and revulsion felt in Belfast. Lake told Pelham that the people of the town had said the authorities would not dare to put the militiamen to death, 'and seem much astonished at the execution'. The rumour circulated that the Scots regiments had refused to provide the firing party, which in the end had to be drawn from the prisoners' own regiment. Hearing it in Dublin, Drennan asked his sister for an account of the procession, and penned some angry, if undistinguished, lines about the high-mindedness of the Scots.[16]

The humiliated regiment lost no time in attempting to rehabilitate its tarnished reputation. The privates and NCOs subscribed to a loyal declaration which they submitted to the local press. The *Northern Star* refused to print it, unless a sentence alluding to Belfast as a town noted for its seditious practices was omitted. On 20 May about a hundred of the soldiers came down from the New Barrack, accompanied by some of the artillerymen, and broke into the newspaper office, destroying books and papers and smashing the type and presses. Eventually Colonel Leslie arrived on the scene, with a guard, and cleared the street. A few minutes later, however, 'a large part of the artillery and some sergeants of the Militia returned arm'd with hatchets, sledges, etc., forced past the guard, attacked the gentlemen in the office, who narrowly escaped with their lives, and then proceeded to finish the entire destruction of all the property on the premises'. The doors and windows were smashed, and the type, having been broken up with the sledgehammers, was thrown down into Wilson's Court. They completed the business about two o'clock in the afternoon, and left the buildings a complete waste.[17]

With its presses destroyed, and its editor in prison, the *Northern Star* finally ceased publication. The authorities were not displeased. Pelham later seems to have believed that the soldiers were punished, but no military punishment is recorded. When, on 2 September, the proprietors claimed £4,000 in damages for 'the destruction of their printing press and property by men in military dress', the claim was put aside as not coming under the relevant act.[18] By then another case was attracting most of the public's attention and adding immeasurably to the bitterness.

THE WAKE OF WILLIAM ORR

William Orr was a prosperous young farmer living at Farranshane, a mile or so from Antrim in the direction of Donegore. A Presbyterian of New Light views, he had been an active Volunteer, and sometime after 1794 he became a United Irishman and an occasional contributor to the columns of the *Northern Star*. He was suspect to the government for this reason alone. On 15 September of that year Orr was arrested on a warrant issued by the Reverend George Macartney, the vicar of Antrim, charged with administering the United Irish oath during April to two soldiers of the Fifeshire Fencibles, Hugh Wheatley and John Lindsay. For some time before his arrest Orr had been in hiding near his home, and it was when he risked a return there to see his dying father that he was apprehended. That evening he was marched off under a guard of dragoons to Carrickfergus, where he was to be imprisoned for a whole year without trial.

There is a good deal of evidence to suggest that Orr's trial in September 1797 was deliberately engineered by the government, or at least by Castlereagh, in order to frighten the New Light Dissenters.[19] From the authorities' point of view, however, it proved a disaster from the outset. The initial depositions of Wheatley and Lindsay were confused and unconvincing. The Antrim historian Samuel McSkimmin says that they were two 'ruffians' whose connection with the United Irishmen came to light accidentally when some papers were seized in Derry where they were stationed. This is corroborated by their commanding officer, Colonel James Durham, who was the first to interrogate them.[20]

They told him that on their way to Derry on 24 April 1796

they were billeted in the inn of John Hyndman at Antrim, where a man stood them a drink. On the following day 'John Campbell of Sixteentowns' gave them further entertainment at his house, and then conducted them to a field where a man they now believed to be William Orr was engaged in sowing flax-seed. This man assembled a number of persons they assumed to be a committee of United Irishmen. The whole party went to Orr's house at Farranshane. Orr then placed a book in Wheatley's hand and desired him to swear that he would be a United Irishman. Wheatley refused at first, but after being threatened by Orr and the others he took the oath.

The trial judge was Barry Yelverton, the first Baron Avonmore, the same Yelverton who had been a prominent Volunteer and Patriot MP before 1782. Orr's defence was arranged by James McGuckin, a Catholic solicitor whose office was in Fountain Lane in Belfast.[21] McGuckin had become a United Irishman in 1796, and he frequently acted for the society. (He was to be arrested in Liverpool in 1796, and to become an informer.) McGuckin instructed John Philpot Curran and William Sampson as Orr's counsel. The prosecution was led by Arthur Wolfe, who (as Lord Kilwarden) was to die under the pikes of Robert Emmet's followers in 1803.

The jury, in spite of being packed, could not agree on their verdict, and they were locked away from seven o'clock in the evening until six o'clock the next morning. The foreman, Archibald Thompson of Cushendall, County Antrim, a timid elderly man overwhelmed by his responsibility, then declared that 'they left the prisoner to his Lordship's mercy'. As this was not a proper verdict, they were sent back, and eventually Thompson, with obvious reluctance, announced a verdict of 'Guilty' with a recommendation to mercy. This verdict Yelverton at once transmitted to Dublin.

Two days later, when sentence was to be pronounced, Curran moved for an arrest of judgment on some legal points. He contended that the Insurrection Act had expired and that the judge's mind ought to be the repository of the law as it existed and not as it *had* existed. He also argued that the state had no right to wage war on the subject under false colours: Orr had been arraigned for high treason, but not under the appropriate treason statutes. Yelverton, with the assistance of Judge William Tankerville Chamberlain, considered these points carefully and dismissed them. Curran then produced two extraordinary affidavits. Thompson swore that he had been intimidated by certain persons to agree to a verdict contrary to his opinion. He and another juryman also swore that two bottles of whiskey had been passed in to them through the window, and that some jurors had been very sick and vomited before the verdict was given. Yet another juryman swore that he was resolved to acquit Orr, but was induced to agree to the verdict on being assured that the punishment would not be death. (Mary Ann McCracken told her brother in a letter dated 27 September 1797 that Thompson appeared 'quite distracted' at the idea of someone being condemned to death because of his [Thompson's] ignorance, as it seemed 'he did not at all understand the business of a juryman', and that he had held out from the forenoon until six o'clock the following morning.)[22]

The two judges ruled that these subsequent affidavits were no reason for refusing to pass sentence. Yelverton, who was a classical scholar and a translator of Livy, quoted his favourite author to the effect that laws had no hearts to feel nor ears to hear. Nevertheless, when he passed sentence he became very emotional, and afterwards he sank his head between his hands and burst into tears. Not surprisingly, this made a deep impression on those who witnessed it, but Drennan, when he heard of it, was disgusted. 'I hate those Yelvertonian tears,' he told his sister.[23]

The government was left to decide whether it would be decent to hang a man after the verdict of such a jury, and in view of all the evidence of subornation and false testimony it seemed for a time highly likely that Orr would be reprieved. But the ministers feared that if this happened, it would be impossible to convict in similar cases, and the military commanders, it need hardly be said, were of the same opinion.

The execution was fixed for 7 October, but it was twice postponed as new evidence came to light. On 3 October the Reverend James Elder of Finvoy, near Rasharkin in County Antrim, swore an affidavit that in April 1796 Hugh Wheatley had attempted to commit suicide and had confessed to him as a Christian minister that he had been prevailed upon to swear a false oath against some prisoners. He had other sins on his conscience, including seduction and murder. On 7 October Captain MacNevin of Carrickfergus wrote to Cooke at Dublin Castle that he had interviewed a man who had been with Wheatley and Lindsay at Rasharkin, and that Wheatley was 'deranged in his understanding'. He added that one day there were two ministers of religion attending him at Mrs Huey's. 'This information,' wrote MacNevin, 'I communicate lest you should be impos'd on very much by Wheatley.'[24]

Meanwhile other desperate efforts were being made by Orr's family to save his life. His brother drew up a memorial appealing against the execution, for submission to the lord lieutenant. Even the Reverend William Bristow, the sovereign and high sheriff of Belfast, agreed to sign it if Orr confessed his guilt. A signed confession duly appeared in the *Belfast News-Letter*, but Orr immediately repudiated it in a letter to the lord lieutenant. His brother was obliged to admit that, failing to persuade the prisoner to sign, he had forged the name himself. Support for Orr reached high levels in society. Lady Londonderry was moved to intercede with the lord lieutenant, but in vain. Dr Alexander Haliday wrote to Lord Charlemont, the governor of Armagh, that every exertion had been made 'by most respectable people, and on strong grounds', to save Orr, but that he feared he would hang, 'leaving behind a character without reproach ... a broken-hearted wife and six helpless children'. He added, 'Our dear countess has done all that it was possible for her to do, but, as it appears at present, with as little success as the rest.'[25]

Orr was executed at 2.45 p.m. on 14 October 1797 on the open common a mile from Carrickfergus, between the Belfast road and the sea, where for over a century there had stood The Three Sisters, an ancient multiple gallows of three stone columns supporting a triangle of wooden beams.[26] It was said that the streets of Carrickfergus were deserted, as the townsfolk expressed their contempt for an act of shameful injustice, but if that is so, most of them had gathered on the Gallows Green.

Extraordinary precautions had been taken by the military authorities, a sign of the importance attached to this execution as a warning to the country people. Infantry were drawn up round the gallows, and a detachment of cavalry was kept moving on the outside of them, while Colonel Lucius Barber of the artillery placed two field guns to command the road. He recorded that Orr 'spoke nothing but to his clergy', and that he was allowed to go to the gallows in a chaise, without being pinioned or having the noose placed round his neck. Beside him in the chaise sat two ministers, the Reverend William Staveley and the Reverend Adam Hill of Ballynure. It might at first seem strange that Orr, who was a New Light Presbyterian, should be attended by Staveley, a minister of the Reformed sect called Covenanters, but there were at least two reasons for Staveley's presence. His wife's farm lay alongside Orr's, so that it was in part an act of neighbourliness. And Staveley himself had just been released from prison, after being falsely charged with storing arms in his meeting house near Belfast.[27]

Orr had at first refused the offer of a carriage, fearing that he would be deprived of the company of his friends, but the three men were allowed to go together, reading the 23rd Psalm, and the concluding verses of I Corinthians 15:55, 'O Death, where *is* thy sting? O grave, where *is* thy victory?' Before Orr mounted the scaffold, 'a poor Catholic tenant of his own stood weeping by his side, to whom he stretched out his hat, presenting it to him as a token of friendship and remembrance'.[28]

At the gallows foot Staveley prayed aloud, the friends embraced for the last time, and Orr ascended the ladder. After the rope had been placed around his neck he exclaimed, 'I am no traitor. I die for a persecuted country. Great Jehovah receive my soul. I die in the true faith of a Presbyterian.' As the bolts were withdrawn a huge sigh went up from the watching crowd, a sound of mingled pain and menace, which over the next seven months was to resolve itself into just two words – 'REMEMBER ORR'. His dying declaration, which had been thoughtfully printed in advance, was widely distributed and found a place of honour in many a humble cottage. In it he denounced the way in which his trial had been conducted, and asserted his innocence, while making it perfectly clear that he was a United Irishman.[29]

He was buried in his sister's grave in the old Templepatrick churchyard at Castle Upton. The headstone, shaded by a yew tree, did not bear his name. Mourners lined the entire route of his funeral through Ballynure and Ballyclare to the place of interment. In the spring which followed his execution a posthumous daughter was born to him and christened Wilhelmina. A mourning card was circulated, 'sacred to the memory of William Orr ... an awful sacrifice to Irish freedom on the altar of British tyranny'. There was a brisk trade in relics, locks of his hair and what were alleged to be fragments of the hood in which he was executed. Gold rings were engraved with his name. Henry Joy McCracken was to wear one at the Battle of Antrim, and on the eve of his own execution he bequeathed it to his mother Ann.[30]

William Drennan, with a passionate intensity which sometimes outran syntax, sat down to write 'The Wake of William Orr', lines which are often regarded as his best:

> Write his merits on your mind,
> Morals pure and manners kind,
> In his head, as on a hill,
> Virtue placed her citadel.
>
> Why cut off in palmy youth?
> Truth he spoke and acted truth,

Countrymen, Unite! he cried
And died – for what his Saviour died.[31]

The Presbyterians had their martyr.

Then, rather unexpectedly, in the final months of 1797 the danger in the North seemed to subside. The French had not come in the summer. It was known, even in Belfast, that Bonaparte was completely sceptical about the prospects of an Irish revolution, and Wolfe Tone was kept cooling his heels in Paris. In the rest of the country, where tension remained high, there was talk of an insurrection on Christmas Eve, but few believed it. The diminution of serious outrages in Ulster became very marked. Much had happened during 1797 to undermine the elevated political sentiments which had once sustained the public-spirited merchant class of Belfast. The town was on the very brink of a rapid commercial expansion which would transform it early in the nineteenth century into a modern seaport, and one of the most enterprising, if the youngest, of the cities of Britain's industrial north. The siren voices of the Industrial Revolution called men away from the Rights of Man doctrines of the American and French revolutions, and within twenty years clandestine political clubs of working men would become illegal combinations to fight their employers, the first trade unions.

There was, besides, a disturbing development taking place, in the north of Ireland especially, which not only negated the alliance between Protestant and Catholic but threatened to create a worse animosity in its place. 'The most alarming feature of the movement,' wrote Camden in April 1798, 'is the appearance of the present contest becoming a religious one.'[32] Loyalty in Ireland was beginning to rally round the new standard of Orangeism, and both communities were drawing energy from religious passion.

Early in 1798 there was a shake-up in the military command. Sir Ralph Abercromby, a distinguished Scottish soldier, had taken over from Lord Carhampton as commander-in-chief in Ireland in 1797. He was not entirely happy about taking up the post, and his worst fears were rapidly confirmed. 'On my arrival here,' he told a friend, 'I found an army of upwards of 40,000 without any arrangement for its subsistence.' It was in a state of total unpreparedness for military action. None of the artillery was in a condition to move – even the guns were unprovided with horses, and there were no proper magazines. The cavalry were in general unfit for service. Most alarming of all to Abercromby's experienced eye was the way in which the regular troops were scattered through the Irish countryside in small detachments, especially in the disaffected North. In December 1797 he impressed upon Lake 'the absolute necessity' of concentrating the troops in larger bodies; otherwise they ran the risk of being corrupted, disarmed and taken prisoner.[33]

Abercromby was determined to put the army on a proper footing, and on 26 February 1798 he issued a general order to all his officers, instructing them to enforce discipline and restore the army's good name. Standing orders, he pointed out, expressly forbade troops to act on their own initiative against the disaffected. They must act only when called upon by the magistrates, or when they were themselves attacked. With Scottish directness, however, he startled everyone by declaring that the army was 'in a state of licentiousness which must render it formidable to everyone but the enemy'. This pronouncement was resented by the officers, but even more by the Irish landed classes, whom it thoroughly alarmed. Their reaction was soon conveyed to the Cabinet in London, and Pitt wrote to Camden to ask if he had really authorised such an order, which the prime minister thought 'almost an invitation to a foreign enemy'.[34]

Abercromby ignored the furore and went off to inspect the North, and then the rest of the country, before reporting to Camden. He admitted that the order was strong, but he was convinced that it was necessary. Camden had absolute confidence in him, but when the order became generally known, he was obliged to carpet him. The interview was painful for all concerned, and Abercromby at length said that if he did not enjoy the confidence of the government, he would prefer to resign. The Cabinet greeted this offer with something like relief, and since parliament was by then 'in a smothered flame' and the Opposition unable to believe its good fortune, Pitt put pressure on Camden to accept it. Abercromby's only other ally, Chief Secretary Pelham, fell ill at this juncture, and Abercromby was allowed to go.[35]

The difficulty was to know how to replace him. Dalrymple, who had preceded Lake in the North and now had the southern command, was considered unsuitable, and was still sulking at being passed over for commander-in-chief in 1797.[36] Lake, who had seniority, was not exactly suitable either, but he was appointed *faute de mieux*. The northern command now went to Major-General George Nugent.

HENRY JOY McCRACKEN

The suspect who slipped through Castlereagh's net in September 1796 did not remain at large for long. He was Henry Joy McCracken, a young Belfast cotton manufacturer, and his name, which he always used in full, indicated pride in the two very respectable Presbyterian families from whose union he sprang.[37] His father, Captain John McCracken, was a mariner by profession and an entrepreneur by instinct. At the time of his marriage he commanded a ship trading with the West Indies, but in later years his name is to be found associated also with some of the town's most progressive commercial and philanthropic ventures. Ann Joy was descended from a Huguenot family which was settled at Killead in County Antrim in the late seventeenth century, but subsequently made its mark on the history of Belfast. Her father was an attorney who left Killead in 1737 and made a modest fortune by founding the *Belfast News-Letter* and extensive paper mills. The Joys were a public-spirited family of Whiggish outlook, and closely associated with the rise of the Volunteer movement in Belfast.[38]

Henry Joy McCracken, the fifth of Captain McCracken's progeny, was born at 39 High Street on 31 August 1767, though the family later moved to Rosemary Lane (now Rosemary Street). He showed an early talent for mechanics, but he eventually went to learn the business of cotton manufacture – the entire family were connected in one way or another with the textile trade. Politics was his ruling interest and he rapidly became one of the most active of the young radicals in the 1790s, sharing many of his ideals with his favourite sister, Mary Ann. In 1795 he was sworn in to the fifth society of United

Irishmen in Belfast, and his sanguine and impulsive nature ensured that his activities soon attracted the attention of the authorities. By 1796 he was marked down as one of the more dangerous of the conspirators and a warrant was issued for his arrest.

Two of his brothers, Francis and William, shared his political views, but for John, the youngest, politics was an activity to be avoided at all costs as one likely to lead to discomfort and danger. John was, in Mary Ann's words, 'designed by nature to be a painter', and he was also fond of drawing and music, sailing and yacht-racing. While still young, he married a beautiful wife and became one of the town's most prosperous cotton manufacturers. Henry had an instinctive sympathy for the humbler people working in that industry, and with Mary (as she was usually called in the family) he concerned himself about their welfare and education. He had opened the first Sunday school in Belfast, to teach boys and girls reading and writing, on the same principles as those advocated by Robert Raikes in England a short time before. For this purpose he had found a room in the old market house in High Street, but the Reverend William Bristow arrived one day with several ladies 'with rods in their hands as badges of authority', and putting 'to flight the humble pioneers', they closed the school down.[39]

McCracken used the pretext of travelling about Ireland to sell his cottons as a cover for his United Irish activities, and he was away from home on one of these expeditions at the time of the September arrests. The McCracken house was closely watched. Bristow wrote to Lord Downshire:

> I fear that McCracken has had some notice from Dublin or here of the intended proceeding against him – Atkinson the High Constable, who lives opposite to McC's Father's house assured me he was not there. Mr Skeffington, Mr Brown and I agreed not to go to the house until we were certain that he had returned to it as that might defeat the whole business. I watched in Atkinson's house for five hours, and Atkinson watched the greatest part of the night. Mr Skeffington and Mr Brown

patrolled the streets in hope of seeing him but he never appeared.[40]

Presumably McCracken did return, for two days later, on 10 October, he was arrested and taken to Kilmainham prison in Dublin. He spent the rest of 1796 and most of 1797 in Kilmainham, fretting at the enforced inactivity, and intensely bored, since there was 'very little variety of incident in a jail' – the high point of every day was the ball game they were allowed to play in the prison yard. As far as they were able, the members of his family in Belfast supplied creature comforts, 'a new pair of blankets, an old under one, a pillow and a quilt lined with diaper, 2 pillow cases, one bolster case, one pair pantaloons & a pair of red slippers', but Kilmainham was a damp and gloomy place, and despite his youth, he developed severe rheumatism.[41]

In April 1797 he was joined as a prisoner by his brother William, one of Newell's victims, arrested as he sat with friends in a Belfast tavern. William had a more placid temperament, and soon made the best of a bad job, finding lucrative employment in copying legal documents in his neat clear handwriting. His mother sent word that Henry was to look after him, and guard him 'like the apple of your eye, and keep him and whatever might injure him at a distance from each other'. In transmitting this message, their sister Mary Ann was hoping that the responsibility might have a good effect on Henry, as she had heard 'you all make a great deal too free with yourselves. Could you not find more amusement in reading than drinking, now that you subscribe to a circulating library?' Obediently, Henry began to read Fénelon in French, with the help of a French prisoner arrested for spying.

The arrival of new prisoners from the North helped to cheer up McCracken. He was put out of his room to accommodate the Reverend Sinclair Kelburn and Dr Crawford. Later these two were very closely guarded, but McCracken and his friends were able to push papers under their door and sometimes get in for a chat with them. The rest of the new prisoners were working men, including James Burnside, a weaver who had worked for McCracken and was one of the most trusted of his United Irish associates.

The effect was to bring together, with ease of communication, some of the more determined of the northern conspirators. McCracken's rheumatism got worse, however, and the state prisoners began to quarrel among themselves. A 'deep cutting quarrel' developed between McCracken and Neilson, who had begun to drink heavily. In 1796 the prisoners had vowed that they would not seek individual release, and the ill feeling appears to have arisen over efforts to secure the release of Neilson, Charles Teeling and Henry Haslett. Though McCracken accepted that there might be motives '*beside the justice of the thing*', he was furious none the less, and the row led, on at least one occasion, to physical violence. As far as possible, they tried to keep their families in the North out of these feuds, and Mary Ann, who was closely in touch with Mrs Neilson, at length persuaded her brother to make up the quarrel.

Teeling was eventually released on bail because he was ill with fever. McCracken made no application for release, but his cousin, the lawyer Henry Joy who lived in Dublin, went to considerable trouble to try to have him and some of the others brought to trial as quickly as possible. When these efforts came to nothing, and his rheumatism grew worse, McCracken allowed his application to go forward. On 6 December he and William were released on bail. William at once returned to his wife Rose Ann in Belfast, but Henry stayed in Dublin for a few days to contact friends.

When finally he returned to Belfast, he collapsed almost at once and was seriously ill for weeks. His convalescence was slow, but just as soon as he was able to get about, he involved himself again in the plans of the United Irishmen, cheered by rumours that another French expedition would be ready by April or the beginning of May. At the end of February, the Ulster executive secretly chose him and Robert Hunter, a well-to-do Belfast shipbroker, as their delegates to contact the national executive in Dublin and to bring back their decisions. McCracken had scarcely arrived in the capital when the government, on the information of Thomas Reynolds (whose wife was Tone's sister-in-law), arrested fourteen members of the Leinster directory at Oliver Bond's house, and issued a warrant for the arrest of Lord Edward Fitzgerald. This was a severe blow to the New System at its highest level, but Fitzgerald and Neilson remained at large, and the northern delegates were assured a fortnight later that the supreme executive had survived the shock and confidently expected the French on 1 April.

The cautious northerners waited and watched. The truth was that the national executive was reduced to Lord Edward, the two Sheares brothers, Henry and John, Neilson, who was by now alcoholic, and Francis Magan, later revealed to be a government spy. Under cover of carrying on the family textile business, McCracken, with Neilson and a dozen other northerners, went on co-ordinating plans for a United Irish–Defender uprising to coincide with a French landing. Writing from Dublin on 12 May, he told his sister, 'I have said nothing about going home, however that does not make it the more distant. You know it is one of Godwin's principles, make no promises.'

McCracken was now tugged by conflicting duties. His father was dangerously ill and Mary Ann clearly wanted him to return to Belfast. 'You all think I have acted wrong in staying away so long. It would at least appear so, but perhaps when I explain what has keep't me, you will acquit me of a charge of want of affection which I feel at present my conduct *appears* to discover.'[42] In the same letter he reported that the soldiers were searching every day through Dublin for pikes and shafts, and carrying off all the timber that might be converted to that use. A few days later he returned to Belfast and reported to the Ulster leaders the final plans drawn up by the national executive. The day chosen for the uprising was 23 May, and the signal for simultaneous mobilisation of United Irishmen all over

Ireland was to be the stopping of the mailcoaches from Dublin on all the main routes – to Belfast, Cork, Athlone and Limerick.

The stratagem of the mailcoach signal was an idea credited to Neilson, and its beauty was that it would turn one of the government's most powerful weapons against it. The well-run system of the mailcoaches on major routes was not only an efficient postal service but 'a finely-spun web of communications that held the country together'. By interrupting it, the United Irish leaders hoped to paralyse government at the very moment when thousands of their followers would rise to seize the capital and other strategic centres throughout Ireland.

In the event, the first mailcoach signal was bungled, despite the most elaborate preparations. Four of the five mailcoaches passed unscathed through the insurgent pickets. The fifth, the Belfast coach, was stopped by a trick at Santry and burned. By then Lord Edward Fitzgerald, the chosen commander-in-chief of the rebel army, had been taken, overpowered and mortally wounded in a desperate struggle at his lodgings on 19 May, and Neilson, becoming hopelessly drunk in the process of mobilising the Dublin insurgents, had wandered to Newgate, where Lord Edward lay a prisoner, and had been instantly arrested.[43]

The plan which they had jointly worked out to surround and occupy the capital failed before it had begun, and for a moment the government was able to hope that the whole United Irish conspiracy might have collapsed, for the initial outbreaks in Leinster were rapidly contained, but three days later a huge popular uprising broke out in County Wexford, led by a Catholic priest, Father John Murphy. It had the fervour of a religious crusade, fuelled by ancient hatreds of class and creed, and the pikemen carried all before them until 5 June, when they were repulsed in the attempt to take the town of New Ross. For a while the fate of British government in Ireland seemed to hang in the balance. No one had expected rebellion in Wexford, where there was little United Irish organisation. What really puzzled the authorities was the lack of any outbreak in Ulster.

JAMES HOPE

'The quiet of the north is to me unaccountable,' wrote Undersecretary Edward Cooke, 'but I feel the Popish tinge in the rebellion and the treatment of France to Switzerland and America has really done much, and in addition to the army the force of Orange yeomanry is really formidable.' The army of the French Directory had invaded Switzerland in a time of peace, crushed all resistance with military force and destroyed the ancient Swiss constitution. This action, following the French destruction of the Dutch Republic, had undoubtedly alienated the Ulster Protestants, and when France came close to declaring war on the United States over shipping disputes, many of the northern radicals finally turned against their erstwhile ally.[44]

When the mailcoach was burned at Santry the northern United Irish leaders ignored it and made no move, waiting perhaps to hear that the capital was safely in insurgent hands. The adjutant-general for County Antrim was the Belfast merchant Robert Simms. These military terms were used very loosely in the New System, but presumably the rank indicated the relationship to the commander-in-chief, Lord Edward Fitzgerald. After his death on 4 June the adjutant-generals acted as independent chief commanders in their respective counties, but, confusingly, there was sometimes mention of more than one. Robert Simms and his brother William were the well-to-do owners of a paper mill at Ballyclare. William had been secretary of the first society of United Irishmen in Belfast in 1791, and both brothers were among the founders of the *Northern Star*. Both had been imprisoned briefly in 1797. Simms was elected as adjutant-general at a meeting in William

Tennent's house in Waring Street in Belfast in November 1797, but he had accepted the post reluctantly, pointing out that he had no military experience.[45]

Simms did not summon his officers after 23 May until one of them, James Hope, warned him that a spontaneous outbreak on the part of the people could hardly be prevented. Only then did Simms agree to call a council of war at Parkgate in south Antrim for 1 June. Hope was a very remarkable man, a pioneer socialist before socialism had been articulated as a political creed. Born at Templepatrick in 1764, he was of Covenanting stock, and claimed that his father had been driven from Scotland by religious persecution. At the age of ten he received fifteen weeks of schooling, and was then employed by a local farmer named Bell, a kindly man whom he recalls with affection in his *Autobiography* because he continued his education:

> The first three years I earned my bread with William Bell of Templepatrick, who took every opportunity of improving my mind, that my years would admit. In winter he made me get forward my work and sit with him while he read in the Histories of Greece and Rome, and also Ireland, Scotland and England; besides his reading and comments on the news of the day turned my attention early to the nature of the relations between the different classes of society.

Other employers later also took an interest in his education, until he could 'read a little in the Bible, though very imperfectly'.[46]

At fifteen he was apprenticed to a linen weaver, a trade he was to follow in many places for the rest of his life. Before he was thirty he married Rose Mullen. At about the same time he joined the Roughfort company of Volunteers, and in 1795 he became a United Irishman, sworn in at Lowtown near Mallusk. He was elected a representative to the central committee in Belfast and made the acquaintance of Neilson, Russell and Henry Joy McCracken. Hope was interested above all in improving the conditions of the working man in town and country, though the United Irishmen, steeped as they were in the afterlight of the *philosophes'* Rights of Man theories, were surprisingly unconcerned with this aspect of human relationships. The landowner was the radicals' natural enemy, for a variety of political reasons, but Hope was almost alone in targeting the manufacturer as well.

This, he argued, was an additional problem which the men of Ulster had to worry about, 'manufacture and commerce, fictitious capital, fictitious credit, fictitious titles to consideration . . . the numberless interests of the few, in opposition to the one interest of the many'. He had hard words, too, for 'a pensioned clergy, puzzling its followers with speculations above human comprehension, and instigating them to hate each other for conscience sake, under the mask of religion'.[47]

The message which Hope was now bringing to Simms was one of frustration, the impatience of the younger members of the organisation with middle-aged leaders, and of working men with middle-class decisions. Even the government did not appreciate the extent to which the leadership of the northern United Irishmen had been demoralised by the disarming of Ulster, the change in public opinion and the course of the rebellion in the South. The attitudes of the Ulster and the southern United men were now reversed. In 1797 the Ulster delegates had advocated a rising without an invasion by the French, and had not been supported by the men of Leinster. Now that rebellion had broken out in Leinster, the Ulstermen were hanging back. What was left of the northern command structure adopted a policy of waiting on events. Until 29 May it made no preparations of any kind.

On that day, however, there was an abrupt change of mood. A provincial meeting of delegates was convened at William Campbell's inn in Armagh, at which a young shopkeeper from Belfast, Thomas Bashford, denounced the Ulster directory for its inactivity, saying it had betrayed the people by failing to carry out the North's part of the national plan. It was voted out of office and a new executive was elected. Bashford then took a list of all the military establishments in the province and asked the delegates if they thought they could disarm the military in their respective counties. Derry and Donegal thought they could, Armagh and the upper half of Tyrone thought they could not. Asked if the people they represented would act, they all said they would, except Down. It was then resolved that the adjutant-generals of Down and Antrim should meet next day and agree an overall plan of insurrection. If an insurrection was not agreed on, they would all return to their occupations and 'deceive the people no longer'.[48] What these earnest conspirators did not know, however, was that every decision they made was being conveyed to the government by highly placed informers.

Nicholas Mageean was a young Catholic living at Lessans, two miles from Saintfield, on the old road to Belfast. He joined the United Irishmen some time after 1795, and being an active and intelligent member, he was elected to the Down provincial directory, and appointed a colonel in the military organisation. Soon after this appointment he became a paid informer, regularly transmitting details of the meetings he attended to the Reverend John Cleland. How Mageean was first recruited is not known, but there is evidence which suggests that he was threatened with death or transportation after being arrested in a meeting of United Irishmen at Moy, County Tyrone. He reported the proceedings of all the meetings he attended between 14 April 1797 and 31 May 1798, and was far and away the most important of the northern informers. His information enabled General Nugent to dispose his force – at a time when it was much weakened by detaching to the South – so as to attack the rebels at their points of assembly and to gain an advantage over them before their strength was collected. He was well paid for his services, and he was not suspected until after the Rising. As late as February 1798, his house was attacked by drunken yeomen.[49]

The other informer who occupied a vital place in the northern command structure was a Protestant, the Belfast bookseller, John Hughes. His shop was at 20 Bridge Street, near the premises occupied by Samuel Neilson and Thomas McCabe. He became a United Irishman in 1793, and renewed his oath in 1796. He, too, was eventually elected to the Down committee, but Hughes was not a courageous man, and, after his arrest at Newry on a charge of high treason, he was easily forced by threats to provide valuable information to Colonel Lucius Barber, who combined his command of the artillery with being head of intelligence. It was from Hughes that the government learned why the United Irishmen had not risen in 1797. He revealed that the County Down colonels had been in favour of action then, but that those in Antrim had been unwilling to commit themselves without foreign aid, and the other northern counties were unprepared.[50]

Between them, Mageean and Hughes were largely responsible for the breakdown of efforts to co-ordinate the mobilisation of Antrim and Down on the eve of the insurrection, and they contributed materially to its ultimate failure. They were arrested and imprisoned in 1798, both to preserve their cover and in the hope that they would elicit further incriminating evidence from their fellow prisoners.

When the meeting of the Antrim colonels assembled at Parkgate on 1 June, most of the county committee managed to attend, and they were just about to get down to business when the sentries they had prudently posted reported that a party of dragoons was approaching rapidly from the direction of Antrim town. The dragoons rode through the village without halting, but the committee had already dispersed in alarm. It reconvened in a straggling manner in nearby Templepatrick, where Simms abruptly announced his resignation.

The other members of the committee were stunned by this sudden defection. There was no obvious candidate to take his place. After much debate three names were proposed – Henry Munro, a linen draper from Lisburn, John Coulter (the proprietor of a bleachgreen at Collin) and 'a gentleman belonging to the neighbourhood of Larne'. None of these was actually present, and the committee reached the extraordinary resolution that the post should be offered to the first one met by the delegates appointed for the purpose. After this shaky arrangement, it was agreed that the final decision on whether to rise or not should be taken two days later by the colonels, meeting on the northern side of the Ballyboley Mountain, at a secluded spot called the Sheep-Ree.[51]

Some days before these dramatic events, Simms had dispatched Hope to Leinster, with orders to go to a secret United Irish camp north of Dublin and find out what was happening. Hope dutifully obeyed, but on his way he met McCracken coming out of Belfast. 'You mustn't go,' McCracken told him. 'There is no camp on this side of Dublin; there has been some fighting at a place called Clonee, near Dunboyne, but the men have marched for Tara, and are defeated and dispersed.' He added that Simms had attempted to conceal the signal for the Rising from the committee, 'and must be watched, or the hope of a union with the South is lost'. Hope said that if Simms was acting from cowardice or treachery, he would see that he was court-martialled for disobeying the order. 'Let him try me' was McCracken's reply. 'Go home until you hear from or see me.'

They parted and McCracken returned to Belfast, where he was nearly taken by a party of yeomen who recognised him in Hercules Street near the Shambles, a collection of butchers' stalls. He was saved by the wife of a butcher, who rushed out of her shop brandishing a large knife. The yeomen thought it prudent to leave the street and did not return. She concealed McCracken in her house until nightfall, when he got away by a back entrance. He at once contacted Hope and next day they heard the news of Simms's resignation and the curious method of selecting his successor. They decided to keep a close watch on the colonels and McCracken began to suspect that the Defenders must be left to look after themselves.[52]

When the Antrim colonels met again on 3 June, the delegates reported that they had not been able to find one of the proposed leaders – this was hardly surprising – and the familiar agitated debate began on what to do next. One party argued that the Rising must begin at once, without waiting for foreign aid, another that any move without the support of French regular troops was doomed from the outset. Eventually a vote was taken, and it was decided once again to postpone action until the French arrived. A few protested violently at this procrastination and withdrew from the meeting in disgust. In the Antrim village of Ballyeaston, McCracken and some of the subordinate officers and their followers were waiting to hear the result of the meeting, and when it arrived the crowd burst into an uproar, shouting that their leaders were aristocrats, despots, cowards, villains and traitors. A new meeting was convened, this time with McCracken in the chair, and the decision taken at the Sheep-Ree was reversed.[53]

It seems probable that the final decision was taken in a public house in Templepatrick, owned by one Dr Agnew, on Tuesday 5 June. By now the colonels were only too glad to put all the responsibility on to McCracken's shoulders. He was elected adjutant-general for the county of Antrim, and since the rest of the provincial executive appeared to be in disarray, he became by default commander-in-chief for the whole of the North. The Rising would begin on Thursday, just two days later. McCracken's hand was forced by the fact that the magistrates has been summoned by Lord O'Neill and were due to assemble in Antrim town on 7 June, and the chance of seizing them as hostages in the strategic centre of the county was too good to miss. Hastily he began to work out a military plan for taking control of the key towns, a plan which he hoped would be followed simultaneously in County Down, and, if possible, the other counties. Each important centre would be occupied by the United Irishmen in the locality; the militia could be relied on to defect in large numbers and the garrisons would fall one by one. McCracken would lead the main force in the attack on Antrim. On Wednesday he issued his battle orders to the most trusted colonels in Antrim: 'Army of Ulster, tomorrow we

march on Antrim; drive the garrison of Randalstown before you
and haste to form a junction with your Commander-in-Chief.
1st year of liberty, 6th day of June 1798.' The colonels would
be responsible for calling out the United men in their own
areas, and leading them to secure and occupy the towns and
villages. Leaving a small garrison in each, they would march the
rest of their men to agreed assembly points, of which the principal was to be Donegore Hill near Antrim. The assembly there
would provide a large reserve force to be employed once
Antrim was taken. These actions would be co-ordinated with
similar operations which, it was assumed, would be taking place
in County Down.[54]

Unaware that the adjutant-general for Down, the Reverend
William Steel Dickson, had just been arrested, McCracken
dispatched Hope to Belfast with a letter to him, bringing the
news which the Down men so eagerly awaited. It was early
morning when Hope reached Belfast and very few houses were
open. He met an associate, a coppersmith called William
Stewart, in North Street, and they went to Hughes's house
together. Hughes was only just awake and came out of his room
half-dressed and wringing his hands in apparent agitation. 'It is
all over,' he told them. 'Our leaders have sold us . . . There is but
one way to stop their treachery, and that is to have them
arrested; you have done much for the cause, but no service
equal to that of lodging information against them.' Hope was
not prepared to listen to that kind of talk. He took a pistol from
his pocket and put it to Hughes's chest. 'If you were not so near
your wife and children,' he told him, 'you would not speak
those words again.'

However, Stewart took Hughes's part. They began to laugh,
and told Hope they were only testing him. Hughes then sent
Hope to a house in Church Lane, where he said Dr Dickson
would be expecting him. Hope waited at the house for some
hours but Dickson did not come. Then Hughes sent him across
the river to Mountpottinger, but again there was no sign of
Dickson. When Hope made his way back to Bridge Street,

Hughes told him to come into town again next day, and this time to bring a man and a horse with him, as he had some things 'which Harry would need'.

When Hope returned next morning it was to find Belfast strongly guarded at every entrance, and the atmosphere already very tense. It was easy enough to get into the town, but getting out was another question. Hope recalled:

> When I got to Hughes in Bridge Street, they were preparing to flog men in High Street. Colonel Barber and some officers were walking up and down in front of the Exchange; we could see them from Hughes's window upstairs and Hughes seemed greatly agitated. One of [his] clerks came up and said they were flogging Kelso, and in a little while the servant girl ran into the room in haste, and said that Kelso was taken down and was telling all he knew. At this time we could see the military moving in small parties in different directions through the street in seeming haste, and Barber and his officers coming towards Bridge Street. Hughes exclaimed 'They are coming here; what will become of my poor family?' 'What ails you, Hughes?' said I. 'You need not be so frightened.' 'Oh, look here,' said he, taking me into another room, where he showed me a strong linen ticken bag with better than a stone weight of musket balls and some packages of gunpowder.

Hope immediately gathered up the bags and ran downstairs with them. The clerk followed him to the hall door, exclaiming, 'Hope, if Barber sees you, you will be hung on an iron lamp.' The weaver's coolness was indeed almost beyond belief. Picking up yet another sack, he put all the bundles into it, and made his way through the jostling soldiers to a carman's yard in North Street, where he hastily 'put some old things together – two swords, the colours we afterwards fought under at Antrim, and a green jacket'. The sack was left untied, with a few weaver's heddles projecting from it, and then thrown carelessly on a cart. Hope took the cart out of town, driving behind a troop of yeomanry, as if for protection. Once outside the town, he gradually drew away from the yeomen, and striking off the road at Shankill, got safely into the mountains.[55]

III

THE
BLUE HILLS
of
ANTRIM

O that a man might know
The end of this day's business ere it come!
JULIUS CAESAR, ACT 5, SCENE 1

THE SUMMER DAWN

The county of Antrim was created in some moment of primeval drama when the process of plate tectonics caused molten lava to burst through the surface limestone of this corner of Ireland. Cooling, it sagged towards the centre to form the great basin which is filled by Lough Neagh. The basalt layers all tilt in that direction and are much eroded, but the outer scarp of the plateau, along the coast, is a rampart of ragged black heights, running from just north of Belfast to Fair Head, where the Atlantic and the North Channel meet. It provides one of the most magnificent stretches of coastal scenery in Europe, on account not only of the cliffs themselves but of their ever-changing colour in sunlight and shade, the dark grandeur of the basalt contrasting with the white limestone at its foot. Between Benbane Head and the town of Bushmills the basalt crystallised into the distinctive hexagonal columns of the Giant's Causeway, which eighteenth-century scientists regarded as one of the wonders of the natural world.

Inland, the plateau had at that time flat and desolate areas of bog-land, but it was intersected by broad, fertile valleys, where the main pattern of settlement was to be found. The character of the whole region was profoundly Scottish, not just as a result of the plantations of the seventeenth century, but because of a largely uncontrolled influx of population over much longer periods. Part of its character was to be seen in the population of the nine great glens which run more or less diagonally towards the coast. Here the people, of mixed Scots and Irish ancestry, remained Catholic when the rest of the county filled up with Dissenting Protestants, Presbyterians in the Scottish mould.

The southern edge of the plateau ends abruptly in the precipitous slopes of Cave Hill, which looks down upon Belfast. On its summit there is a prehistoric earthwork called McArt's Fort, not too difficult to reach from the town, and in earlier times a favourite excursion for the townspeople. From this eagle's perch on a fine day one can see the whole of eastern Ulster, from the distant Mournes in the south to Slemish and the mountains of Antrim and Derry in the north. Below lies Belfast and the waters of the lough, and over the sea horizon rise the outlines of Scotland, Cumbria and the Isle of Man. To that summit, one day in June 1795, as every Irish schoolchild knows, Wolfe Tone climbed with Russell, Neilson, McCracken, the Simms brothers and 'one or two others', and there they solemnly swore never to desist in their efforts until they had subverted the authority of England over their country and asserted her independence.[1]

Long before daybreak on Thursday 7 June, Hope and his men had begun to assemble at Craigarogan fort, a Norman motte-and-bailey near the straight road between Glengormley and Templepatrick. They were mostly, like Hope himself, former members of the Roughfort company of Volunteers who had been sworn in as United Irishmen in the locality. Roughfort crossroads was also the site of the Four Towns Book Club, which had disseminated radical propaganda in this whole area of south Antrim. As the sun came up they kept their rendezvous with McCracken and the men from Belfast. A white mist covered the fields, and the air was warm and still with the promise of a perfect summer day.

McCracken raised the standard of revolt by planting on the summit of the mound the green flag Hope had smuggled out of Belfast. Then they waited for news that the general order had been obeyed. For a time there was anxiety and uncertainty as shadowy figures came and went in the mist, and then at last a horseman was heard approaching from the direction of Carnmoney. He was John McKinney from Sentry Hill, and he brought word that the whole country was in insurrection. The patriots of Larne had led the way, defeating the town garrison and forcing them to surrender. This news was greeted with cheering, and messengers were immediately sent out to all the adjoining districts.[2]

By now more and more men were arriving, armed with pikes and muskets, among them a contingent from Carnmoney led by a young farmer called Joseph Blackburn. Three companies formed up and moved off to rendezvous with the men of Templepatrick. As they marched off in the summer dawn they began to sing the 'Marseillaise'. One company was commanded by Hope, who would emerge as the hero of that day. The second was led by McCracken's brother-in-law, Big Jim McGladdery, with William McCracken trudging along somewhere in the ranks. The lead company was commanded by Henry Joy McCracken himself, tall, fair-haired, an inch under six feet, and just past his thirtieth birthday. He wore the uniform of the old First Belfast Regiment of National Volunteers, a green jacket faced with yellow, green waistcoat and white breeches.

Somewhere along the road Hope struck up another air, a popular song called 'The Swinish Multitude'. It was a defiant response to an unguarded reference by Edmund Burke to the common people, and what would happen to civilisation if they ever rose in rebellion.[3]

The first objective was to form a junction with the all-important Templepatrick company – the most determined and reliable of the insurgents that day would be drawn from the broad valley of the Sixmilewater, with Templepatrick as its natural rallying point. The Templepatrick men had been paraded early in the morning by their colonel, James Rusk, who originally hailed from the Bohill behind Divis. He said that he would follow them to Antrim, but he did not do so, and the command was taken by John Gordon, a carpenter of Donegore. Templepatrick's most important contribution, however, was the raising of the Blue Battalion's guns.[4]

When the Volunteers were finally disbanded in 1793, six brass cannon belonging to the Belfast Blue Battalion (its nucleus was the old élite Blue Company) were spirited away in Belfast and not surrendered to the authorities. Four of them were recovered not long before the insurrection, but the other two were hidden so ingeniously on business premises that they eluded all searches made for them. They had been put into the charge of Rowley Osborne and James Gault (a Templepatrick man), both of whom had been members of the Blue – the 'Blue' in the title of some Volunteer corps generally meant that they were Masonic. Shortly before the turn out, the guns were brought from Belfast 'in Mr Blow's carts' to the Dunadry paper mills, and thence to Dr Agnew's inn in Templepatrick, from which they were taken by night and hidden in Templepatrick meeting house, under the seat 'occupied by Mr Birnie of the bleach green'.

The cannon were raised, but only one of them was taken to Antrim. It was mounted on the wheels of an old chaise belonging to Lord Templetown, one which was used to draw timber on the estate, and the gun crew consisted chiefly of James Burns and his father. Burns, who was then about twenty-six, was a deserter from the Royal Irish Artillery, and as such deemed to be knowledgeable about guns. He was one of those young Presbyterian men of the district who had formed a cell of Defenders, and taken a modified version of their oath, as well as becoming a United Irishman. This was very unusual. The cannon had neither slow match nor portfire, and one of the gunners had to carry an iron pot full of burning peats.[5]

By now the column, consisting of the Carnmoney, Roughfort and Templepatrick regiments, had been joined at Muckamore by men from areas farther south, mainly Crumlin and Killead, and it filled the whole road, the pikes appearing above the hedges as far as the eye could reach. As they approached the eastern outskirts of Antrim, they were further reinforced by parties of those who had assembled on Donegore Hill, though many of the insurgents would arrive there too late

for the battle. Those who joined McCracken came by the old
Ballynure road, which met the Templepatrick road just to the
east of the town. The force was now divided. The main column
would enter the town by the Scotch Quarter, while the
Donegore battalions would move to the right and attack the
town through Patie's Lane.[6]

In the east Antrim villages of Ballyclare, Ballyeaston and
Ballynure, the insurgents had mustered that morning in considerable strength. There were nevertheless many absent faces,
those of 'esteemed veteran patriots, who, for years previous, had
declared their highest ambition was to serve the army of the
Irish republic'. When enquiries were made about the defaulters,
'some were reported to have been suddenly seized with violent
bowel complaints, others with cramps or rheumatic pains; the
wives of several were given out as at the point of death; some
only the night before were said to have had their ankles
sprained, but for the absence of the greater number, not even
a pretext was assigned'. Search parties were immediately sent
out to look for the deserters. Some were found in their hiding
places and compelled to turn out, while others protested that
they would not go to fight, even if they had to die where they
were. A few of these were, 'notwithstanding their piteous
wailings', forced into the ranks; the rest were given up in
despair.

The Ballyclare commander was one Henderson, a wheelwright, who had as his right-hand man an ex-soldier. At about
10.30 a.m. he was joined by a regiment from Ballyeaston and
Ballyboley, 'under the orders of a respectable dealer of the
former place', a man called Hay. The joint force was divided
into small sections, each under a leader, and they marched off
in high spirits on the road to Antrim, singing and cheering.
They carried the standards of the old Volunteer companies of
their districts, flags and colours reverently preserved since 1793.
The Ballyeaston flag had in large letters: LIBERTY AND OUR
COUNTRY.

The Ballynure regiment (FEAR NO DANGER) took a different

route, turning east to join up with the contingents from Larne. In command, at the front of the line and brandishing a rusty sword, rode Larry Dempsey, a deserter from the 24th Dragoons. Dempsey was a foreigner in these parts, a Catholic from Munster, and in the exaltation of the moment he exclaimed, 'By Jasus, boys, we'll pay the rascals this day for the Battle of the Boyne.' This sentiment caused consternation in the ranks, and though attention was diverted by the joyful union with the Larne force, it continued to excite sour comment until they reached Donegore, when 'the novelty of the scene changed the conversation'.[7]

The fertile valley of the Sixmilewater bisected the plateau between Antrim and Ballyclare. Donegore Hill, the assembly point for the Army of Ulster, was the most southerly spur of the upper massif, rising by very gentle slopes to a flat summit, where naked outcrops of rock showed through a light covering of moss and soil. According to one observer, there was 'not a better position for the encampment of ten or twelve thousand troops anywhere in Ireland', and it was probably chosen by the executive in the early stage of its overall plans – such sites were favoured by the United Irishmen elsewhere in the country. Donegore's advantage was that, though not high, it commanded a view in all directions. No military force could approach it unobserved, and it was here that all the insurgents, except those initially earmarked for the attack on Antrim, were to repair after the seizure of the main towns. In the event, its occupation by the people was to be brief, scarcely a day, and evidence about what happened there is tantalisingly sparse, apart from one graphic poem. But, for a few hours at least, the camp 'overawed Antrim and Carrickfergus and frightened Belfast'.

Like so many such eminences in Ireland, it still had in 1798 traces of extensive prehistoric cairns and chambered tombs, which have long since been obliterated by the plough. These places had a peculiar fascination for the United Irishmen, perhaps connected to the conscious striving to identify with, or re-create, Ireland's cultural heritage. The contemporary version of that past, owing much to the misdirected researches of antiquaries like General Charles Vallancey, differed considerably from the interpretation of modern archaeologists. Donegore was described as having been the 'court of the Brehons, or highest chiefs', and the local United men were in the habit of meeting there, long before 1798. Its lonely situation guaranteed security; 'the witches and other supernatural things expected to be seen there kept the women and children away', especially after dark.[8]

Among those who came to Donegore Hill on 7 June was a rustic poet, with a merciless eye for the human attributes on display there. James Orr was later to enjoy local fame as the 'Bard of Ballycarry', and he arrived at the assembly point with the insurgent corps from Broadisland in the east of the county. County Antrim at this time boasted several bards, inspired by the example of Robert Burns and eager to emulate him by expressing their thoughts in the vernacular. Few of them had any conception of the extent of Burns's erudition or approached the cunning of his art, but Orr's best dialect poem describes his experiences from the preparation for the Rising to the moment when (paraphrasing the Psalmist) 'ilka cauf turn'd his backside, an' scamper'd aff'.

> While close-leagu'd crappies raised the hoards,
> O' pikes, pike-shafts, forks, firelocks,
> Some melted lead – some saw'd deal boards –
> Some hade, like hens, in byre-neuks:
> Wives baket bannocks for their men,
> Wi' tears instead o' water;
> An' lasses made cockades o' green
> For chaps wha us'd to flatter
>   Their pride ilk day.[9]

Orr's verses (written long afterwards) were sardonic and disillusioned, but a clear-sighted attempt to describe the scene as it really was. There were men on Donegore who had been alternately heartened or scolded by their worried womenfolk, and who promised to elude the leaders and guards and return home as soon as possible, leaving it to 'the daft anes' to pursue the campaign; there were some who went behind a dyke to answer a call of nature and never came back; some who had fortified themselves with 'two rash gills from Herdman's quart' (from the inn in Ballycarry). And there were others, the truly brave, who passed by 'weans and mithers', thinking on the red fields of war, and how the rabble might later ravage their quiet dwellings.

The first thing which made an impression on the poet when he reached Donegore was the sheer noise of the excited host, as if a beehive had been suddenly overturned:

> When to the tap o' DONEGORE
> Braid-islan' corps cam' postin',
> The red-wud, warpin', wild uproar,
> Was like a bee skap castin'.[10]

It was an extraordinary sound and sight for a man of a philosophic turn of mind, with an admiration for Rabbie Burns:

> ... *Leaders*, laith to lea the rigs,
> Whase leash they fear'd was broken,
> And *Privates*, cursin' purse-proud prigs,
> Wha brought 'em balls to sloken;
> Repentant Painites at their pray'rs,
> An' dastards crousely craikin'
> Move on, heroic, to the wars
> They meant na to partake in,
>   By night, or day.[11]

Here on the summit of Donegore perhaps as many as seven thousand men awaited the outcome of the attack on Antrim. More continued to arrive in the course of the afternoon. Sixty-five years later, James Burns told the Reverend Classon Porter, the historian of the Kilwaughter congregation, that 'a large party of United Irishmen, 15,000 as he describes them, never took part in the fight at all, but stood at the outside of the town, being on their way to the appointed rendezvous at Donegore

Hill'; but with the confused memory of old age (he was then in his ninety-second year) he places Henry Joy McCracken and Samuel Orr, the brother of William Orr, with this party. It reflects the undoubted reality that hundreds of insurgents were still on their way to Antrim and Donegore when the action was decided.[12]

When the drums beat to arms in the New Barrack in Belfast at dawn that day, Colonel James Durham had already been awake for several hours. At 4 a.m. he had been roused by Captain George Peacock, General Nugent's aide-de-camp, with the message that Nugent wished to see him at once. He found Nugent in his quarters poring over a clutter of maps and intelligence reports in the candlelight. Among the papers on his desk lay an urgent missive from a mole planted deep in the United Irish provincial directory. It told him that by daylight the whole of eastern Ulster would be in rebellion against the Crown, that the town of Antrim would be attacked by a large insurgent force, and that the magistrates summoned to meet there would be taken hostage. There was no doubt about the genuineness of the message; it was written by Nicholas Mageean, the man who was entrusted with the rebel mobilisation of County Down.[13]

Contrary to popular belief, reinforced by many a graphic school lesson, communications in Ireland at the end of the eighteenth century were good and improving rapidly; the mailcoach system had been developed to a remarkable degree. It carried passengers and mail to the main centres throughout the island, and the mail included all but the most sensitive military information. The Dublin mailcoach usually reached Belfast at one o'clock in the morning, tearing in along the old Malone Road, through Sandy Row, and over the Blackstaff into Barrack Street, *en route* for its final stop at the Donegall Arms. Colonel Durham later recalled that at the barracks the officers were in the habit of sitting up at night until the mail arrived. It told them that all was well and quiet in the capital, and brought the GOC his latest instructions.[14]

On the night of 23–24 May the mailcoach had not come in, and soon orderly dragoons from the South brought the news that the coaches leaving Dublin had been stopped and burned 'by the mob', the signal for a general 'rising of the people'. In the event, only the coach to the North had been burned, but by noon on the 24th Nugent knew that Ireland had exploded.

George Nugent was the illegitimate son of the Hon. Edward Nugent, a colonel of the 1st Foot Guards. His grandfather, the Earl Nugent, had become fabulously rich by marrying a succession of very wealthy widows, a talent so marked that Horace Walpole had coined the word 'nugentize' to describe it. Born a Catholic, the Earl apostasised to Protestantism, but returned to the bosom of the Church at the end of his life, 'a jovial and voluptuous Irishman who left Popery for the Protestant religion, money and widows'. George Nugent inherited little of his grandfather's flamboyance; his character may, indeed, have been formed in reaction to it. A first-class soldier, who had the undoubted advantage of influential family connections, he was also a prudent and considerate man, possessed of imagination, humane in his treatment of the vanquished, and diplomatic in his relations with the local population.

Educated at Charterhouse and the Royal Military Academy, he had entered the army as an ensign of the 39th Foot. At the age of twenty he was in America, taking part in the expedition up the Hudson, and the storming of the forts of Montgomery and Clinton. When the American war ended he had reached the rank of lieutenant-colonel, and returning home, he became aide-de-camp to his relative, George Nugent-Temple-Grenville (afterwards the Marquess of Buckingham), who was appointed lord lieutenant of Ireland in 1787. In 1790, as a lieutenant-colonel of the Coldstream Guards, Nugent campaigned in the Netherlands and eventually commanded a brigade. In that year, too, he was returned as an MP for Buckingham. Promoted to the rank of major-general, he held several commands in the south of Ireland before his transfer to

Belfast, where in November 1797, he married Maria Skinner, the daughter of the attorney-general of New Jersey.

Cortlandt Skinner was an American of Dutch-Scottish ancestry who had felt obliged by virtue of his office to take the side of the Crown when the colonies revolted, and later had raised a corps of loyalist volunteers known as 'Skinner's Greens', which, with the rank of brigadier-general, he led into action at Springfield and elsewhere. Hounded out of New Jersey after 1776, he and his family moved to Jamaica, and then to Britain, where they were warmly received. One of his sons, also called Cortlandt, settled in the north of Ireland, and his name appears with Nugent's on lists of the County Antrim magistrates in 1797 and 1798.

'General Nugent is much liked,' Mrs McTier told her brother, 'and always *was* in this town; and I believe in my soul will act with all the forbearance the nature and difficulty of his station will allow.' Prudent and diplomatic handling of the ex-Volunteer middle class in Belfast had secured the surrender of four of the long-hidden Volunteer cannon in Belfast, and other arms were coming in daily, without recourse to the savage methods employed by his predecessor, General Lake.[15] Nugent was indeed sensitive to the complex alteration of sentiment which had overtaken the North in the last two years. There remained the worrying question of his thinly spread, outlying garrisons in Antrim and Down. If he had to move too many troops to go to their aid, or if the French should land, then the Belfast story might take another turn.

The contemporary military strategy for dealing with the United Irish threat, which with hindsight seems hardly appropriate, was to scatter troops very thinly over the areas thought to be disaffected. Some of the small provincial towns like Larne, Carrickfergus and Randalstown in County Antrim, or Comber and Ballynahinch in Down, had very small garrisons, often of only company strength, and they were isolated and vulnerable. The town of Antrim, where the magistrates were to meet on 7 June, was guarded by Major Daniel Seddon and a troop of the 22nd Dragoons. At some point after midnight, Nugent decided on a calculated gamble. He would test the strength of the northern rising on its first day by sending two columns to meet the rebels head-on at Antrim, and possibly, if he was lucky, nip the whole enterprise in the bud. He dispatched riders posthaste to Blaris camp with orders for General Tom Goldie there. Then he sent for Colonel Durham. Take what force you like, Nugent told him, and march immediately.[16]

By now the short summer night was ending, the sky beyond the narrow windowpanes growing lighter. All the signs were that it would be a fine, warm summer day. In the dawn the drummers were called out to beat to arms. The assembling of the mixed force which Durham led out of Belfast was a complicated and lengthy process, and the sun was well up before it was complete. An infantry force of 250 men of the Monaghan Militia was mustered at the barracks. The cavalry consisted of a troop of the 22nd Dragoons commanded by Major Smith, backed up by Captain Alexander Colston of the Royal Irish Artillery and two field guns. Then the Belfast Yeoman Cavalry had to be called out, a body of loyalist citizens, merchants mostly, who were eager to see action. They were under the command of Captain William Rainey.

Had James Durham been a more imaginative man, he might, as he crossed the barrack square that summer morning, have reflected on the vagaries of military life which had led him to be in Belfast at that time. A Durham of Largo in Fife, he is rather in the shadow of his more distinguished brother, Admiral Sir Philip Durham. Admiral Durham's rise to high rank owed something to the fact that he was one of only a handful of survivors of the sinking of the *Royal George*, in the century's worst naval disaster. When the entire bottom fell out of the ship off Spithead in 1782, Rear Admiral Richard Kempenfelt and more than eight hundred people drowned. Durham, who was the officer of the watch, had the good fortune to be rescued after half an hour in the water and taken on board the *Victory*.[17]

Though James Durham's adventures were less dramatic, his life had also been touched by great events, and neither brother was to be cheated of old age. When he was over eighty, the soldier took a large business ledger, interleaved with pink blotting paper, and began to set down his memoirs. The rambling narrative, with some obvious inaccuracies and highly individual spelling, presents in the main the portrait of a very conventional soldier and country gentleman, who had the good fortune to have coal discovered on his estates, but his early career was not without interest. Disgruntled by lack of promotion, as almost all officers are, he travelled quite extensively on the Continent, watching the Austrian army at manoeuvres, under generals with Scottish and Irish surnames, and witnessing the early stages of the French Revolution at first hand.

For a year he and his wife lived at Lausanne in Switzerland, which was rapidly filling up with the fugitive French aristocracy. When they decided to return to England in 1790, a lady who had been maid of honour to Marie Antoinette begged them to take her with them to Paris, so that she could be reunited with the Queen. She was afraid to travel in her own French berline, so the Durhams took her to Paris in their sturdy English postchaise and delivered her safe to the Queen, who was then virtually a prisoner in the Tuileries. On the Sunday following, the Durhams were found a corner in the gallery, and the Queen, as she passed through on her way to mass, made a low bow to them.

In 1794 Durham accepted the government's invitation to raise a fencible regiment in Fifeshire, and in the following year he took it to Ireland. The Fife Fencibles went first to Derry and then to Carrickfergus before coming to Blaris and Belfast. It was to Durham, as their commanding officer, that the privates Wheatley and Lindsay had first made the confessions which provided the evidence against William Orr, and now on this warm June morning he was riding at the head of his column as it made its way uphill past Carnmoney Moss. From all directions reports were reaching him of a considerable force of rebels in arms.[18]

★

Nine miles away at Blaris, dispatch riders had brought orders to General Goldie to assemble a similar force and send it to Antrim by a different route. Goldie was a landowner in south-west Scotland, the 'Colonel Tam' whom Burns mentions in one of his ballads.[19]

Goldie, an inveterate card-player, hardly allowed the Rising to interrupt his favourite pastime,[20] but on the morning of 7 June he ordered Colonel Henry Mordaunt Clavering to take command of 2 companies of the Armagh, Monaghan, Dublin, Kerry and Tipperary Militia, 150 of the Light Dragoons and suitable artillery – 2 six-pounders and 2 of the latest howitzers – and head for Antrim. The militia had a longer trek ahead of them than Durham's men, for they had to skirt the Antrim plateau to the east, through Crumlin and across the open flat country which is now Belfast International Airport. Accordingly, Clavering sent the artillery and cavalry, commanded by young Lieutenant-Colonel William Lumley, an Old Etonian and the seventh son of the Earl of Scarborough, racing ahead of him. They reached Antrim in the early afternoon.[21]

Patrick Heron, the MP for the Stewartry of Kirkcudbright, was the patron of Goldie and his aide-de-camp, Captain William Newall. Heron, a scion of an ancient Nottinghamshire family, was married to the daughter of Thomas Cochrane, eighth Earl of Dundonald, and his seat was at Kirroughtree, beside Newton Stewart. Lady Elizabeth Heron, who was a talented amateur musician, had composed an air for Burns's 'Banks of Cree', and Burns greatly admired Heron's political outlook, to the extent of composing ballads to support his election campaigns in 1795, even adapting 'A Man's a Man' for the purpose. He described Heron as 'The independent patriot/The honest man, and a' that.' During the early days of June 1798, Newall wrote copious letters to Heron from Blaris, giving him news of how the Rising was developing.

On that Thursday morning he wrote:

I have only time to say in this instant [we] have had information that six thousand Rebels are to assemble near this today and to make a grand attack on the Town of Antrim. We have this moment sent a detachment consisting of a hundred of the 22nd Lt. Dragoons, a Battalion of Lt. Infantry, two curricle guns and two Howitzers to attack them. If they fall in with the Rebels it's not unlikely but we may move with all our force some time to-day or night to the assistance of them sent out.

Reinforcements were desperately needed from England and Scotland, and they were astonished that they had not yet arrived. In Newall's opinion, the rebels meant 'to rise everywhere about us'. The military were taking every precaution to prevent them from assembling in force, 'but I imagine all won't do'.[22]

The usual route north from Belfast to Antrim and the interior of the county followed the Shore Road as far as Greencastle, and then struck north-west through the gap between Cave Hill and Carnmoney, where the M2 motorway now runs. This, the line of Durham's advance on Thursday morning, took him through Mallusk and Templepatrick; he was following close on McCracken's heels, two hours later.

Three columns were now converging on Antrim – McCracken's rebel force, strengthened by levies from the localities on the immediate line of his advance, and two well-equipped army detachments of cavalry and infantry. But to the east an enormous rebel force was assembling at points along the coast and further inland. It would be remembered, and long remembered, as 'the Turn Out'.[23]

THE TURN OUT

The turn out had begun, untidily enough, on the evening of Wednesday 6 June at Larne, a small port on the east coast. Here, as elsewhere in south Antrim, it had its strongest support among the local Presbyterians. The origins of the old Larne and Inver congregation are to be traced in that period of Scottish history when ministers of outspoken Presbyterian views were sometimes obliged to flee for sanctuary to Ulster, where nevertheless they accepted ordination from the Irish bishops. One such was George Dunbar, twice ejected from Ayr by the High Commission, and eventually settled as pastor in 1627 'at Inver, near Lochlairn in Ireland'.[24] His successor, Thomas Hall, held on to Larne for forty-nine years, surviving the Commonwealth, Protectorate and Restoration, no mean achievement, for none of these régimes was favourable to the Presbyterians, and even Cromwell contemplated transporting them to Tipperary. Among those listed for this ethnic redistribution were many of the name of Agnew.

Ministers like Hall were constantly on the move between Ulster and Scotland, and Hall was sustained by the tithes of the Larne parish. In 1668, however, the congregation took a high-minded decision and 'forsook their ministers as to maintenance'. Later ministers were understandably apt to comment on this decision with some feeling. One of them observed dryly that if the congregation denied their pastors bread, they at least gave them stones, for a brand-new meeting house was built at 'the head of the town', and as the Head of the Town congregation it has been known ever since. A stubborn righteousness was built into its very fabric.[25]

By 1798 Larne was one of the Nonsubscribing, or New Light,

congregations of the Presbytery of Antrim. The Nonsubscribers were the Presbyterians who, early in the eighteenth century, had initiated an acrimonious debate in the General Synod of Ulster by the refusal of their ministers to sign the Westminster Confession of Faith, or any 'man-made' definition of their belief. The Church was divided, and peace was achieved only by a compromise: the Nonsubscribers were allowed to constitute the Presbytery of Antrim, as a kind of devolved assembly, remaining on good terms with the parent synod. The minister of Larne in 1798, the Reverend James Worrall, was, uncommonly, a native of Limerick and a defector from the Church of Ireland. The congregation then included many of the leading inhabitants of Larne and its neighbourhood, among them the local landowner, Squire Edward Jones Agnew of Kilwaughter Castle, George Anson McCleverty, a magistrate who lived in the village of Glynn, James Agnew Farrell and Dr George Casement. All of these persons were to figure prominently in the events about to take place.[26]

Casement was a respectable but unpopular citizen of Larne who took no part in active politics. He had indeed a particular incentive to keep a low profile, for he had been one of the jurors at the trial of William Orr in 1797. By simply doing his duty, as he saw it, he had been unlucky enough to draw down on himself the anger of 'these people called the United Irishmen'.[27] On the Sunday evening after the trial he had been attacked by a party of men on the road near Larne and thereafter he lived in constant fear of assassination. Nevertheless, Casement had no special reason for apprehension when he went to 'the Scramble' in Larne on the evening of Wednesday 6 June. This was the name given locally to a kind of dance and social gathering which the Larne people held from time to time in public rooms in the town.

Unknown to him, members of the executive committee of the Larne United Irishmen were at that moment assembling at a house in the town. They had received McCracken's orders to seize the garrison at first light on the following morning, and they decided to commence action at once with the shooting dead of Dr Casement. One of the conspirators had an uneasy conscience, however, and conveyed this information to a friend. The friend was Casement's brother-in-law, Malcolm McNeill of the Corran, the sickle-shaped spit of land running out beyond the harbour. McNeill went to the Scramble, and on coming out managed to put Casement on his guard.[28] Not surprisingly, the doctor was very agitated, concerned not only for himself but for the safety of his wife and family. It was now about ten o'clock in the evening and there seemed little chance of organising their escape from the town. He contacted four of his most trusted friends, and they agreed, with Casement and his two sons, that they would stand or fall together.

The tiny garrison in Larne consisted of twenty men of the Loyal Tay Fencibles, a detachment of the regiment stationed in Carrickfergus. They were billeted in a private house and under the command of Lieutenant Andrew Small. It seems likely that Small had already received some warning, for he had begun to reconnoitre the town with a sergeant and a few privates and was enlisting the aid of loyal citizens who could arm themselves. Among those eligible was Casement's son, John, who was pro-collector for the port of Larne; a few days earlier Colonel Anstruther, the commander at Carrickfergus, had granted him a permit to keep arms. With these, and a plentiful supply of ammunition, the little party of loyalists now prepared to assist the military to withstand whatever onslaught the night might bring.

As the patrol passed through the old town a light was seen in the upper storey of one of the houses, though it was by now some considerable time after curfew. The soldiers demanded entry but were denied. They then tried to force the door open and failed. It had been barricaded on the inside and they could hear a great noise of people running down the stairs and escaping by the back of the house. Sergeant Aiken and Mr Hill were in time to cut off some of the fugitives and two were taken prisoner. Then the rest of the patrol succeeded in forcing the door and went up to the lighted room where they found a pitchfork, a pike head and a number of fir poles ready to be fitted with heads. Two men were found in their beds and taken with the other prisoners to be placed under guard at the fencibles' quarters. Then, astonishingly, Small allowed the rest of his detachment to retire for the night.

He would scarcely have done so had he known that the United Irishmen he surprised had reconvened in the open air behind high hedges at the bottom of the town. And Casement would have been even more agitated had he known that chief among those who were plotting to make him the victim of the first shot fired in the Rebellion was his own minister, Mr Worrall.

Worrall had been educated at Trinity College, but when he embraced Presbyterianism he gravitated north, becoming in due course a tutor to the family of Mr Turnly of Rockport. James Agnew Farrell was connected to the Turnlys by marriage and he was a prominent member of the Larne congregation. It was through his recommendation that Worrall received a call from them in 1796.[29] Both men were ardent radicals, and, by 1798, sworn United Irishmen. Farrell was the chosen colonel of the Larne regiment and as such he received McCracken's orders on 6 June.

Farrell had summoned the secret meeting, but when the conspirators assembled, he was not in his place. He was sent for, but was nowhere to be found. It was not until later that his friends learned that he was already on board a boat bound for the Isle of Man, and not until much later that they knew that his copy of McCracken's orders was on General Nugent's desk in Belfast, before they had even begun to move. It is not clear to what extent his duties devolved on Worrall, if at all. For the moment all was confusion. Probably the younger men seized the initiative, as they were to do elsewhere, and decided to rise immediately and to eliminate the unfortunate Dr Casement. Worrall was a man of delicate health (he suffered from asthma) and he is described, even by those opposed to his politics, as amiable and accomplished, but one could scarcely disagree with Classon Porter's judgement that 'as a recognized leader of the insurgents in this neighbourhood, he was cognizant of measures contemplated, if not perpetrated, against hearers of his own, which should never have been connived at, or silently observed, by a minister of the Gospel of peace'.[30]

For Casement and his friends, unaware of the United Irishmen's problems, the hours passed slowly, but the summer night was short and by three o'clock they knew it would soon be light. They relaxed and took some refreshment. Casement was aware that his friend McCleverty intended to go to Antrim that day to the magistrates' meeting, and he now wondered if he and his son should attempt to reach McCleverty's house and put him on his guard. But before they could do so, there was a sudden alarm and they heard the sound of people climbing over a gate near the house. Casement went outside and saw two men hurrying along the street called The Point. He recognised one of the men, Andrew Darragh, and hailed him, but both men ran off.

The loyalists then began to hear a great lamentation of women's voices coming from the direction of the old town. Now Casement's first concern was that Lieutenant Small and his men must be awakened, and to this purpose his son and the solitary soldier left with them as guard set out for Small's lodgings at the head of the new town. Almost at once they collided with a large body of rebels, who fired on them and mortally wounded the soldier. Thinking the man already dead, John Casement took his weapons, which providentially saved his life, for the rebels assumed that he was one of their number. He succeeded in reaching Small, who was already alerted and in the process of mustering as many men as he could free from guarding the prisoners, and, together with the loyalists, they began a spirited sally into the town.

They fell straight into an ambush. Two soldiers were shot dead and the lieutenant and a corporal were wounded, for the loss of one of the rebels. Small was helped back to his quarters, while his sergeant mustered the rest of the Loyal Tay Fencibles and retreated to their barracks as the most eligible place to defend.

After the military had concentrated their dispirited force, they expected a fresh attack at any moment, but there was a diversion. McCleverty had been taken prisoner at his home in Glynn, and he was now brought in to Larne. It was proposed to send him to the barracks with a party of insurgents at his back and a message demanding instant surrender. This scheme was rejected as inhumane and the message was sent by another hand. It was returned unopened, the officer declaring that his men would defend themselves to the last. That retort 'seemed to paralyse the exertions of the insurgents'. They retired to the Mill Brae, where McCleverty at once attempted to use his influence with them. He tried to persuade them of the folly of the whole enterprise and advised them to disperse and return home. He promised that if they did, he would use his utmost endeavours with the government to secure their pardon. He also sought, and obtained, their permission to send for the local squire, Edward Jones Agnew of Kilwaughter. When Agnew arrived he added the weight of his counsel to try to persuade the people to give up their arms. His advice and entreaties were set aside, but he was permitted to return to Kilwaughter.[31]

Casement's little party meanwhile returned to his house and again took stand there. They were mostly young and active men and their mobility had given the rebels the impression that their numbers were greater than they were. Casement later learned from two renegades that the rebel body had seriously contemplated an attack on the house, and had carried out a reconnaissance before abandoning the plan. The loyalists now considered the feasibility of getting a message through to Colonel Anstruther and the main body of the Loyal Tay Fencibles at Carrickfergus. A horse was found, and a soldier called John Watson volunteered to make the attempt. He managed to pass the rebel guard on the Larne bridge, but half a mile farther on he ran into a party of United men. He was shot through the lung and piked in the shoulder before they took his weapons and his watch.

Casement knew nothing of Watson's fate until noon on Thursday, and the taking of the soldier's belt and musket were to have implications elsewhere. After daybreak, as everything seemed quiet, Casement moved his wife and the younger children to a safer house which was overlooked by both the military and his own party. They decided to make another attempt to communicate with Carrickfergus, either through Islandmagee or by water, and to this end a letter was written and sent down to the harbour, addressed to Mr Reade, the port surveyor. The letter reached Reade about 5 a.m., but during the next hour there was no sign of activity in or about the harbour, of which their situation commanded a clear view. At six o'clock a second message was sent to Reade by Mr Hudson, one of the tidewaiters, but still Reade did nothing as far as Casement could see. Gradually he came to realise that the main body of rebels had evacuated the town. They were, in fact, on the way to Donegore Hill with McCleverty as prisoner. They were in high spirits, for news had reached them (quite false, as it turned out to be) that Carrickfergus Castle had been seized, with its entire arsenal.

At noon a much-relieved Casement and some loyalists moved their families down to the Corran. The rebels had at no point occupied it. There they could be put into boats with the help of friends and taken to some other part of the Antrim coast where they would be safe. The operation was just getting under way, when to his horror Casement saw a large contingent of pikemen coming into view on the adjacent hills of Islandmagee. That they were pikemen was bad enough, but that they were from Islandmagee made his heart skip a beat. 'Then we thought our situation desperate in the extreme,' the doctor recorded, 'the savage disposition of these people being particularly dreaded.'[32] There was nothing for it but to cast off the boats and scramble back up to the town where his arms and ammunition were. Once again they determined to sell their lives as dearly as possible.

The sixty or so pikemen whom Dr Casement saw on the hills of Islandmagee were only a portion of the insurgent force which had mobilised there during the night, but crossing the narrow stretch of shallow water which separated them from Larne would present no difficulty to men who had been doing it all their lives. However, it soon appeared that this was not their intention, at least for the present. Islandmagee was, despite its name, a peninsula, seven miles long and one or two miles wide, joined to the mainland by a low flat isthmus and curving in to enclose the waters of Larne Lough and almost touch the coast again at Larne. In the eighteenth century, and for long afterwards, there was a ferry at this point.

Like most peninsulas, however accessible, Islandmagee suffered the imputation of being the home of weird people, inbred, suspicious of strangers, and isolated from the cultural mainstream. Jack London, who set one of his stories there, claimed that Islandmagee seamen always came back to the Island to find their wives, and that 'a poor creature of a schoolmaster once married a woman from the far side of Larne Lough and even he lived under a cloud all his days'.[33] These were romantic notions. Islandmagee was no more isolated in 1798 than it is today, and it has one attribute at least which is known throughout the seafaring world, and probably explains why Jack London knew of its existence. For some reason it produces more master mariners per square foot than almost any other part of the globe.[34]

Islandmagee's connection with the Magee clan, which gave it its name, was all but lost in the murk of time. A massacre of Catholics, including the last of the Magees, was reputed to have taken place in 1641, in retaliation for the wholesale massacre of Protestants in the North that year. There was, however, no doubt about the solidly Scottish and Presbyterian character of Islandmagee by 1798. The Ordnance Survey of the 1830s recorded that the inhabitants 'to a man were descendants of Scottish settlers of the seventeenth century, and still retained in their habits, manners, dialect and religion, the characteristics of the country of their forbears'. These origins were manifest in their names, and in their massive old furniture and family Bibles with dates from the century of emigration.[35]

Probably no reason beyond the homogeneity of the Islanders need be adduced to explain their response to the turn out. It was for them, as for others, 'the logical outgrowth of the economic experience, social attitudes and ideological instincts of the people'.[36] It was not significant that these people were 'very honest, but shrewd and cunning', showed 'little taste for reading', or that the farmers were sometimes seen staggering as they came from Sunday morning service. As the survey officers solemnly recorded, 'a space of half an hour, termed "intermission", elapses between the two services in Presbyterian churches during summer. On retiring for this space, they were in the habit of adjourning to a convenient ale-house, and there remaining during the second service, until they became quite drunk.'[37]

The two public houses which existed in Islandmagee in 1798 had done roaring business on the night of 6 June, refreshing the teams of men who worked in relays in the forge of the blacksmith, Jamie Adams, helping to make the pikes. Lookouts had been posted on all the approach roads, and here at least they were secure from surprise. Early on the Thursday morning a large body of men assembled at the Knowehead Brae, under the command of William McClelland, a well-to-do young farmer of twenty-two, whose family had fifty-eight acres at Portmuck. His second-in-command was William Curry of Ballycronan.[38] They were working to a general plan. With contingents from other parts of Islandmagee, they were to muster before Redhall, near Ballycarry in the neighbouring parish of Broadisland. This was another prosperous Ulster-Scots farming community, and according to the Ordnance Survey memoirs, the inhabitants 'to a man took a more or less active part' in the turn out. Among them, that bright hot morning, was the poet, James Orr. If Orr is to be believed, there was not a great deal of enthusiasm, once the call had come, but enough of them had turned out, at least, to ensure an early military victory at Redhall.[39]

The hall was a modest seventeenth-century house which had seen a succession of proprietors, each with his own decided views on architecture, but it has managed to preserve to this day a fine Jacobean plaster ceiling, one of the very few left in Ireland, and the ghost of a white lady who wanders in the grounds at night. The house stood 250 feet above sea level, with a fine view of Larne Lough and the sea beyond. Near it was the Mill Glen, a steep ravine carved in the limestone by a cascading stream. At its foot lay a little space of grass that became a carpet of wild flowers in summer, and at the top was the 'Madman's Leap', so called because a seventeenth-century rapparee had eluded his pursuers by jumping from one side to the other. (In the adaptable Irish way, the legend has now been transferred to a rebel escaping the yeomen in 1798.)[40]

On 7 June the insurgents were less interested in Redhall's romantic setting than in the contents of its gun room. The two columns from Islandmagee converged at the causeway near Ballykeel Point and went on to join up with the United men from Ballycarry. The Islandmagee rebels knew that the owner of Redhall, Richard Gervase Ker, had a plentiful store of weapons and this was their main objective. At the entrance they were received by the butler, who informed them that Mr Ker was not at home. (He had prudently withdrawn to Carrickfergus.) They broke open the gun room and distributed the muskets found there, only to discover that, before his departure, Mr Ker had had the foresight to remove all the firing pins. Nevertheless, they shouldered the muskets, and with the horses rounded up by sixteen-year-old Willie Nelson, they pressed on, encouraged, like the Larne men, by the false report that Carrickfergus had fallen.[41]

At the little village of Glynn, on the shore of Larne Lough, they met the victorious contingent coming out of Larne. Most of the rebel force moved off towards the assembly point at Donegore in the course of the morning, but small bodies were left behind, presumably to hold the occupied territory. In particular, a party of about sixty Islandmagee men were ordered to take post on the hills facing Larne. These were the men who so alarmed Casement.[42]

Eight miles north of Larne, at the point where the first of the Glens of Antrim reached the coast, lies the village of Glenarm. Before the building of the splendidly scenic Antrim Coast Road, the cluster of small cottages, the homes of fishermen and farm labourers, was somewhat isolated, and the approach to it was from the landward side through the glen. Hidden in the trees, across a shaded river on the north side, rose Glenarm Castle, the residence of the Earls of Antrim. A solid Jacobean mansion, of the kind often described as 'a commanding pile', the castle had its own deer park, waterfall and salmon leap. The Earls of Antrim were the Macdonnells, close kindred of the fabled Lords of the Isles, who for centuries had ruled a fiefdom on both sides of the North Channel, in the days when sea communications were more important than national boundaries. When the Scottish McDonalds of Islay came under pressure from their enemies, they took refuge with their kinsfolk in Ulster, and vice versa. At its narrowest point the sea was only thirteen miles across, and in clear weather they could see each other's signal fires.

Glenarm Castle was a monument to one of the tamer aspects of the Macdonnells' complicated history. As the inscription on the barbican proclaimed, it had been built in 1636 by Sir Randal Macdonnell, 'with the leave of God', as he piously conceded. This Macdonnell had been a thorn in the side of Elizabeth I at the close of the sixteenth century, and had joined Hugh O'Neill in his rebellion against the English, but a few months before the Queen's death, he had adroitly changed sides, thereby securing the future of his clan. The Scottish King James who shortly afterwards ascended the throne of England wished to make Ulster an anvil on which to hammer his recalcitrant Highland subjects, and in 1603 he granted Sir Randal Macdonnell by deed patent the Route and the Glynns of Antrim, without regard to the indigenous Irish.

In time this produced an interesting mixture of population. Most of the Glensfolk were Catholics of Scottish Highland or Irish origins, but in the seventeenth century the convulsions in Scotland drove great numbers of Lowlanders across to Antrim. Presbyterians though they were, Macdonnell was happy to receive them as his tenants, to the satisfaction of his sovereign, who made him a viscount in 1618 and Earl of Antrim in 1620. The fifth earl, who succeeded to the estates in 1721, was brought up a Protestant, and by the end of the eighteenth century the Macdonnells were well and truly part of the Irish Protestant ascendancy. The sixth earl resided for most of his life in Dublin, and having three daughters and no son, he petitioned the Crown to allow the titles to go forward in the female succession. The petition was granted, and when he died in 1791, his eldest daughter Catherine succeeded as Countess of Antrim in her own right. She was not in residence in Glenarm on 7 June.[43]

From an early hour that morning, large crowds had begun to assemble on Bellair Hill behind the castle. The hill was a low eminence with gently rising green slopes between Glenarm and Glencloy, and many of the men came from Carnlough and the area 'at the back of the hill'. The rallying point was near the farm owned by the Reverend Robert Acheson, who had come to Glenarm as assistant minister to his uncle, the Reverend Thomas Reid. Acheson had been born in Clough, County Antrim, and his first ambition was to be a doctor. He had pursued a full course of medical studies at Edinburgh University, and practised for a time in Coleraine, County Derry, where he married his cousin, Elizabeth Smith, but he then decided to devote himself to the Christian ministry. He was a New Light minister whose views were sometimes at odds with the Old Light opinions of some of the local congregations and he found it difficult to become established, one reason why his uncle, who was now elderly, had taken him as assistant.

Acheson was ardently political, and it was reported that he had been seen drilling men in the fields behind Glenarm. On the Sunday before the Rebellion he preached a stirring sermon in Glenarm meeting house on the text: 'Be not afraid of them that kill the body' (Luke 12:4).[44] On Thursday morning, when the insurgents began to gather on Bellair Hill, the Glenarm Yeomanry, commanded by Captain George Stewart, and the small detachment of Tay Fencibles billeted in the village, decided upon a pre-emptive strike. They seized Acheson and two other potential leaders, William Coulter and Hugh McCoy, and occupied the castle as the best place of defence.

This strategy had not been completely thought out. The insurgents at once started to round up the wives of the local yeomen and take them as hostages to Bellair Hill. They planned to attack the castle next day and force the yeomen to surrender by placing their wives in the forefront of the action. Sixty years later, Andrew McKillop, a native of Glenarm, recalled that both his grandmothers had been taken as hostages to the insurgent camp. His maternal grandmother was set free, through the intercession of a friendly rebel, but his paternal grandmother, with her twelve-month-old baby in her arms, was detained with the rest of the women all night on the hill. The baby was McKillop's father.

During the morning some loyalists who had escaped from Larne had the bad luck to seek sanctuary in Glenarm. They, too, were made prisoners and taken in triumph to Bellair, where one Rourke told them that they would be shot 'by authority of the Republic' if Acheson and the others were not released. Rourke had come from Larne himself and he had the cartouche and musket of one of the soldiers killed there, which gave great weight to his pronouncements. He confidently asserted that he had seen Dr Casement hanged between the shafts of a cart at his own front door.[45]

Kilwaughter Castle was situated a mile or two to the west of Larne. There, one dark day at the end of November 1798, Squire Agnew sat down to write an account of his experiences on the morning of 7 June and the hours which followed. 'This account I shall put away from the eyes of man for a generation,' he wrote, 'when no man can come to any harm thereby.' And he added that in his house at Kilwaughter and that of Henry Shaw, his cousin at Ballygalley, the hunted rebels had been given shelter and many afforded a safe passage to America.[46]

The squire had been born Edward Jones, the son of Valentine Jones, a West India merchant who was a leading figure in the commercial and political life of Belfast. Valentine Jones was one of those concerned citizens who assembled in a tavern in 1752 to plan the town's Charitable Society as a shelter for the old and infirm poor. Their building still stands, probably the oldest and finest in the city, and a headstone in the Clifton Street burial ground nearby records that 'Mr Valentine Jones, of the town of Belfast, merchant, lived respected and died lamented by numerous descendants and friends.' He was ninety-four when he died in 1805, and it is said that on one occasion when he danced in a quadrille at the Assembly Rooms, the other three men were Valentine Jones, his son, Valentine Jones, his grandson, and Valentine Jones, his great-grandson.

He married, as his third wife, Eleanor Agnew, the only daughter of the 'Old Squire' of Kilwaughter, William Agnew, and Edward Jones was a son of that union. When he succeeded to the estate, Jones complied with his grandfather's will, and took the name Agnew. He was, to the day of his death in 1834, a member of the Presbyterian congregation of Larne. That he inclined to popular, and therefore, in the eyes of the government, dangerous, political views is indicated by the fact that his name on a list of County Antrim grand jurors in 1797 is marked 'disaffected'.[47] He and James Agnew Farrell were second cousins.

Early on Thursday morning one of Agnew's servants, John Hunter, told him that thousands of rebels had gathered in arms at Glenarm, and that Mr Acheson, the Presbyterian minister there, had been arrested and taken away under a strong guard of the Tay Fencibles and the yeomanry. Agnew's own sympathy with the radicals and the popularity of the old squire combined to give him a certain immunity from rebel attention, and he therefore resolved to ride over to Ballygalley Castle and consult with Henry Shaw. At Galbraith's crossroads he encountered forty or so of the insurgents, many of whom he recognised as his own tenants. They were dressed in their Sunday-best clothes. Two of them wore green tailed coats, cut in military fashion, with brass buttons and yellow facings, and nearly all of them sported green ribbons. He saw some firelocks and pistols, but most of the men were carrying burnished pikes.

Two men, whom he did not know, ported their pikes across the road and ordered him to dismount, but as he left the saddle and came to the horse's head, one said. 'You are Squire Agnew?' He replied that he was. 'You are held to be a level-headed man,' said the insurgent. 'May I ask what has you here in these troublous hours?' Agnew said his intention was to call on Squire Shaw. The two men conferred with the others and then told him to remount and pass. 'All's well in the name of the Republic.' It was nearly four o'clock in the afternoon when Agnew reached Ballygalley and found his cousin in earnest conversation with Father Devenny, the Catholic priest, and Mr Boyd of Mount Edwards.

They were all in grave mood and Agnew had hardly sat down when news arrived that the rebels had taken several loyalists from Larne to Glenarm and were threatening to shoot them on Bellair Hill if the fencibles and yeomen did not at once release Mr Acheson, along with William Coulter and Hugh McCoy of Glenarm. One of the Larne men captured was believed to be Samuel Baillie of the Larne Yeomanry. It was hastily decided that Agnew and the priest should ride over to Glenarm to see what they could do to mediate.

When they reached Glenarm, Agnew was relieved to find that the officer in command of the fencibles was 'an easy Scot', who at once agreed to parley with the rebels for an exchange of prisoners, 'and so it was that Mr Acheson and Coulter and McCoy were exchanged for the Larne men'. Agnew says that he did not catch the officer's name, but this was perhaps a tactful lapse of memory in view of what happened later. After a friendly glass of punch with this agreeable soldier, Agnew returned to the shelter of his cousin's house at Ballygalley and was allowed to pass freely by all the posts along the way. The Scots officer might have been less amenable had he foreseen that Acheson, immediately on his release, would don full regimentals and take command of the rebel host on Bellair Hill. And Agnew would have been considerably agitated had he known that Father Devenny was an informer in government pay.[48]

THE LONG AFTERNOON

The first part of McCracken's strategy went exactly according to plan. Randalstown, a little market town on the River Maine, not far from where it flows into Lough Neagh, is about five miles north-west of Antrim. It is a town with some history, the manor having been granted to Rose, Marchioness of Antrim, by Charles II in 1683 and renamed for a contemporary Randal Macdonnell. On 7 June 1798 it was garrisoned by fifty foot and twenty cavalry of the Toome Yeomanry, commanded by Captain Henry C. Ellis, who had no orders how to act if the town were attacked. On the previous evening Ellis had received reports of United Irish mobilisation in the neighbourhood and during the night he sent out a mounted patrol to reconnoitre the road north to Ballymena. The patrol was surrounded and captured.

Early on Thursday morning separate rebel forces from the direction of Ballymena, Ahoghill, Portglenone and Toome converged simultaneously on the town, following a concerted plan of attack. They carried a variety of colours. The United Irish flags were mostly green, those of the Defenders green edged with white or yellow and with a large yellow cross. Some were emblazoned with a harp without the crown, and one at least had the device 'REMEMBER ARMAGH'. Their numbers were estimated at nine thousand, but they were probably a good deal less. Ellis had drawn up his yeomanry in the main street and they began firing on the first of the rebels to reach them, but when the size of the advancing force was realised, they withdrew into the market house, secured the gates and took post in the upper storey.

The firing continued for about forty minutes, after which a

woman brought forward some burning straw and pushed it through the iron gratings. The fire was fed with more and more straw, and soon the whole building was enveloped in thick smoke and flame. The yeomen were now in immediate danger of suffocation and Ellis had no option but to surrender. As the stairs had burned through, the yeomanry had to be evacuated by ladders placed against the upper windows. Ellis and his lieutenant, Jones, were lucky to be among the first loyalists to be taken prisoner that day; there was no sign of a desire to take savage retaliation against them. Casualties had been light on both sides. The prisoners were disarmed and marched away to the insurgent camp at Groggan Island, a defensible area almost encircled by marsh. On the following morning the two officers would be sent under escort to Ballymena, which by then was being regarded as the insurgent headquarters.[49]

At Randalstown the victorious rebels now divided their force. A small party was posted to hold the town. Another party, consisting mainly of men from Duneane and Grange, was dispatched to destroy the vital bridge across the Bann at Toome, the link between east and west Ulster. The main force, assembled under the command of Samuel Orr, George Dickson, and two men named as John Magennis and Halliday, set off, as arranged, to join McCracken in the attack on Antrim.

The men from the Toome area had gone about a mile and a half in the direction of home when they were met by a messenger who told them that some cavalry from County Derry had already crossed the bridge and were heading for Randalstown. At this the insurgents left the main road and took post in the fields. The cavalry soon afterwards came in sight; they were a troop of the Salterstown Yeomanry and as soon as they became aware of the rebels they slackened pace and then wheeled about. As the troop retreated in haste, one of the rebels fired a single shot from a long fowling piece and brought down a yeoman. His frightened horse left him and galloped after its companions, and, with wild yells, the rebels rushed upon the man and began to strip him, fighting among themselves over his boots and buckskin breeches. He was a young man called Hall from Magherafelt, and he died of his wound a few days later.

The insurgents continued on their way, and reaching Toome, began their work of demolition about six o'clock in the evening. It proved to be much more difficult than they had anticipated, the solid masonry resisting all their efforts with crowbar, spade and pickaxe for fourteen hours. It was just after 8 a.m. on Friday when the central arch fell into the river with an enormous crash.[50]

On the other side of the Bann in County Derry several thousand men had gathered at Maghera, intending to march on Antrim and join McCracken. About a tenth of them had firearms; the rest were provided with pikes, pitchforks and turf spades. Elaborate plans had been made in the spring of 1798 to attack the towns of Moneymore and Magherafelt and disarm the troops there, but when the time came, there was little movement elsewhere in the county. At Kilrea, on the evening before the Rising, one of the United Irishmen joined the yeomanry and turned informer, effectively stifling any action in that area. There was what McSkimmin describes as a partial rising at Garvagh. 'The turn out was disappointing, their leaders abandoned them, and soon afterwards they dispersed.' At Maghera, too, the rebels were soon to disperse, on hearing that Brigadier-General John Knox was moving towards them with his troops from the direction of Dungannon, and that the Boveagh Yeoman Cavalry, commanded by Captain Langford Heyland, would cut off their retreat. The rebel leader William McKeiver was the first to leave the ground, and the other leaders soon followed him. That was effectively the end of the Rising in south Derry.[51]

The little town of Antrim is situated at the north-eastern corner of Lough Neagh, the largest expanse of inland water in the British Isles. It is eighteen miles from Belfast, ten from Ballymena, and almost twelve from Toome, where the stone bridge across the River Bann was the only northerly land communication with the counties of Tyrone and Derry. The mailcoach from Belfast to Derry ran through Antrim, and it commanded all the routes to the northern and western districts. The town then consisted chiefly of a single wide street, beginning at the Belfast end by what was called the Scotch Quarter and ending at the wall of Lord Massereene's residence, Antrim Castle, at the other. Here it was joined at right angles by a long narrow thoroughfare called Bow Lane, leading out into open country.

The wall still stands there and is known as the Battery Wall. By climbing the bank behind it and looking through the embrasures, one can see the main street much as it appeared to the yeomen who took up post there on that June day. Now the scene is one of heavy traffic and busy supermarkets, but the essential topography has hardly changed. The wall commanded half the length of the street, which ran parallel to the river, the Sixmilewater. Facing the castle wall, and plumb in the middle of the street, stood the market house, which today still houses the court of petty sessions and is the oldest courthouse in use in Northern Ireland. Built in 1726 by Sir Clotworthy Skeffington, fourth Viscount Massereene, as a session house for the grand jury, it was an impressive edifice of classical, almost Florentine, elegance. Access to the courtroom on the first floor was by a double flight of steps. The ground floor, with its open arches between sturdy pillars, was used as the market hall. Like the market houses of many other Ulster towns, it served in the eighteenth century as a jail, or guardhouse, where prisoners could be confined.

On the south side of the street, near the centre of the town, stood the parish church of All Saints. The church and its churchyard were on ground above the level of the street, and the surrounding wall has been an obstacle to road-widening schemes in recent times. In June 1798, however, the strategic advantage it offered was obvious. Still farther along the street, but on the other side, stood the First Antrim meeting house of the Presbyterians, firmly in the Scotch Quarter. The building, with 'its heavy creaking doors, with old-fashioned latches, its broad aisles, and still more roughly-hewn supports . . . and the high pulpit with its massive sounding-board' was erected in 1726.[52] First Antrim was a leading New Light congregation and it had been at various times the charge of a succession of intellectual ministers whose theological opinions were known far beyond the confines of the county – in Dublin, in East Anglia, the Netherlands and New England. In 1981 the church was presented to Antrim Borough Council and its congregation (now Unitarian) joined the Nonsubscribing congregation of Templepatrick.

The Antrim garrison, commanded by Major Seddon, consisted of one troop of the 22nd Dragoons, a company of the Antrim Yeomanry raised by Lord Massereene, and about forty armed civilians. A messenger brought Seddon an urgent dispatch from Nugent at about 9 a.m. on Thursday. It warned him that the town would be attacked that day and promised that reinforcements would reach him. The general alarm was heightened when it was discovered that many of the townsfolk had already left home to join the insurgents. Seddon ordered all inhabitants to remain in their houses. The street was patrolled and a search begun of the Scotch Quarter, which was notoriously disaffected. On finding some pikeheads in one of the houses, Arthur Macartney, the son of the vicar and a lieutenant of the Royal Irish Artillery, 'took a coal and put it into the thatch and immediately the house was in flames'. Neighbours tried to put the fire out but without success, and by the forenoon it had spread to several of the other houses, which were eventually destroyed. The owners dragged as much as they could of their furniture and possessions into the gardens.

By then the first of the magistrates were beginning to arrive in the town, among them James Moore and Robert Gamble, who had come from Ballymena with a yeomanry escort. All had been quiet there when they left, though they had seen armed men near Kells. Others arriving in the town had a different story to tell – that the people were everywhere in arms and concentrating in great numbers on Donegore Hill. At half past one the sentries on lookout on the high ground suddenly reported that they could see hundreds of armed men advancing along the Ballyclare and Templepatrick roads. Their glittering pikes appeared above the hedgerows as far as the eye could see.[53]

McCracken had planned his strategy with care. Four columns were to advance on the town simultaneously but from different directions. His own force, consisting of men recruited from the districts between Belfast and Antrim, was to enter the Scotch Quarter along the main road, while a second column, collected from Ballynure, Ballyclare and Doagh, was to march in by the Carrickfergus road. It was the joining up of these two columns which the lookouts had seen. A third column, from the Connor, Kells and Ballymena areas, was to enter the town by Patie's Lane, which branched north from the main street between the church and the market house. A fourth body, from Shane's Castle, Randalstown and Dunsilly, was to come in by Bow Lane at the head of the town and under Lord Massereene's wall.

Seddon had selected the wall and the market house as the strongest points to defend and he disposed his troops accordingly. To the surprise of the garrison, however, the two insurgent columns converging on the Scotch Quarter halted on the edge of the town and remained stationary there for half an hour. It was an unexpected piece of luck for Seddon, since he knew that every precious minute was bringing the relief force nearer. McCracken may have been puzzled or cautious because of the blazing houses, but it is more likely that he was making sure that the Patie's Lane force, led by the Belfast printer John Storey, was in position and ready to move in conjunction with him, for messengers were seen scurrying backwards and forwards across the fields on either side of the town. There was another matter which was causing him concern. Though Randalstown was only four miles away, there was as yet no sign of Samuel Orr's column. Eventually part of the Ballyclare division was ordered to move along the north side of the town and occupy Bow Lane.[54]

It was 2.45 p.m. before McCracken gave the order to advance.[55] The Templepatrick, Carnmoney and Roughfort Volunteers marched in to the street with some ceremony, preceded by fifes and a single drum. The musket men went first, about eighty in all, then the solitary Volunteer cannon on its makeshift carriage. Finally came the rest of the force, armed with pikes and pitchforks. According to one eyewitness, they carried several stand of colours, some green and some green and white. 'We marched into Antrim in good order,' says James Hope, 'until our front arrived opposite the Presbyterian meeting house.'[56] The advance party of musketeers were then told off into sections for firing.

While McCracken's force had been halted at the entrance to the town, Colonel Clavering's and Colonel Durham's columns had joined up a mile or two to the south. Durham had sent Smith with his light cavalry two miles in his front to reconnoitre, under strict orders not to quarrel with any of the country folk unless they were attacked. He found Clavering, approached the town and saw that it was in rebel hands, and he heard Colonel Lumley, commanding the dragoons, say that he proposed to ride on and enter the town sword in hand.[57] Lumley kept his word, and at the very moment when McCracken's men were advancing down through the Scotch Quarter he entered the town at the other end by the old Dublin road. He crossed the Massereene Bridge and wheeled his two curricle guns in to the main street. Then he opened fire at two hundred yards' range on the advancing rebels.

The street was full of thick smoke from the burning houses and the bombardiers had little chance to take aim. The canisters of grapeshot should have been devastating in the close ranks of the insurgents, but in the event they did little damage beyond casting up showers of gravel in the street. The insurgents rushed to take cover, clambering over the wall of the churchyard, which was only a few feet high at that end. A slight current of air carried the smoke towards the military, and one of the bombardiers was killed by a rebel musket ball as he was in the act of laying one of the guns again.

Lumley gave the order to cease firing and lined up eighty of his dragoons. The time had come to give these rustic would-be soldiers a taste of cavalry warfare. He ordered the yeomanry, who before his arrival had been bravely preparing to advance, to flank off to the sides of the troop and support him. Then, raising his sword, he led the charge up the street.

As the horses gathered speed James Burns fired the first round from the old Templepatrick brass six-pounder. His father had loaded it with two tins of musket balls and two and a half pounds of shot. The second time they used three pounds of shot and the gun was fired again just as the leading cavalrymen reached it, but this time the recoil lifted it clean off the carriage and it could not be used again.[58] It, too, had done little damage because it had no elevation, but the dragoons suffered heavily from the deadly rebel musket fire as they passed the churchyard wall. The rebel pikemen flanking the sides of the street then closed in, stabbing with their long weapons at the horses, while they kept out of range of the dragoons' sabres. Cornet Dunn was among the first to fall; then Lumley was slashed across the ankle and his Achilles tendon severed.

James Magee was looking out from a window directly opposite the point where the soldiers and rebels came into contact. He watched horses going down and some running riderless with their entrails exposed. He saw the quartermaster, whose name he learned later was Simpson, engage a tall rebel who had been helping to work the cannon, one William Kelly. The soldier reined his horse towards the man and at every opportunity aimed cuts at him which the other dexterously parried. Unable to keep his ground, Kelly retreated, stabbing his pike viciously at the horse until it sank to its knees. Simpson dismounted and then, finding himself instantly surrounded, he handed over his sword in hopes of mercy. Kelly took the sword and brought it down across the quartermaster's face, cutting off his nose and most of his cheek. Shocked by this act, Henry Campbell, one of the insurgent leaders, tied his handkerchief over Simpson's face and carried him into a lane. His nose was hanging down over his mouth. He kept saying that he had left a wife and seven children that morning in Lisburn, and very soon afterwards he died. On his way back up the lane Campbell was shot in the back. He was carried into a pig house where he lay until Saturday, and was then barbarously put to death by the yeomen who found him.[59]

Lumley's dragoons had been raked by gunfire from the houses on either side as they passed along the street. Now they were hopelessly entangled in a mass of pikemen in the Scotch Quarter. Swords were of little use when ten or twelve pikes were thrust at a single horse or rider, and it was soon clear that only a swift retreat would save them from annihilation. By now, however, James Hope's men from Templepatrick had occupied the churchyard and the cavalry again came under fire, and suffered further loss as they passed back along the street.

The military were not unmindful of the fact that they might be attacked in the rear and surrounded while they were engaged with the main body of rebels in the street. That was indeed precisely McCracken's plan. Before the charge, Lieutenant Lawrence Neville of the Royal Artillery had positioned his two curricle guns well beyond the market house at a point almost opposite the end of the Massereene Bridge, and flanked by the yeomanry and Lumley's dragoons. When the main body of the retreating cavalry wheeled left on to the bridge, the yeomanry were withdrawn past the market house to the shelter of the castle wall, which had a bastion at either end.

The two field guns had been pulled back to the castle wall, but two of the artillerymen had been killed, and it was now decided to abandon them. The rebels in the street rushed forward with wild cheers to seize the cannon, but every one of the party is said to have been killed by fire from the garden, and no further attempt was made. At this, a woman of herculean frame, Peggy Gordon, a well-known character in the town, walked into the street and seized the bridles of the gun horses. Then she yoked them to the ammunition tumbrils and drew them under the cover of the garden wall before securing the guns and, with the help of the one artilleryman still at his post, dragging them alongside the carts. Not a shot was fired at her during this time, and there was hardly an insurgent in sight. Encouraged, twenty volunteers from the Antrim Yeomanry made a sally from the castle gate, led by Dr George Macartney's two sons, Arthur and John, one of the corps' officers. The guns were recovered and at once planted on the castle wall, from where they began to fire round-shot at the insurgents in the street and in Bow Lane.

There now occurred an incident which was afterwards universally lamented. The meeting of the magistrates at Antrim that day had been summoned by Lord O'Neill of Shane's Castle, the governor of the county. As the Hon. John O'Neill, he had been a very popular champion of the independent interest and was well regarded by most of the Presbyterians. On Wednesday he had been in Dublin and had hastened home, passing through Lisburn without stopping, so that he had not received the warning which Nugent had expressly left for him. Accounts of how he came to be at the market house in the thick of the action vary to a surprising degree. One says that he came out of the market house on foot, another that he arrived in the town in a curricle with Lieutenant Jackson, his nephew, but most agree that he was on horseback and supporting the royal forces.

At some point after the retreat of the cavalry Lord O'Neill and Dr Macartney found themselves trapped near the market house. O'Neill was having great difficulty with his horse, which was very restive and refusing to go forward. Macartney stayed with him as long as he dared, and then, when they were completely surrounded by the insurgents, he put spurs to his own horse and galloped through them. He was unable to overtake the dragoons, but he managed to join Mr Staples, one of the MPs for Antrim, on the lough shore. The two men found a boat and rowed right across to the Tyrone side, where they were able to report to General Knox and give him an account of events in Antrim.

O'Neill was left in the street to fend for himself. While he was attempting to urge his horse forward, 'a man in a grey frieze coat' thrust a pike into his side. Some accounts say he shot the man with his pistol, and the assailant was fired on also by yeomen on the wall. O'Neill was only yards from the castle gate and might have saved himself if he had not bravely turned to face his attackers. When they fell back, he was carried into the gardens, but it was soon clear that his wounds were very serious.[60]

Confusion now began to overtake the closely packed ranks of the two rebel columns approaching the town from the north through Patie's Lane and Bow Lane. John Storey and his men in Patie's Lane had been on the point of entering the street when the main insurgent force came under attack from the military, and the fieldpieces on both sides had been fired. The men therefore hesitated, and despite all Storey's entreaties, they refused to leave the safety of the lane. The confusion was compounded when one company of the insurgents in Bow Lane was told off to go to the support of Patie's Lane. There was consequently a great deal of coming and going across the fields between the two lanes.

The Bow Lane men then mistook the bugles of the retreating cavalry for the signal of a new charge, their apprehension increased by the fact that some stragglers of the dragoons and riderless horses had taken shelter in the entrance to the lane. At length these men recovered their nerve and counterattacked, only to be met by a hail of fire from loyalists on the top of the wall, and from the yeomanry, who were in the act of retreating into the castle gardens. So many of the insurgents were killed or wounded that the remainder fell back into the lane, and some kept on running and headed for the open country beyond.

The failure to dislodge the loyalists from the estate grounds was now beginning to sow doubt and indecision in the insurgent ranks. McCracken had chosen the churchyard as his battle station and from there he was attempting to direct operations. The more determined of the Bow Lane contingent were regrouping for a new assault. This time they moved along the back of some ruined properties and re-entered the street farther up, where they had cover from the market house and other buildings and the advantage of covering fire from Hope's sharpshooters in the churchyard. McCracken left Hope in command at the church and went forward to rally his scattered forces. Much depended on the effectiveness of Orr's column which was at last discerned approaching; but the main part of that force now appeared to have halted, and its officers – Orr, Dickson, Halliday and Magennis – were arguing bitterly over tactics. Eventually they convinced themselves that their allies had been defeated and that the town was in loyalist hands. Fearing moreover that they were themselves just about to be attacked by the cavalry, the whole column began to break up.

The scene was witnessed by McCracken, and it was a staggering setback. The panic was spreading to those around him, and he alternately cajoled and berated them, urging them to attack, but 'fair words or threats were equally disregarded'. He seized a pike and threatened to cut down the first one who offered to run away. This only heightened the panic, and when he himself ran forward towards the enemy, two of his lieutenants shamefacedly tripped him with their pikeshafts. John McGivern, an Antrim man who had left the town early that morning to assist in the attack, now volunteered to lead a party against the yeomen. Fifty-three of the insurgents who had muskets came forward and were just about to advance when news came that the army had reached the head of the town.

In retrospect it seems strange that McCracken should have devoted so little thought to the contingency that the army might be close on his heels. No roadblocks or vedettes had been posted on the approach roads to Antrim to give him advance warning. One must allow for his military inexperience and the fact that he did not know how extensively his plans had been betrayed to Nugent by Mageean and the defecting United Irish colonels. He had expected Antrim to fall at once to overwhelming numbers of United Irishmen. Moreover, he believed, justifiably as it turned out, that almost the whole county was by then in insurgent hands. Nugent's decision to send columns from Belfast and Blaris was, after all, a gamble and might have led to a major military disaster, as had happened days earlier in the south of Ireland. Above all, McCracken was under the impression that County Down would have risen also. The fact that it did not gave Nugent a breathing space.

Colonel Durham was still a mile or so from Antrim when he received Major Smith's report of Lumley's ill-fated charge. The rebels were in possession of the town, Smith told him, and had two pieces of field artillery. Durham decided his tactics there and then: he must plan for a siege. He called up Captain Colston of the artillery and told him, 'Captain, I will treat Antrim with respect. I will besiege it. March on. I will choose a commanding position for your two guns.' On arriving at the outskirts of Antrim, therefore, he chose 'a very favourable situation in a grass field on the left of the road commanding the great street of the town', and ordered a bombardment. He instructed Colston 'to fire two or three shots at the crowd of people assembled in the churchyard', a few were killed, 'and the rest dispersed and there seemed to be crowds of men flying out of the town in all directions'.[61]

Durham continued to cannonade the town for half an hour, by which time the main body of insurgents had abandoned it. During the interval Clavering arrived with the Light Brigade from Blaris, and halted on the Dublin road. There was now every possibility that the loyalists in the town would come under fire from the army, a situation averted by the presence of mind of Ezekiel Vance, one of the yeomen defending the wall of the Massereene estate. Vance was a saddler and an Antrim man born and bred. His parents were Quakers, but when he grew up he joined the small congregation of Methodists, established in Antrim after John Wesley's three visits to the town between 1785 and 1789. He lived in the Market Square, and like most of the Methodists he was a loyalist, a 'King and Country' man. On 7 June, therefore, he was in the ranks of the yeomanry. The streets were still filled with thick smoke when the yeomen began to come under heavy fire from the rebels surging along Bow Lane. Vance knew that the main force of the military were now coming into position outside the town, but it seemed likely that they were assuming that the loyalists had been overwhelmed, and they were being very cautious. It occurred to him that some kind of signal might be made to them from the top of the castle, so he stood up and ran towards the building, snatching as he ran a red cloak from the shoulders of a young woman called Abigail O'Neill, who was very angry.

Vance rushed into the hall of the castle. A badly wounded man lay on the floor, desperately pleading for help. Vance hesitated, and for a few moments he kneeled by the man, trying to bind up his wound with a pocket handkerchief. Then he made his way on to the roof, and with the aid of a staff waved the red cloak back and forward as a signal to the army, which he could plainly see on the rising ground opposite. The signal was at once acknowledged. Vance came down again and passed through the hall, observing that the wounded man was now un- conscious or dead. The river was very low because of the hot dry weather, and, on an impulse, he turned and dashed across it, still bearing aloft his red flag, to meet the army and guide them into the town.[62]

James Hope and his men held on to the churchyard to the very end, earning for themselves the title of the 'Spartan Band'. They were now isolated in the centre of the town, and as Clavering's troops entered the main street Hope led his men in a daring feint attack, swinging round suddenly in the confusion created, to withdraw from the town through Patie's Lane on the opposite side of the street. Hope was a courageous and re- sourceful commander, and he managed to rejoin McCracken after the battle.

As the main body of the troops advanced down the street Durham sent files of the Monaghans along the backs of the

houses in the Scotch Quarter to cut off the fugitives. 'The
Monaghan Militia killed many of them,' Durham recalled, and
he admits that the soldiers were soon completely out of hand.
'When out of my sight they killed every man they could get at.
My order of cease firing was not obeyed, nor could I carry it
into effect although riding among them and with my sword
throwing up their firelocks.' He then went down the main
street 'and here I found some men of the 22nd Dragoons lying
dead, and a four-pounder field piece standing in the middle of
the street.' When he reached the market house (which he called
the town hall),

> a great many magistrates ran up to my horse and laid hold of my
> hands and clothes, giving themselves up and begging protection.
> They had been taken prisoner by the rebels and kept in a public
> house. On hearing my cannon fire one man ran out to know
> where the fire came from, another ran out, they all went out,
> none returned. They then came to me.

One of the prisoners was a Lieutenant-Colonel Jackson 'in the
uniform of his Regiment of the Line'. Jackson told him that he
had come into town with Lord O'Neill, 'in Lord O'Neal's
curricle', and that some men had rushed O'Neill and run two
pikes into his body.

Learning that O'Neill had been carried into Lord Massereene's
house, Durham went at once to see him. O'Neill told him that
he had been dressed only by a country apothecary. 'Having two
experienced Army surgeons and Mr Fuller, an eminent surgeon
of Belfast and surgeon to the Belfast Yeoman Cavalry, I sent
them to dress him. On their coming out they told me he could
not live, as the pike had pierced the stomach.' Lord Massereene's
house was full of wounded officers and soldiers, and the greatest
attention was paid to them by Lady Massereene, 'who, I believe,
had been a barmaid at the Inn at Billericay in Essex'.[63]

This startling observation had more than a little foundation
of truth. Lord Massereene's command of the yeomanry during
the action was undistinguished. His most memorable order,

issued several days later, was to shoot twenty-two men who had not made any demonstration on the side of loyalty, a course of action he was dissuaded from by Ezekiel Vance. It was generally accepted that his lordship was slightly insane, the result not only of a fall on his head when he was a child, but of the nineteen years he had spent as a prisoner for debt in the jails of Paris. He married as his first wife the jailor's daughter, Anne-Marie Barcier, who organised two unsuccessful escape attempts on his behalf, before persuading the revolutionary mob to free him from La Force on the same day that the Bastille was stormed in 1789. She returned to Antrim with him, but the couple soon moved to London, where Massereene took up with Mrs Blackburn, née Elizabeth Lane, 'a menial servant in a house immediately opposite his lodgings' who 'possessed a peculiar dexterity of twirling her mop', and twirled it at him when he appeared naked at his window, as he often did. Soon she 'joined the noble peer in adultery', and he installed her at Antrim Castle as the Countess of Antrim. He married her in 1802, two years after his French wife died, at the age of thirty-eight.[64]

Durham went back into the town again and was surprised to learn that Seddon had mounted his half troop of the 22nd Dragoons and galloped out of town with them, leaving Mrs Seddon and her maid still 'hid in a hay-loft', where Durham found them. By now the troops were very noisy and restless, so Durham thought it prudent to order Clavering to march them all off round the lough to Shane's Castle, and take possession of the house, stables and private theatre. In happier days, Lord O'Neill had built the theatre for his wife, who greatly admired the acting of Sarah Siddons. Mrs Siddons was persuaded to give a performance there, and was enchanted by the setting.

Now the chief attraction of Shane's Castle was that it could offer accommodation to two hundred battle-weary soldiers, spread out on the benches and in the boxes of the theatre. The master of the house lay dying at Massereene Castle, struck down, some thought, by his own tenants. Against all expectations, John O'Neill lived until 18 June.

For Colonel Durham it had been a very long day. He went to sleep in the largest bed in Shane's Castle, along with 'Captain McKinnon, who was blown up at the Siege of Badajos, under the command of the Duke of Wellington, and Captain Peacock of the Guards, now Lt General Sir George Peacock'.[65]

Some of the inhabitants of Antrim who had not fled their homes were remarkably little disturbed. A woman named Shaw lived with her daughter in a house at the top of Bow Lane, directly in the line of fire of the yeomen on the castle wall. They came to no harm, though the house was riddled with bullets, and when they were asked afterwards how they had spent the day, they replied: 'At ten o'clock in the morning we heard that there was going to be a battle, and feeling that we might be killed at any moment, we were so terrified that we just went to our bedside, knelt down, and never rose again until ten o'clock at night, when all was over.' Another woman and her daughter had occasion to go out of town in the morning on some business. They returned to Antrim just as the situation was becoming serious. Oblivious to what was going on, they set about preparing their dinner, and later went about various household tasks, notwithstanding the fact that a battle was raging within twenty yards of them. They did not even trouble to look outside their door, but 'minded their business' until all was over.[66]

The inhabitants of the Scotch Quarter were not so fortunate. The scenes which followed the entry of the Monaghan Militia into the town were vividly recalled by James Keen, who later wrote an account of his experiences. After the rebel retreat, bewildered people began to come into the street, or attempted to flee through the gardens at the back of the houses. Some were loyalists, who ran out to welcome the soldiers; others just wanted to get out of the town and away from the fighting. A loyalist called William Eccles ran out to greet the troops, waving his arms in the air. He was instantly shot dead.[67] Keen's married sister wanted to go to their cousins at Boghead, and after vainly trying to dissuade her, her husband and brother decided to go with her. When they got to the foot of the gardens, they could see that a large part of the army was still on the hill, and Keen, alarmed, ran back towards his father's house. There he met his mother and several of her neighbours leaving their houses. He persuaded his mother to go back, and then he and his father went into the garden and sat down by the summerhouse (they may have thought this safer than being found in the house). Twenty minutes later three militiamen burst into the garden.

> One of them came forward in front of the summer house and presented to shoot me. My father aged 77 stepped forward to beg my life. I crouched behind him, those from behind fired and I fell having received a ball through my thigh and through the breast of my coat, while the man in front pressed the muzzle of the piece against [my father's] arm, the contents of which left his arm hanging to a small piece of flesh nearly severed from his body. He died in five days of a mortification. I could not help taking notice of the interposing providence of God upon my behalf, that he did not end my life as was the custom but left me. I remained there for some time. These men shot several others before they left the place. At last my mother assisted me to the house of a yeoman (Wm. McIlroy's) having before assisted my father to his brother's.[68]

Later, orders were given to search the Scotch Quarter for United Irishmen. The intervention of a Quaker, Thomas Chapman, on behalf of his parents, seems to have prevented the razing to the ground of all the dwellings, but they were thoroughly sacked. 'Houses were then entered, doors were smashed, meal and other food thrown into the street, beds ripped up, and their contents thrown through the windows.'[69] That evening the local yeomen, continuing their eager search for the disaffected, came to the house of James Keen's uncle, Alexander Keen, whose loyalty was above suspicion. Ben McCashen, an overbearing man, and possibly by now the worse for drink, said to Alexander Keen, 'Look at that old rogue how he is bleeding to death! Mr Keen you deserve to be punished for admitting such people into your house.' 'I'd have you to mind what you do,' replied Keen, 'for I am as loyal a man as you are.' McCashen had a mallet in his hand and he lunged forward to hit Keen with it but was restrained by his companion, Charles McAlister. There were unfortunately others sheltering in the house. A man called Moore, who, during the fighting, had assisted in putting out the fire in the Scotch Quarter, put his head out when Keen was threatened and was instantly spotted by McCashen. He was dragged out into the street and shot. All this while Alexander McNeeley was hiding at the fireside, shielded from view by his wife, Mr Keen's housekeeper, and Molly Eccles, a neighbour. The women 'stood before and shaded him, else he also would have fallen a victim'.

James Keen remained overnight at McIlroy's. Late that evening one Thomas McCartney and a party of yeomanry came in 'on the search'. McCartney asked, 'Have you anyone in the house except your own family?' 'Yes', said McIlroy, 'James Keen is lying there.' At this a yeoman, Bill Young, said, 'If it be he I will soon know him.' They then brought a lighted candle and McCartney drew his sword. Young came forward and identified Keen, saying that he was 'as quiet and well behaved a boy as any in town'. McCartney then asked him how he came to be wounded, and when Keen told him the circumstances 'he was very civil'.

When James Keen had run home to warn his parents, his young sister and her husband had gone on through the fields to the end of the town where they thought it prudent to lie low for a while. As soon as they were sure that all the army had entered the town they made for the open country, but almost at once a party of soldiers caught up with them.

> My sister threw herself upon her husband while eleven bullet holes were in her petticoats and one through her leg. They caught her by the hair and dragged her from him, and then they shot him through the head. An officer saved her from the soldiers and asked her if the dead man was her brother or her

husband. 'Have you any place you can go to for safety?' he asked
her. 'Yes I have, but the soldiers will kill me.' 'No, do you go,
and I will take care they shall not harm you.'[70]

In concentrating all their attention on the strategic importance
of Antrim both the rebels and the army had overlooked the importance of Ballymena, just ten miles farther north. Ballymena,
the 'middle town', was flanked on the east by a number of
districts with a strong Volunteer tradition, and there was an unexpectedly high turn out of insurgent levies, who were able to
occupy the town and, over the next two days, establish a crude
form of republican government, through a Committee of
Public Safety on the French model.

The Reverend Robert Magill, champion of orthodox views in the Presbyterian Synod and author of *The Thinking Few*, never forgot the sunny 7 June in Broughshane when he was ten years old, because that day the schoolmaster, Mr Alexander, gave his pupils a half holiday. Robert rushed home, and, as his mother was placing his midday meal on the table, he saw John Davis begin beating a drum just across the street. He ran out and asked him what the drum meant. 'You'll know soon enough,' said Davis. A few minutes later Sarah Young and her sister, and some other women, came running into the house, exclaiming hysterically that armed men from Crebilly were marching down to the town with French horns and other musical instruments.

Robert was too young to understand what it was all about, but he sensed the fear of the adults at once. 'The impression made upon my mind by the tears and trembling of the females was very powerful,' he recalled. 'I saw there was something dreadful at hand.' With the attention of the elders distracted, he got together his brother Neill, who was seven, his sister, who was five, and the baby, Nancy, who was only two. Then, hoisting Nancy on his back, he set off with the other two children along the Bucky Brae towards Kenbilly where his aunt and uncle lived. Crossing the river at the wooden bridge, he saw for the first time the armed Crebilly men entering Tullymore by the bridge of Broughshane. The children sat down among the dog roses and watched the pikes and guns glittering in the sunlight as the insurgents formed up in the fields and began to march off in the direction of Ballymena.

When the youngsters reached Kenbilly it was to find their aunt and uncle in tears, for they were loyalists. Hours passed before their mother arrived, distraught for her lost children. She had not seen them leaving home, and it had not occurred to Robert to take any grown-up into his confidence. Meanwhile 'Stringer' Murphy had been spreading alarm through the village by reporting that hundreds of people had been killed in Ballymena.[71]

Ballymena consisted then of four streets radiating from the old market house, along with the Shambles (located in what is now Linenhall Street). The total population of the town was less than a thousand. Early on Thursday morning all but six men of the detachment of yeomanry quartered in the town left to escort two of their officers, who were magistrates, to the meeting in Antrim. The town was thus stripped of military protection at a time when everyone knew that half the population were busy preparing pikes and flintlocks.[72]

During the morning the rumour began to spread that the whole country was up in rebellion. It gained force at noon, when some yeomen rode in with two prisoners they had arrested near Portglenone in the very act of calling the country people to arms. At two o'clock another breathless messenger arrived, to report that the insurgents were advancing on the town along the Broughshane road. (These included the Crebilly men whom young Robert Magill had seen.)

The Reverend William McCleverty, an Episcopalian clergyman who was a magistrate but had not gone to Antrim, immediately took four of the yeomen and rode out to reconnoitre. They soon saw a dense column of men about a mile away and advancing towards them along the road. As soon as they caught sight of the yeomen, the rebels yelled and opened fire on them, whereupon McCleverty's horse took fright and threw him. The yeomen wheeled at once and galloped hell-for-leather back to Ballymena, leaving the cleric to his fate. He was badly winded and apparently injured, and before he could get to his feet the leading insurgents were upon him. He was kicked and beaten, then dragged and carried with them towards the town.

About an hour before McCleverty had set out, the loyal citizens of Ballymena who had volunteered to defend the town had been summoned to the market house. They assembled bravely enough at first, but the news of McCleverty's capture and uncertain fate demoralised them. The small band began mysteriously to dwindle. Of the handful who were left, two were loyal Catholic citizens, Patrick McAleese and Brian O'Rawe, and four or five were yeomen. These men now secured the gateway and arches of the market house and took up their positions in the upper storey, which was reached by a stone stair projecting on Mill Street from the north-east corner of the building. Twelve steps up from the ground, the stair turned at a right angle under the roof, the outer projection being surmounted by a high spiked iron railing. The building had little other claim to strength or security as a place of defence.

The loyalists had barely time to take station at the market house windows when the first of the United host entered the head of the town at Church Street, to the raucous sound of conch shells and tin trumpets. The front ranks consisted mostly of men from the Braid, an area which had been renowned for the number and smartness of its Volunteer corps, and every one of the Braid men carried a musket. Of those who trailed along behind, some carried old unserviceable guns lacking ramrods, and most of the rest carried long pikes. Many had armed themselves with any weapon they could lay hands on – pitchforks, turf spades, scythes, old army bayonets and swords, reaping hooks, and sharpened spindles and harrow pins attached to poles. About 150 had no weapons at all.

For the handful of intrepid loyalists in the market house, it was a terrifying sight. As the rebels surged into the main street they filled it from side to side, and the loyalists contemplated an immediate surrender. However, the lead in their councils had been taken by a schoolmaster from Broughshane, a very brave and intelligent loyalist called Robert Davison. Davison swore that he would never surrender to such a rabble, and he was just explaining that within solid stone walls and with a plentiful supply of ammunition they had nothing to fear, when he was interrupted by the first volley of musket fire from the street. Most of the shot passed at an angle through the windows and lodged harmlessly in the ceiling. The loyalists at once fired back, doing as little damage, but causing utter panic among the attackers who were pressing round the building. Those in front dropped their weapons and fell over others in their anxiety to get away, and within a minute there was a scene of total confusion, under cover of which some men slipped away, and leaving the town, headed by lanes and backways for home. But the majority soon recovered their nerve and took stock of the situation. They had the market house surrounded and they now knew that the loyalists were few in number. The United men were very angry and had a score to settle.

At this precise moment the magistrates' yeomanry escort, which had been returning at a leisurely pace from Antrim, cantered over the Harryville Bridge at the other end of Bridge Street. Astonishingly, they had not the slightest suspicion that the rebellion had broken out or that the town had been occupied. As they crossed the bridge, however, they saw at once that the streets were crammed with people and that some kind of commotion was going on at the head of the town. The yeomen were commanded by a young and inexperienced lieutenant called Hugh McCambridge, who after a fatal moment of indecision led his cavalrymen forward into Bridge Street. No sign of opposition was offered to them until they were completely surrounded; then a yell of triumph went up and a forest of pikes was levelled at them as they were called on to surrender or be massacred. McCambridge gave up his sword at once and was taken a prisoner to a nearby alehouse. His men were immediately disarmed and thrust into the black hole, a small unventilated dungeon on the ground floor of the market house, where the loyalists were powerless to reach them.

Elated by this success, the insurgents renewed their onslaught on the upper storeys of the building, bringing into action the

guns taken from the yeomen. At first they directed a desultory
fire from the corners of the adjoining streets, but finding this not
effective, they then occupied the houses along the north side of
Mill Street, from the windows of which they were able to direct
a more accurate fire. Davison's men were now beginning to
discover some of the drawbacks of the position they had taken
up – the insurgents kept well out of their line of fire and to
depress their muskets sufficiently to get at the men immediately
below meant exposing themselves to the fire from the windows
opposite in Mill Street. Nevertheless, they succeeded in picking
off three of the enemy and were confident that they could hold
on until military help arrived, as it surely must.

Davison was a shrewd and resourceful commander, if an
inexperienced one. Realising that his ammunition would run
out if the attack were sustained, he prised nails from the ceiling
and beams, and filled his blunderbuss, reserving his bullets for
a more determined assault. To the same end, he cut all the
buttons off his coat.

The hot, still afternoon was wearing on, and there seemed no
prospect of taking the market house. Then James Brown, one
of the insurgent leaders, who was dressed in the uniform of a
Volunteer captain, and who that morning had led a company of
insurgents from Broughshane, was heard calling for sledgehammers to smash open the lower gates. 'Get tar barrels,' he
cried. 'Try it with fire.' One McIlhatton got a tar barrel from
the premises of a dealer in Mill Street. The iron gates of the
ground-floor arches were burst in with the sledges and a
fusillade of shots fired up at the loyalists through the intervening
floor.

The memories of Ballymena people in the nineteenth century, the main source for these facts, preserved the details with
great particularity. A man called Cunningham, from the neighbourhood of 'Craigbilly' (Crebilly) was shot dead at the front
door of the premises 'now occupied by the Misses Smyth in
Bridge Street' and carried into the house of a man named
Wilson 'and now occupied by Mr Aaron Rea'. Wilson's house

was next door to the inn, which the United leaders had made their headquarters. The absent landlord, Frank Dixon, was with the loyalists in the market house.

The street cleared, but the tar barrel was brought up under cover and set alight. The problem now was to get a volunteer or volunteers to roll it into the building. Recruits for the 'forlorn hope' were not forthcoming.[73] At some point during the eventful morning an innocent stranger had wandered in to the town on his way from Belfast to his home in the Glynns (the Glens of Antrim). He was carrying a large basket of flax. The stranger was in no way connected with the Rebellion, but the insurgents made him a prisoner and offered him a pike and his liberty if he would join them in the attack on the market house.

He prudently accepted the terms and at this point in the afternoon he was sitting disconsolately on his basket, with the pike lying on the ground beside him. One of the rebels was trying to cheer him up with liberal swigs of whiskey from a jug, and the spirit was beginning to have its effect. Meanwhile Brown was working himself into a fine frenzy of vicarious bravery. 'Are you all cowards?' he yelled. 'Will no-one carry over the barrel before it is burned out?' At this the Glensman suddenly stood up, and seizing the blazing cask, ran forward with it, to the admiring cheers of the crowd. Coolly he placed it below the windows. Then he ran back, picked up his basket and legged it out of town. No one tried to stop him. He had earned his freedom.

The heartened insurgents renewed their attack, heaping straw on the blazing barrel and firing continuously at the upper windows. The flames roared up as the ceiling and the arches caught fire. It was a repetition of the scene at Randalstown; the position of the loyalists was suddenly hopeless. They must surrender or be burned alive. All except Davison agreed to instant surrender. After a few shouted words from the windows, a parley was arranged and they agreed to march out and lay down their arms. The insurgents promised that they might return to their homes. One by one the little garrison filed out and began to descend the stone steps. It was an uneasy moment and when the crowd suddenly surged forward, someone fired two shots either deliberately or by accident. Davison, who was standing at the top of the steps, immediately fired on the culprit, hitting him in the knee.

The men exposed on the staircase desperately tried to regain the shelter of the building, but they were hopelessly vulnerable. Three of them were shot dead – James Raphael, John Logan and a man called Carson. Frank Dixon was wounded by a shot which passed through his forearm and came out at his elbow. It is said that Raphael was killed by a bullet fired from the window of his own house. It entered his body on the left side, a little below the heart, and came out near the spine. His body was taken to his brother's house at Galgorm and buried at Ahoghill on the following day. And it was duly recorded that forty-seven guineas were discovered in his coat pockets.

With quick thinking, four of the garrison who had not yet emerged tried, under cover of the confusion, to make their escape from the back of the building. Rushing past the flames and smoke, they succeeded in dropping down from a back window into the stable yard of the hotel. One who escaped in this way was the town's postmaster, John Laird. He crossed the hotel yard and, forcing his way through another small window, got into Wilson's house. Upstairs he found a little group of loyalist fugitives – a symptom of the confusion which reigned – including 'Mr Brabstone O'Hara of Claggin'. Soon afterwards the house was more thoroughly searched. O'Hara managed to hide, and later, during the night, made his way safely out of the town, but Laird and the others were taken, and lodged in the black hole.

Of the other three who got out of the market house in the same way, one was captured almost at once in Bridge Street. The remaining two, both of them yeomen, were fortunate in meeting the hotel's landlord, Jack Best. Best was an eccentric but good-natured man whose sympathies lay entirely with the United Irishmen, but he agreed to hide the yeomen, whom he knew, in his stable loft, and later, when it was about to be searched, he moved them to a cellar. They succeeded in getting out of the town in the early hours of the morning.

With the last exchange between Davison and the insurgents, the siege of the market house ended. The rest of the loyalists gave themselves up and were pushed in to the dungeon, but surprisingly without further violence. The dauntless school-master refused to surrender, but he was overpowered and disarmed, and dragged to the black hole with savage cries of exultation. The crowd was now wild with delight and strong drink. 'Ballymena's our own!' they yelled. 'Hurrah for the United Irishmen.' Parties of the rebels marched up and down the streets, preceded by horn-blowers, in a kind of ritual celebration. The news quickly spread to surrounding areas.

Towards eight o'clock in the evening one of the rebel colonels, an attorney from Crumlin named James Dickey, rode into Ballymena at the head of his men, mostly from Randalstown but with some recruits picked up in Ahoghill. He was wearing a green jacket and a horseman's helmet and carrying a sabre and pistols. Dickey was an astute man but not one to be trifled with, for he was unbalanced, as succeeding hours would show. He had played a prominent role in the action at Randalstown and somehow extricated himself from the fiasco in Bow Lane at Antrim; he now proposed to take command of the Army of the Republic in Ballymena. His first actions were directed at imposing some kind of military and political order, in view of the volatile atmosphere prevailing in the town.[74]

At about the same time, several members of the provincial directory arrived, their initial prudence overcome by the success of the afternoon's operations in Ballymena. A Committee of Public Safety was set up and Dixon's inn was chosen for its headquarters. At this distance it is not easy to identify all its members, but they were persons of some standing in the local community. They included Dr John Patrick, an obstetrician from Cairncastle who was known to have attended some of the insurgent wounded; Robert Swan of Mount Pleasant,

Ballymena, a farmer and linen merchant; and James Bones, a linen bleacher from Ballygarvey. The brothers James and Samuel Bones were active United Irishmen and had been in the first contingent to march into Ballymena that morning.[75]

A certain ambiguity attaches to the committee's composition. Before setting out for Ballymena the insurgents from Broughshane had made a diversion to Whitehall in search of its owner, Captain James White. White was a magistrate and on the morning of 7 June he had left for the meeting at Antrim, but seeing parties of armed men on the roads, he had turned back. When the insurgents came to his residence, he seems to have been wounded and they warned him 'that he should receive the first fire from any that should oppose them'.[76] He agreed to accompany them 'very reluctantly' and in some sense as a leader – like other magistrates, he was probably trying to exert some kind of influence over them. The rebels were soon to acquire another wounded magistrate in the person of McCleverty: it would seem that both men were co-opted to the ruling junta, and they may later have tried to act as mediators.

The statement which Robert Swan subsequently made, in order to save his neck, is confused and contradictory, and the truth can be discerned only mistily through his efforts at self-exoneration. He begins by declaring that he did not leave his farm until 4 p.m. on 7 June, and knew nothing about the Rising until the evening, when he went into Ballymena with Robert Curry 'to get some smith work done'. On arrival there he was immediately ordered by Mr McCleverty, with several others, into the courthouse, which contained the garrison under arms. Later, when they heard that McCleverty had been killed, and that the insurgents were approaching the town in great numbers, the commanding officer and the garrison decided to surrender. Despite Swan's insistence that he was on his farm for most of the day, this is clearly an account of events in the town during the morning, when many of the loyal citizens did assemble for defence, but then agreed that it might be more prudent to become temporary republicans.

Swan's deposition goes on:

> The prisoners became much alarmed [here some words are
> crossed out] and in order to prevent as far as possible outrages
> being committed, Francis Dixon, James Bones and he [Swan]
> were required to go and [meet?] the rebels, which they instantly
> did, at the entrance of the town. In front were Mr McCleverty
> and Captain White, the former very severely wounded, with
> great danger of being destroyed.

There follows an account of the attack on the market house.
Had it not been for the folly of one unfortunate man, no
blood would have been shed. This man had fired upon them as
they approached the market house to take the surrender, and
wounded Dixon and Bones.

> The insurgents immediately set fire to it, and would have
> destroyed it, with part of the town, had not Robert Swan used
> his exertions to prevent it, a number of men having got a tar
> barrel upon forks, holding it to the tinder which caught fire, and
> the prisoners calling for mercy.

Swan's association of Frank Dixon with Bones and himself is
confusing. Dixon was indeed wounded, but by the insurgents,
not the loyalists in whose ranks he was. It may be that both
Swan and Bones wished to give the impression that they had
acted with Dixon to save the town, and it is possible that Dixon
was recruited to the committee sitting in his inn.

Swan goes on to say that he saw no person exerting any
authority, which was the explanation of what happened next.

> The rebels, immediately after securing the prisoners, were
> proceeding to wreck and destroy the town, when several
> respectable persons stepped forward in order to stop their fury,
> and endeavour to save the place from destruction. R[obert]
> S[wan] was asked by a number of persons, not one of whom he
> knew, why he did not attend. His reply was that he knew
> nothing of the business, and had neither inclination nor abilities
> for such. On making this reply he was threatened with pointed
> bayonets if he continued to refuse. On going to the place

appointed, he was insisted upon to allow his name to be used [as] a means of preserving the Town. Conscious of his innocence in promoting the disturbances, and wishing to assist in preventing bloodshed and the destruction of property, he consented, and continued to assist during that day and on the 8th.[77]

Adam Dickey of Cullybackey, who knew Dr Patrick well (he was the *accoucheur* who had attended his mother at his birth), described him as 'a very peaceful and timid man, honest and truthful, and deservedly trusted', and one of the Committee of Public Safety which sat in Ballymena 'and professed to give all the orders which James Dickey, their General, foolishly executed, like a zealous, impulsive man as he was'. Dr Patrick had never been an officer of the United Irishmen, and he took care to cultivate friends on the opposite side. He took McCleverty into his house, 'who was made a prisoner and slightly wounded in the head, of which he [McCleverty] made the most'.[78]

Some people on the loyalist side were later disposed to be suspicious of the magistrates' complicity. McCleverty and White were probably the persons who were the subject of dark references in letters to Lord Charlemont from the Reverend Edward Hudson, a magistrate originally from Armagh who was proud of the fact that he had kept Portglenone and the surrounding district quiet with the help of the local yeomanry:

> That they [the rebels] had leaders of a higher description than those that appeared, I well know. Whether or no these approved of the insurrection, I do not so well know. But in either case their conduct would have been the same. They would have let the blackguards try the first brush, and then have been determined by the event. Two of these gentry, not quite so prudent as the rest, were forced out on the first day, and had not the rebellion been so suddenly quelled, most of the rest would have submitted to the same kind of gentle ravishment. One of the two has a tolerable fortune in possession, and a larger in expectancy, is a magistrate, a constant grand juror, and lately resigned a company in the militia. He has got a smart wound.

I confess, however, that he seems to have been only the dupe of the other, who is a cunning scoundrel of about £300 per annum, and contrived it so that they were both ravished together, and carried to the rebel army in Ballymena.[79]

The sun was setting now on one of the longest days in Ulster's history. For the people on the coast at Ballygalley it had already touched the rim of the Sallagh Braes and the shadows were racing seawards. At Glenarm and Carnlough they watched it retreat behind the mountains that cradled the Glens. In the centre of the county, at Ballymena, anxious eyes watched it wester towards the distant Sperrins. It was the hour which Antrim folk call the 'dayligone'.

Two miles west of Ballymena, beyond Galgorm, was the tiny Moravian settlement of Gracehill, a piece of continental Europe set down on the bank of the Maine. The warden, Jons Fridlezius, born in Stockholm in 1751, had the duty of overseeing the safety of the settlement during the troubled days of June 1798, along with the minister of Gracehill, the Reverend John Steinhauer. In his diary the latter kept a record of the events of Thursday and Friday:

> Tho' the whole place was under great apprehension of what might come upon them, yet they remained without the least disturbance till towards four o'clock on the morning of the 8th when the fife and beating of a drum was heard. [The United Irishmen] soon marched into our place with pikes, guns, pistols, swords and scythes affixed to long poles and with green flags. Brother Fridlezius met them directly before the Hall [that is, the Church] and received them friendly and respectfully. They directly mentioned their demands, *viz* to deliver up to them all the arms in our place, to search for which they would send two men to each house. But when Brother Fridlezius assured them that they had all been delivered a few days ago to the military in Ballymena, they believed him. They then asked for powder and were led to our shop, but, upon enquiry, believed Brother Coony's word that there was none of it left in the shop. Then they asked for shot, and, as there was some, it was delivered to

them. Upon this they were satisfied, and the Captain told Brother Fridlezius that a Committee of the United Irishmen had met last night to confer in what manner Gracehill was to be treated, and that the result had been that no harm would be done to our place.[80]

Meanwhile, Ballymena had now been placed on a total military footing. Guards were formed and sentries posted on all the roads leading out of the town, and no one was allowed to leave without giving the countersign, which that night was 'Fitzgerald in the dark' – an indication perhaps that news of Lord Edward's death had only then been received.

During the night the streets were patrolled by large bodies of men beating old drums and sounding horns and conch shells. From time to time there were shouts and screams from the multitude, many of whom were by this time blissfully drunk. There was no sleep for anyone sober in Ballymena, loyalist or rebel, and though the summer night was clear, the windows of every house were lighted by order of the committee.

For the loyalist prisoners in the black hole it was a night of torment. They were crammed in to the point of suffocation, the night was warm, and as the hours passed they began to suffer cruelly from thirst. Towards dawn their cries for water and air seemed to move their captors to pity. The door was thrown open, but a strong guard was drawn up in front of it to prevent any escape. What thoughts passed through the mind of Davison can only be imagined. He made no complaint, being anxious, no doubt, not to draw special attention to himself, but his enemies had not forgotten him and some in the crowd were calling for his murder.

Two of them came forward to drag him out. Faint and weak as he was, the schoolmaster had resolved to sell his life dearly. Before leaving the market house he had hidden in his sleeve a small, sharp-pointed engraving tool, and with this he at once stabbed his first assailant, a man called Jamison from Slemish. Six or seven others rushed at him over Jamison's prostrate body, only to fall back bleeding and cursing. But Davison had sealed

his fate. The enraged crowd now demanded that his fellow
prisoners should put him out and threatened that if they did not,
they would all be shot. The result was inevitable. Davison came
out, either of his own volition, or pushed out forcibly by his
terrified companions. He was instantly cut down and a dozen
pikes were thrust into his body. His horribly mutilated remains
were left lying in a gutter and every passing rebel stopped 'to
try his pike on him'. From first to last he had acted with un-
flinching courage.[81]

ON THE COAST

Early on Friday morning, before seven o'clock, Squire Agnew and Squire Shaw went back to the rebel camp at Bellair Hill near Glenarm. They were both on excellent terms with their tenants and were accorded 'the greatest esteem'. In the camp they saw Acheson

in full regimentals, green jacket faced with yellow, white breeches, black hose and silver-buckled shoes. He was in great spirits, and was wildly cheered by his little army of more than 2,000, and there were many women on the field, some cooking an early meal on the camp fires and others moving around with jugs of fresh milk and oat cake for the citizen army.

It was a most beautiful June morning, Agnew recalled, as the sun climbed above the hilltops and the mist lifted like a great white sheet in the valley:

I returned to Ballygally with a sad heart as I, like the ancient Greek, so deeply pondered on the fate that lay ahead of these worthy common people of this Kingdom. It came all too true, for the rebellion in Antrim, in which the greater rebel army was engaged, was broken by a great military force, but the news of it prevented many of my tenants advancing into battle to meet the same bloody fate.[82]

What Agnew does not mention in his memorandum is that he and Shaw used their utmost efforts to dissuade Acheson from this desperate enterprise and to save his skin, efforts that were crowned with success. No doubt they acquainted him first with the news of the defeat at Antrim; then they managed to persuade him to seek a pardon for himself and use his influence to ask the people to disperse. The truth can be glimpsed in a letter two days later from Captain George Stewart, who commanded the Glenarm Yeomanry, to the magistrate Edmund McNaghten of Beardiville: 'The prisoner Mr Acheson was with the rebels on Bellair Hill on Thursday, 7th inst. and on Friday morning sent me a message that they would wish to treat . . .' There was another exhange of prisoners, and then 'Mr Acheson and Mr Butler and another of the rebels had a meeting, and agreeable to the terms I offered they agree to lay down their arms and hand them in by twelve o'clock on Monday, some of them comply within that time and several after, and as far as I know Acheson advised them to submit entirely to their capitulation.' Acheson and all the others who fulfilled the engagement were to be forgiven 'without any reserve' for the events of Thursday, except any who had committed an atrocious crime, 'such as murder or burning houses'. Stewart adds that he is writing at the instance of Acheson, who is the bearer of the letter. 'I should be sorry that he should suffer, as he has my promise of safety for this offence, and has as far as I know complied with his engagements.'

There can be little doubt that Agnew and Shaw were behind this capitulation, but Stewart was offended because they had not thought fit to take him into their confidence. 'Several of the greater culprits have escaped as yet, as the gentlemen who came up did not consult, nor even acquaint me they were in the country.'[83]

One Andrew Stewart of Drumnacole, a yeoman, made a deposition on 14 July 1798 that on Saturday 9 June he had seen Acheson on the brae at Carnala among a company of insurgents 'addressing himself particularly to those who, he thought, had the greatest influence among them, and heard him repeatedly advise them to avail themselves of the benefits of the treaty made with Captain Stewart, otherwise they would be sorry for it afterwards'.[84]

The turn out at Glenarm had collapsed. Several of the leaders were, however, put on trial in Belfast in late July. At his court martial Acheson conducted his own defence, and was 'singularly pertinent and effective' in cross-examination. He was acquitted, chiefly it was thought, because of the lenity of the president of the court, who was (of all people) Colonel Leslie of the Monaghan Militia, and the influence of his uncle, the Reverend Thomas Reid, 'who was an important officer in the Masonic Order'.

Acheson certainly regarded Leslie as the man who had saved his life and they later became firm friends. Acheson had his only son named Leslie in the colonel's honour. Reid felt that Acheson should not return to Glenarm, and he eventually accepted a call to Donegall Street congregation in Belfast, where he was installed in 1799. He remained there for the next twenty-five years, contributing regularly to the *Belfast Magazine*. He died in 1824, aged sixty-one.[85]

When Dr Casement and the loyalists of Larne left their families on the shore at the Corran and hurried back to defend the town they had steeled themselves for another rebel onslaught, either from Islandmagee or from inland. On the way back to town, Casement looked along the road towards Ballycarry and was much surprised to see a party of cavalry on it. This turned out to be Captain Ellis and part of his troop. The sight, which delighted Casement, had the opposite effect on the Islandmagee rebels, 'who immediately dispersed'. However, Casement found it very sad that 'there did not appear to be any joy exhibited by any of the principal inhabitants of the town on the arrival and very martial conduct of Captain Ellis and his men'. The cavalry did not stay long; Ellis had heard only by accident of the plight of the Larne people, and, though on essential service, had volunteered to ride to their rescue.

The serious attempt to take control of Larne had been abandoned when the main body of insurgents had left the town for Donegore Hill, but Casement in his account emphasises the continuing danger. There was at that time no certainty of the success of the army in the interior of the county, and it was believed that a general turning out would take place again on

Friday night. For whatever reason, he allowed himself to be persuaded by family and friends to proceed to Carrickfergus by water. He freighted a small vessel, and 'leaving the sergeant in Larne a quantity of gun-powder for his defence', sailed from the Corran about seven o'clock in the evening and arrived safe in Carrickfergus in the morning, 'where we met a very different scene, every face presenting loyalty and friendship'.[86]

Carrickfergus, with its imposing Norman castle and convenient harbour, was a key strategic position, and Colonel Anstruther had held it in a tight grip since 9 a.m. on Thursday, when the drummers of the Tay Fencibles had beat to arms, word having been received that the whole country was in open rebellion. The shops were immediately shut, and about fifty suspected persons were rounded up and confined in the castle. Guards were placed on all the roads leading from the town, and no one was allowed to depart without the written permission of the mayor or the commanding officer. About 150 of the inhabitants at once came forward, asking to be formed into a yeomanry corps under the command of gentlemen from the neighbourhood; their only uniform was a black cockade worn on the hat.

That evening a large crowd had assembled on the green outside the town, close to the scene of Orr's execution, but they dispersed on hearing the news from Antrim. Over the next few days the garrison ventured out to scour the countryside, burning houses and making arrests. By 13 and 14 June reinforcements of fencible cavalry were arriving from Scotland, and it was observed that many of the country people were wearing red ribbons as a sign of loyalty.[87]

NORTH ANTRIM

Owing to some failure of communications, the United Irishmen in the north of the county had not begun to move until Friday morning. The main body of insurgents then began to assemble on Dungorbery Hill, in the parish of Kilraughts. Samuel McAndless of Ballyclough later deposed that he had been roused from his bed at three o'clock in the morning to go with the others to Ballymoney. There is a good eye-witness account of events at Dungorbery by James Clark, a revenue officer, who was taken there as a prisoner. Clark had escaped from Ballymena, and during the night he made his way by cautious stages to Clough, but on leaving there to reach Ballymoney, he ran into the insurgents who took him to Kilraughts. He was brought before their commander, Richard Caldwell, and charged with being a spy. Caldwell had no time to deal with the case, but gave orders that the prisoner was to be closely guarded. Clark was left sitting on the back of a ditch, from where he watched Caldwell drilling his men on the hill above Kilraughts meeting house. They were armed with pikes, guns, graips, pitchforks and scythes tied upon sticks. Other witnesses testified that Samuel Adams of Ballymoney and James Hamilton were among the insurgent officers marching their men round the hill to the sound of fife and drum.

Clark also saw John Gunning of Ballymoney acting with authority as a person who had command, making his men march and wheel as soon as the sun was up. The intention of the United force was to attack Ballymoney, but they changed their minds. When they heard that the army were already there, there was confusion for a time and then the whole company marched off towards Ballymena, Caldwell walking in front with a drawn sword in his hand. Later Caldwell was mounted on a black horse, while Samuel Adams kept the men in ranks during the march. Clark was left sitting on the ditch on Dungorbery Hill. He watched the retreating column until it was a mile off. Then he got up and walked calmly into Ballymoney.[88]

A society of United Irishmen had been founded in Ballymoney in 1795, meeting in the house of one Willoughby Chesnut. Its members included Dr A. Hamilton, the two attorneys John and James Parks of Bushbank, and a schoolmaster, David Shearer of Newbuildings. Richard Caldwell and John Gunning were appointed military officers. Caldwell's two sisters Flora and Catherine were married to the Parks brothers. John Nevin of Kilmoyle was also a captain, in the parish of Ballyrashane and drilled men at Derrykeighan in a field which was afterwards known as 'the drilly knowe'.[89]

The Caldwell family had long been settled in the Ballymoney area. In 1718, during the first great wave of emigration from Ulster to America, a Caldwell had taken part in the founding of one of the most celebrated of the Scotch-Irish settlements. John Caldwell, Richard's father, recorded:

> Among the survivors of the Siege of Londonderry were my two great-uncles Thomas Bell and William Caldwell, who with various others, principally from the town[land] of Ballywatick in the parish of Ballymoney, some of whom had shared with them the hardships of the siege, not liking the aspect of public affairs in their own country, sought an asylum in America, and in the year 1718, when their average age might be about 48, migrated to Boston, and from there made their way to Nutfield, as it was then called, listened to his first sermon from their minister Rev. James McGregor, under an oak on the east shore of Beaver Pond, purchased their title from the Indians and built the town of Londonderry.[90]

John Nevin of Kilmoyle was active in attempting to persuade regular soldiers to desert, or take the United Irish oath. John Wright, a deserter who was later recaptured, was to recount how, in the autumn of 1796, he was decoyed to Willoughby

Chesnut's house and persuaded to desert. His club of hair was cut off and he was given money and clothes and passed from house to house until he came to reside for three weeks with Nevin, who told him that the entire Kerry Militia in the Coleraine garrison were United Irishmen.

In June 1797 a weaver approached the magistrate Edmund McNaghten, claimed His Majesty's pardon, and revealed that he was deeply implicated in the United Irish plans. He told how he had attended a meeting after sunset in a corn kiln belonging to the Nevin family. It had lasted for an hour, most of the time being taken up by John Nevin reading the *Northern Star* to the company. On other occasions Nevin had read out the constitution of the United Irishmen and laid it on a table. Those who wished to be sworn in then took it up and read the oath aloud. He further alleged that Nevin was one of the men chosen to give notice of the Rising to the United men in the parish.

Reporting all this to the authorities in Dublin, McNaghten added that had it not been for Nevin's efforts there would have been very few United Irishmen in the parish where he lived. 'He is one of the richest Countrymen in this Neighbourhood, and has several tenants under him.' Nevin wished to seek the cover of having taken the oath of allegiance, but dared not approach any of the local magistrates to give him a certificate. Instead he travelled upwards of forty miles to Belfast, where he got a magistrate to give him a certificate that he had taken the oath and entered into a recognisance. But by November 1797 McNaghten was reporting with satisfaction that Nevin had been arrested and sent to Carrickfergus.[91]

In April 1798 the provost of Campbeltown in Scotland wrote to McNaghten that 'we are very much pestered with the people from your side of the water and we are at some loss how to treat them'. Clearly, McNaghten told Lord Castlereagh, 'these villains have societies here and in Argylshire which hold communication with each other'. On 23 May 1798, the day the Rebellion broke out in the South, he wrote again to Castlereagh

to say that John Caldwell (Richard's brother) had been arrested
and was now in Dublin Castle.

> All his family and connections are notoriously disaffected.
> Although I cannot bring *any proof* against any one of them I
> know very well they have been all very busy in forwarding to
> the utmost of their power all the mischief that has been going
> on of late – Caldwell's sister is married to one John Parks an at-
> torney – This Parks has written an account to his father-in-law
> of the arrest of his son and has told him that he was taken up
> merely because he was an inhabitant of Belfast. Old Caldwell has
> been reading the letter to almost every person here.[92]

Two years before the Rising, and with no thought at all of
Ireland in his mind, a young Scotsman called Robert McKerlie
accepted an ensign's commission in the 2nd Royal Manx Regiment of fencible infantry, which had just been raised by Lord
Henry Murray, the younger brother of the Duke of Atholl.[93]
McKerlie left his home in Galloway on 4 May 1796, bidding a
tearful farewell to his ninety-two-year-old father, whom he did
not expect to see again, and took ship for the Isle of Man, only
to find on his arrival that the regiment was in garrison at
Scarborough. He kicked his heels for a while in Douglas, then
crossed to Liverpool and made his way to Yorkshire. On 20
June he presented himself to his commanding officer at
Scarborough and was at once posted to Whitby, where three of
the battalion companies lay. Young McKerlie had existed for
two months on the twelve pounds he had brought from home.
He was fed up and homesick, and was overjoyed to find that
one of the other ensigns was an old schoolfellow.

Under the sergeant-major's direction he made such progress
in drill that he was soon judged fit to appear on parade in
regimental uniform for battalion officers – a long coat with royal
blue facings, cocked hat with white feathers tipped with black,
white breeches, long boots, and at his side a steel-mounted
basket sword. But the occasion proved to be one of intense
humiliation for him. He had celebrated with his comrades in the

usual way the night before and was spectacularly sick on parade, 'a salutary lesson for such consummate folly'.[94]

In September the regiment was marched by stages to Liverpool and embarked for Dublin, where, after an uneasy crossing, they were kept penned up in the transports for a whole day, at the end of an immensely long pier. At last they were disembarked and marched to Drogheda, and since it was Sunday ('a belting day') McKerlie took the opportunity to sneak off to see the site of the Battle of the Boyne. Next day the regiment moved slowly to Monaghan, and then on to Omagh and Derry. Finally McKerlie found himself part of the garrison at Coleraine, a congenial post since the area provided plenty of fishing and shooting.

By the summer of 1798 Lord Henry, 'a tall handsome man ... with a penetrating eye',[95] was in command of the entire Coleraine garrison – two troops of dragoons, a battery of field artillery, a body of the Somerset Militia and his own regiment, the Manx Fencibles. To back them up he could call on the local yeomanry corps from Dunluce, Dunseverick and the Giant's Causeway. He had taken elaborate steps to put the town in a state of defence. As elsewhere, the market house in the town centre was chosen as the obvious place in which to make a stand, but Murray went further by blocking all the streets leading to it. Colonel Andrew Small, a zealous and experienced field engineer, had the streets trenched, and built breastworks across them, protected by abatis of sharp stakes. Outside these fortifications the streets were torn up and large stones left lying around.

On 7 June, when news reached him of the attack on Antrim, Murray's instinct was to sit tight behind this miniature Maginot line and guard against surprise. On Friday morning he sent out reconnaissance patrols which found some United Irishmen and chased them in the direction of Kilraughts. (These were, presumably, Caldwell's men.) Thursday and Friday had passed with no sign of an attack on Coleraine, so by Saturday morning Murray felt sufficiently confident to issue from his headquarters with a force of 220 regulars, four corps of yeoman cavalry and two curricle guns. Having intelligence that the rebels were assembling to the south-east, he marched along the right bank of the Bann and then cut across country to Ballymoney which he found almost completely deserted.[96]

As he belonged to the Light Company, McKerlie was ordered to the front of the column, with a detachment for skirmishing if necessary and with the duty of scouring a plantation on the line of march, not far from the hill on which the enemy were believed to be in position. Suddenly a man started up like a frightened hare from the bog on their left and fled into the undergrowth, where it was hopeless to try to pursue him. The corporal instantly levelled his musket and fired but without hitting him, much to McKerlie's relief, for he was sure that the man was perfectly innocent.

When they reached the outskirts of Ballymoney the regiment formed in columns of section on the road. The rebels, seeing the approach of the force, had left the town and were concentrating on the hill towards Kilraughts, so there was no opposition as Murray's soldiers entered the town. He was not in a mood to show clemency and began at once to set fire to the houses of known or suspected insurgents. Anyone who was unable to produce a certificate of having taken the oath of allegiance was liable to have his house marked for burning. McKerlie wrote:

> I cannot say precisely what could have been the reason for wreaking our vengeance on this devoted town. Our commanders were perhaps informed that the inhabitants were rebels, or partly so, but, from whatever cause it proceeded, they did not hesitate to make a signal example of this unfortunate place. The town was speedily set on fire, and misery in an appalling form was no doubt the consequence of doing so.

On Sunday Lord Henry marched his men out to devastate the countryside, burning farms and cottages in all directions in the parishes of Bushmills, Ballintoy, Billy and Ballyrashane. 'The scene was dreadful, an unresisting people driven from their homes, their houses in flames and the women screaming and in distraction, no doubt crying for mercy, endeavouring to save their bedclothes and other articles belonging to them...What dreadful effects from civil war.' McKerlie was genuinely shocked at the severity of the military action, but even more by the fact that it was being perpetrated on the Lord's Day. 'Such proceedings could hardly fail to harden the mind.'[97]

Murray did not stay away from his garrison headquarters longer than was necessary to punish the surrounding country-side. His foray had been a calculated risk. Before leaving Coleraine he had authorised the issue of guns to inhabitants of proved loyalty and appointed officers to command them, reckoning that these loyalists could hold the fortified town centre if attacked, long enough for the regulars to return and relieve them. The trusted loyalists included John Galt, a member of an old Coleraine business family, who had become a Methodist lay preacher and kept a diary of events. All day on Sunday messages arrived in Coleraine that the enemy were moving in large bodies towards the town, and that evening Galt went on parade with the rest. He recorded:

> Among our townsmen there is one who has talked more about his loyalty, and what ought to be done, and what he would do, than many others put together, but when it came to the trial it was quite different. On seeing the arms given out, he skulked home, and while we were marching past his door I and the others saw him peeping out of his window at us.[98]

At Harmony Hill John Caldwell, the father of the insurgent captain, was having his breakfast on Saturday morning when Major William Bacon arrived with an order, signed by Lord Henry Murray, to burn the house and property, allowing only five minutes to bring the children to safety. The Caldwells, who owned a gristmill and a bleaching house, gathered up what possessions they could and assembled on the lawn, where they were forced to watch their home and outhouses, the work of generations, burned to the ground. Suddenly in their distress they became aware of their neighbour, James Hunter, running across the fields from his house half a mile away. Hunter was a Quaker and 'his countenance portrayed sympathy and bene-volence'. He brought them words of comfort and, like the Good Samaritan he was, wine 'to reanimate the heart, which but for the unprotected family around, would most probably have ceased to beat'.

They all sat down together on the grass where they were soon joined by another neighbour, Mrs Pery, who had driven out from the village when she saw the flames 'to bring comfort and a supply of various refreshments, wisely guessing how much they would be needed'. For the next few days the family lived under a carpet thrown over two hedges, until the bleaching house, which had been spared, could be fitted up as a shelter.[99]

THE COMMITTEE OF
PUBLIC SAFETY

Friday had begun badly in Ballymena with the murder of Davison. Worse was to follow as Dickey left the town to complete some unfinished business at Kells. Samuel Parker was colonel of the Kells men, but on the previous day he had not turned out with his contingent; and since he had been present at the Templepatrick meeting in Dr Agnew's public house on 5 June when the decision was made to seize the Antrim magistrates, it was now believed that he had sent a warning to Seddon. For this treachery Dickey confronted him on his own doorstep and stabbed him to death. Afterwards, towards noon, Dickey returned to Ballymena, intent on searching out more evidence of betrayal.[100]

Among the prisoners in the black hole was William Crawford, a town constable who lived in the porter's lodge of Ballymena Castle demesne. The rumour had spread that he was a government informer, and the accusation was apparently considered by the Committee of Public Safety. At twelve noon Dickey arrived at the black hole and the unsuspecting Crawford was brought out. Dickey put the charge to him and immediately stabbed at him with his sword. Crawford begged for mercy and tried to run away, but he was knocked down with a pike. Dickey then inflicted a blow on his neck which almost severed the head from the body.[101]

After this murder the committee decided to put all the remaining prisoners on trial, on the grounds that they had broken the terms of their agreement to capitulate when they had fired on their captors from the market house steps. Fortunately for the prisoners the trial was postponed and about one o'clock attention was distracted by the arrival of a large contingent of the United men from the neighbourhood of Ballymoney, under the leadership of Caldwell and Gunning. They were received with tremendous cheering. Johnny Wham the bellman had been posted as a sentry on the tower of the market house to warn of any approach by the military. No soldiers came, but for hours he had been able to encourage the patriots with repeated announcements of fresh levies coming in from all parts of the surrounding countryside. His earlier cries of 'Friends from Clough', and 'More friends from Clough', became a legend, and entered into local speech as a form of greeting. He now triumphantly announced the arrival of the army of north Antrim.[102]

Caldwell's men were well armed and they brought with them several cars loaded with provisions and choice wines and spirits, looted from the houses of gentry and prosperous farmers they passed along the way. These were destined for the camp at Donegore, but, as McSkimmin records, 'no part of this good cheer reached that depot'. Instead, 'the hampers of wine were soon emptied of their contents, the heads of bottles struck off, and the wine drunk and spilled in the streets'. The hams and other provisions were disposed of in the same way. The quality of some fine vintage wines plundered in the town itself from the cellars of Mr Adair did not appeal to all the consumers, some of whom swore they would rather have buttermilk, or 'bunny-ramer'. Thus did the Quartier Saint-Antoine come to Ballymena's Church Street.[103]

The Ballymoney force had been augmented along the way by bodies of men from Killymorris, Loughguile and Clough, and their respective neighbourhoods, all of whom had assembled on the hill of Drumlurg, which thereafter was known as Pike Hill. Further reinforcements from these areas were promised, and continued to come in during the day. The insurgent army in Ballymena now numbered something in excess of ten thousand men, armed with pikes and muskets, in a state of great excitement and persuaded that 'Ireland was their own'. The

Committee of Public Safety knew that this was not so, and they endeavoured, as far as they were able, to keep news of the débâcle at Antrim from the crowds in the streets. Some, believing the cause to be lost, had already stolen away to arrange alibis for themselves or to seek means of fleeing the country.

At about three o'clock a well-dressed stranger rode into the town and asked to be taken to the committee on urgent business. He was assumed to be 'an eminent insurgent general', and after a short while he re-emerged in the company of several members of the committee. A general muster and review of the rebel forces then took place, and various pike and musket exercises were carried out under the stranger's orders. Finally, accompanied by two of the committee, the stranger set off to inspect the outposts. On the pretext of selecting a better position he rode some distance beyond the line of sentries on the Randalstown road, when, suddenly putting spurs to his horse, he galloped away and was seen no more. This unforeseen development caused great consternation and something close to panic in the committee.[104]

Later that afternoon, about five o'clock, the remains of Robert Davison and William Crawford were thrown on a car and drawn to the churchyard. Still in the blood-stained clothes in which they died, they were lowered into a pit which had been specially dug a few yards to the left of the entrance gate. A man called McCready leapt into the grave and placed the arms of the murdered men around each other's necks. Since they had been such close associates in life, he said, they should 'lie like lambs together now'.

In the evening some fugitives from Antrim began to straggle into the town from the direction of Kells. One or two of them bore unmistakeable signs of the action they had been in, and the news of the dispersion of the United army soon spread through the insurgents who crowded round the newcomers to hear every detail. The mood of the summer afternoon had given way to a sullen quiet, punctuated by the occasional yell of defiance. The mass of pikemen, under no particular discipline, began to break up into debating societies. At length one group, which had clustered in the north-west corner of Castle Street, rushed to the inn and confronted the committee, peremptorily demanding an outline of the situation and future prospects. 'The faces of the rebel junto were deadly pale, and their lips were evidently quivering with apprehension.' One member 'attempted to sustain the delusion which they had practised with impunity throughout the day'. He represented the defeat at Antrim as a slight and temporary setback, which had been counterbalanced by triumphant success in every other part of the county. There was some truth in the latter claim, but he went on to tell his audience that the garrison at Carrickfergus had been surprised, and the castle captured with its great store of arms, artillery and ammunition.

At this there were a few half-hearted cheers, but the statements were not entirely believed. However, after further prolonged discussion it was agreed that they should await the issue of the next day in their present position. In other words, like every other body of United Irishmen in the county, they were waiting to see what someone else would do. As night advanced, the guards were doubled on the roads leading to Kells, Antrim, Randalstown and Toome, but the boisterous patrolling of the streets was given up. The atmosphere was in sharp contrast to that of the previous night, and nothing disturbed the silence but the odd dismal blast on a cow horn. Every sheltered nook was occupied by the dark forms of the insurgents, 'some sleeping beside their pikes and guns, some smoking, some drinking, some in whispered consultation, but all thoroughly frightened, and many anxiously discussing plans to avoid the anticipated consequences of their actions'. It was the night before Agincourt, but without Henry V.

At midnight more fugitives, who had been hiding in the fields all day near Randalstown, reached the sentries on the Randalstown road. They assured them that the military who had encamped at Shane's Castle on the previous evening would soon begin their advance on Ballymena and cautioned them not to be taken by surprise. The guard were very grateful for this timely intelligence. They had no intention of being taken by surprise, or by any other means, while they had legs to carry them. Their captain was Ned McCormick, and at ten o'clock next morning he was seen cutting turf in Slanesallagh Bog, halfway to Carnlough.[105] The disturbing news that the army was actually on its way soon reached the town, adding to the terror and confusion there. Any sign of a disposition to come to grips with the regulars was conspicuously absent, and by the early hours of Saturday morning there were unmistakeable indications that a rout was beginning.

THE BRIDGE OF TOOME

The Reverend Edward Hudson gives an interesting commentary on these critical hours in his correspondence with his old patron, Lord Charlemont. He was not impressed by the level of communication among the military high command. Hudson reported that according to Nugent, Durham had pursued the rebels towards Randalstown, in which direction they had fled. However, according to Hudson,

> they did not fly that way, nor did Durham send a man until next day. If he had sent any force there before ten o'clock at night (which he might easily have done) he would have found the rebels drunk and rejoicing. He seems to know nothing of the affair at Randalstown, nor how the troops of the yeomanry were taken. He speaks of a body of rebels entrenched at Toome, and that Clavering and Knox were advancing to attack them. Clavering did move from Shane's Castle [to Ballymena] about two in the morning, on Sunday 10th, privately, and would I suppose have attacked them but that they were not there. The fact is, and this I speak confidently, that after Thursday the 7th, when a mob assembled there to break down the bridge, there never was a rebel force at Toome exceeding twenty men, amongst whom there were but three firelocks. Knox sent to reconnoitre the pass, but I believe was not much the wiser, and I fancy General Goldie is likely to incur some censure for not giving the detachments of yeomanry in the various posts some orders how to act in case of being attacked by a superior force.[106]

Hudson was particularly concerned about Randalstown, because Captain Ellis was his son-in-law. Ellis had commanded fifty foot and twenty dragoons, and with proper tactical planning they would have been sent to Antrim, four miles away, to reinforce Seddon. In Hudson's opinion this would have saved Lord O'Neill's life. Instead, Ellis had been taken as a prisoner to the rebel camp at Groggan Island, and from there to Ballymena.

On Friday morning Clavering did in fact turn his attention to Randalstown, after some tidying up in Antrim. Hundreds of pikes and other weapons were collected, and the dead rebels disposed of – 'Sent a party to throw the dead bodies into the lake,' Captain John Slessor recorded in his diary (in fact they were buried in shallow trenches on the lough shore where the Sixmilewater flowed into it). 'A large detachment went out reconnoitring as far as the village of Randalstown; saw some rebels on the hills, but they took care to keep out of range of shot; three were taken prisoner, and we were on the point of hanging them, when it was thought more prudent not, they having in their possession two yeomanry officers, whom they had taken prisoner in a smart skirmish the day before.'[107]

Hudson says that after detaching the party to break down the bridge at Toome, about eight hundred of the rebels took post about two miles away 'in a place surrounded almost entirely by bog, where they passed that night and almost the whole of the next day'. Meanwhile 'the grand army' of about seven thousand rebels had taken possession of Ballymena. 'Very early in the morning of Friday Clavering advanced from Shane's Castle to Randalstown, from whence he sent out a small party of dragoons to reconnoitre the tentless camp of the rebels.' He declared that he would burn Randalstown 'unless the rebels ... would give up Mr Jones's son and my [Hudson's] son-in-law whom they had taken prisoners'.

'Upon this,' writes Hudson, 'an intimate friend and brother-in-law of mine, who is extremely popular (though he was never a United Irishman) wrote to the commander of the rebels (one Henderson, a colonel and a wheelwright) stating the destruction that impended and strongly recommending submission.' Henderson and his men proved unexpectedly pliant; they said that if their lives and properties were secured, they would submit. This answer was carried to Clavering who gave the written assurance they required. The emissary returned to the rebel camp, this time taking with him two gentlemen for added security. After haranguing the men for some time he perceived signs of great discontent among even the most desperate of them, on which he turned his horse, crying out, 'Let those who would save their lives follow me', and about three quarters of them did, and delivered up their arms. Two hundred stayed behind, and after firing some shots at their departing comrades, they marched off to Ballymena, whither they had already sent their prisoners.[108]

Clavering's threat was carried out, since the prisoners had not been released. 'Colonel Clavering received orders to burn Randalstown,' wrote Slessor. 'It fell to my lot to set fire to it, which was soon effectually done by sending artillerymen in different directions with portfires. The houses, being mostly thatch, were soon ablaze. Only those who witness such distressing scenes can form any idea of them. How far such measures are politic, Government ought best to know.' Slessor adds that only with the greatest difficulty could the officers restrain the men from plundering and committing all kinds of excesses. Their painful duty performed, they returned to Shane's Castle.

The entry in the diary of Pastor Steinhauer for 9 June reads:

> A very turbulent day. Randalstown was seen in flames and the U.I. there, tho' willing to surrender arms, would not give up their leaders. The King's Army was marching to Ballymena, where there were thousands of U.I. and many women and children with cart loads of possessions came for shelter, Gracehill being the only safe place now in these parts. We were willing to shelter the women and children, but would not harbour the men, who had orders to present themselves in Ballymena.

Late that night (Slessor puts the time some hours earlier than Hudson) the soldiers marched the nine miles to Toome to make an agreed rendezvous with General Knox. The rebels were gone, but they had plundered the village and 'broke a beautiful arch across the Bann which prevented our junction for the time'. They had also cut trenches across the roads to impede the cavalry and artillery.

If the Toome rebels are remembered at all, it is because of Roddy McCorley. A young Presbyterian from Duneane whose family had been evicted from their farm after the death of his father, he was in hiding for nearly a year after the Rebellion before being betrayed, tried by court martial at Ballymena, and hanged 'near the Bridge of Toome' on Good Friday, 1799.[109]

SLEMISH

Dawn on Saturday 9 June found the Ballymena insurgents demoralised and on edge. Clavering's force was moving slowly towards the town and the scouts reported that a military attack might be expected about noon. It now became apparent that a great number of men, perhaps as many as five thousand, including several members of the committee, had defected during the night. 'The main body of rebels now understood that all was lost, and, as the day advanced, they left the town by hundreds, without any ceremony, and scampered homeward in every direction, like frightened hares.'[110]

Clavering, with the 64th Regiment of Infantry and detachments of the Monaghan Militia, arrived within sight of the town about 1 p.m. and formed a temporary camp on Ballee Hill. The colonel had made it clear that his intention was to burn the town, and some of the principal inhabitants came to a rapid agreement with the more level-headed insurgent leaders that a deputation should be sent to him at once, to negotiate security for the property of householders on the unqualified submission of all who had been in rebellion. They took the familiar line that the citizens themselves were innocent of any concern in the insurrection, and that Ballymena had been invaded by strangers 'of whom they knew nothing, and with whose objects they had no sympathy'.

The deputation was headed by Dr Wilson of Cullybackey, a respected local figure and 'a man of moderation and intelligence'. Wilson was undoubtedly a United Irishman, but he had taken no part in the violent incidents in the town and had exerted himself to protect the lives and property of loyalists. He had succeeded by his influence in saving the lives of two of the magistrates, David Leslie of Lesliehill and George Hutchinson of Ballymoney. On their way back from Antrim on the seventh they had been dragged from their carriage and would have been piked on the spot had it not been for Wilson's intervention. To protect them further he had accompanied them all the way to their respective homes. This was a strong card in the negotiator's hand.

It was apparently Wilson who succeeded in persuading Clavering to offer a general amnesty (for which the colonel was afterwards much criticised in some quarters)[111] on condition that all the rebels would instantly lay down their arms, and evacuate the town within the next four hours. It was a considerable gamble on Clavering's part, and one which, fortunately for him, was successful. The terms were eagerly accepted by the great majority of the rebels, who threw down their weapons on the spot. During Saturday evening these were collected by the cartload and deposited in Dixon's yard, where they were later surrendered to the military authorities. The roads leading out of Ballymena were now crowded with men intent only on reaching their homes as speedily as possible, and the ditches were filling up with discarded pikes. On Sunday morning the streets of the town were deserted. Few of the inhabitants dared to venture out of doors, and no stranger was to be seen.

Clavering entered Ballymena at ten o'clock on Monday morning, at the head of his entire force, which paraded along Bridge Street and Castle Street, before being drawn up and halted on the spacious lawns of the Adair mansion. The inhabitants were ordered to provide refreshments for the troops, and when this order was not immediately complied with, were told that the soldiers would be permitted to find provisions for themselves. This had the desired effect and the provisions were immediately produced. A few soldiers were left to garrison the town and in the evening the rest were marched back to their field quarters at Ballee. Some days later the whole camp was moved to the racecourse at Broughshane, where it was to remain for many months after the Rebellion.

The military occupation of the district continued for over a year. Clavering and his troops retired and were replaced by the 12th Royals under Colonel Greene, along with Anstruther and the Loyal Tay Fencibles. Soldiers were billeted in almost every house, to the great annoyance of the inhabitants. The parish church and the Presbyterian meeting house were appropriated as winter quarters for some of the troops, with the usual consequences. The interiors of the churches were stripped, every piece of wood except the roof and the windows being broken up and used for firewood. During that time public worship for both denominations was either suspended or conducted in private houses. The market house was left in ruins, and the petty sessions court was held in the military guardroom.[112]

In Broughshane the days following 7 June were filled with confusion. At one point on Friday all the women and children fled to Coreen Hill on a false report that the military were approaching. On Saturday morning Robert Magill heard 'Captain' Duffin ordering his men on the streets of Broughshane to wear green cockades, and he had the inexpressible joy of seeing his schoolmaster marching at the head of a company of rebels. The children cheered and waved green branches as they passed. Magill remembered, too, the handing over of the arms on Pike Sunday. The guns, pikes and swords were piled high on carts. His father even gave up his grandfather's sword, which had reputedly been worn at the Battle of the Boyne: 'I was exceedingly grieved to see it removed from the home.'[113]

Not all of the Ballymena men had surrendered on Saturday. After Clavering's offer of amnesty, some of the leaders urged the people to continue resistance. At twilight the shout was raised, 'Let those who are for the camp at Donegore hold up their hands.' After a good deal of noise, about two hundred men, all of them still bearing firearms, eventually agreed to strike across country and join Henry Joy McCracken at the camp on Donegore. They marched out under cover of the dark and camped that night at Kells, where it would seem McCracken was able to rendezvous with them. On a report that the army was advancing from Antrim, plans were made for an ambush, under the direction of the redoubtable Larry Dempsey. But the army did not appear, and instead they heard the dismal news that the camp at Donegore no longer existed, all the rebel host there dispersing on the morning of the tenth. Next day McCracken found his small force still further reduced by desertions. Only ninety-seven of the most dependable remained with their leader, and they now decided to take refuge on Slemish.

A plug of volcanic rock rising dramatically from the surrounding landscape, some eight miles to the east of Ballymena, Slemish was the mountain on whose slopes legend insists Saint Patrick tended his sheep, when first brought from Britain as a slave. As a lookout perch, it was unsurpassed in the county, and from it the movement of a military column at any point of the compass would be seen at a great distance. For the moment they were safe from surprise. The small band included the most trusted of McCracken's associates, in all probability the men who had most vociferously pressed for an immediate rising at Templepatrick on 5 June, among them James Hope, James Dickey, Samuel Orr and James Burns.

They were to spend the next week on the mountain (how they were supplied with food is not recorded), and during that time they became very bored. Burns says that they just lay there in the summer weather, 'and cracked, and tumbled and rolled about'. One day McCracken, prodding the ground at the foot of the hill with the point of his sword, uncovered a well, which is called 'McCracken's Well' to this day. Early one morning Samuel Orr got up before it was light and stole away to Ballymena, where he threw himself on the mercy of Colonel Greene, and told him about the United Irishmen still on Slemish. Greene at once dispatched an orderly dragoon to them with a letter to say 'if they did not get out of that, he would bring the guns and blow them into the air'. This letter was read out to them, and they decided that it would be prudent to keep on the move.

Most of the men made for Little Collin, over by Glenwherry.

This was the area where, during the Killing Time in Scotland in the seventeenth century, the Covenanter Alexander Peden had taken refuge. The United men remained on Little Collin for the next fourteen days. Then the Reverend William Holmes, the Seceding minister of Ballyeaston, got to hear about them and sent word to Sergeant 'Fogy' Lee in Carrickfergus that there was 'a set of robbers' on the top of Wee Collin, and called on him to send troops to disperse them. (The 'Old Fogies' was the name given to a company of veterans which MacNevin and Lee commanded.) At this, another Old Fogy, John Magill, gave a boy two shillings to take a letter to the men on Collin and warn them of their danger. After that they finally dispersed, each man taking his own road.[114]

McCracken, however, had not lost hope of County Down and was determined to try and reach it. On the evening of 14 June, exactly one week after the Battle of Antrim, a man named McCann had actually managed to reach Slemish from the camp at Saintfield and had given a glowing account of the state of affairs in Down. McCracken seems to have decided to try to retrace the circuitous route by which the messenger had come. Among the men who accompanied him was George Dickson, who was to become celebrated in legend as 'General Halt'. He earned his nickname by an exploit which showed extraordinary courage and initiative. Alone and unaided, he disarmed five of the Tay Fencibles and their sergeant at Sandy Braes, between Connor and Parkgate. The soldiers did not at first see the band of thirty or so United Irishmen, and Dickson said he would go forward alone and make them lay down their arms. His companions tried to dissuade him, but to no avail. He walked up to the sergeant, seized his sword with one hand and with the other presented a loaded blunderbuss to his head, saying that he would blow his brains out if he did not at once order his men to lay down their arms. The bluff succeeded, and the disarmed soldiers were allowed to proceed on their way back to Ballymena. The arms, Burns thought, 'were given in charge to some woman', but he did not know what eventually became of them. Dickson was afterwards hanged, but not before a song had been made about him, and how he was 'the general who made us all halt'.

The evidence suggests that the band concerned was that of McCracken, as he attempted to pass just west of Ballyclare in hopes of crossing the Lagan at Shaw's Bridge. It had now dwindled to thirty-two, and the rumour that they intended to organise another turn out caused all the men in this district to flee to the hills. The road leading into Ballyclare was guarded by sentries, and McCracken was incensed to see that some of them were men he knew, who had failed to turn out on 7 June. He was worried because one of his most trusted men was missing, and he feared that the man might have been taken by the sentries. He overpowered and disarmed them and afterwards he and his men 'went on towards Roughfort'. (This could be a garbled version of the Dickson incident, or be connected with it in some way.) McCracken had almost reached Derriaghy when at last he heard the dreadful news from Down. There was nothing for it now but to return to the mountains.[115]

In the three days following the Battle of Antrim harsh retribution fell on the towns and villages thought to be the centres of disaffection. Refugees flocking into the Moravian settlement at Gracehill reported seeing Randalstown in flames. Clavering was said to have allowed his troops two hours for plunder before setting fire to the town, but Slessor says that the officers restrained their men from looting, though with great difficulty. Lord Henry Murray's overhasty incendiarism at Ballymoney obliged the government to meet a large bill for compensation from loyalists. Templepatrick was razed to the ground by the Monaghans while the inhabitants dragged their furniture and possessions into the street. Dr Agnew's inn was specially marked out for vengeance, but Agnew was sheltered by the Presbyterian minister, the Reverend Robert Campbell, and was eventually able to make his escape. Looting by the rebels had been general since dawn on 7 June. 'Law and authority being in abeyance, honour and honesty were left to take care of themselves.' In Antrim and Ballymena most of the shops and all of the public houses were pillaged.[116]

The celebrated Four Towns Book Club at Doagh was sacked by the yeomanry. It had been founded in 1770 by the village schoolmaster, and ten years later Edward Jones Agnew had given the members a site on which to build a substantial school-house for the Sunday school they had established, and a library in which to meet. Reading societies became popular in the parishes of south Antrim, and the desire to read was taken, in official circles, to be clear evidence of disaffection. In June 1798 the library was completely ransacked:

> The books were trampled under foot or torn asunder, the wainscotting dashed from the walls, and the globes broken to atoms . . . A soldier, unable to destroy in an instant a volume of 'Gibbon's decline and fall of the Roman empire', proceeded to kick it down the stairs leading from the club room to the street, when one of his comrades endeavoured to dissuade him and calm the fury of his rage, offering to purchase the volume at its full value . . . The only work saved on this occasion from the general wreck was 'Robertson's history of Charles the fifth', which the adjutant who was with the party, purchased, when about a quarter of a mile out of the village, from a drummer.[117]

People moving through the county on their lawful occasions were inevitably caught up in the turmoil. Two young women of the Moravian sect, travelling from the 'single sisters' house' in Dublin to visit their parents in Gracehill, reached Antrim on 7 June. Warned of the danger ahead, Ann Cossart and Elizabeth Carmichael 'turned off the road, and slept that night at Boyds', who belong to our people'. Next day they saw the bodies of men and horses still lying in the street and in the fields. They were delayed for several days before being given a pass to reach Gracehill.[118]

There was at that time a road for wheel traffic from Corbally and other townlands on the north-eastern shore of Lough Neagh to the mouth of the Sixmilewater, which it crossed by a ford and joined the road from Antrim to Randalstown. On 7 June Arthur McConnell left his parents' home at Corbally, with a manservant and two conveyances to fetch turf from a moss just north of Antrim. They had crossed the Sixmilewater and reached the Randalstown road when they had the bad luck to fall in with Orr's men flying pell-mell from Antrim. They allowed the servant, being old, to go free, but young McConnell was carried off to their camp at Groggan Island. During the night he escaped, but fearing to return home by the same route, he struck northwards across country towards Ballymoney, where his married sister lived. Tired and hungry, he reached her home next day. Meanwhile, his father sent the old servant back to Antrim on Friday to seek news of Arthur, or recover his body, for they feared that he might have been killed among the insurgents. The servant was detained by the military and made to assist in burying the dead. As travelling remained dangerous, Arthur McConnell stayed at Ballymoney for some considerable time, and he may have considered that he had fallen out of the frying pan into the fire. He found no means of communicating with his parents, who gave up hope of ever seeing him again. When at last he returned home, he was received as one who had been dead and was alive again.[119]

When the Rebellion broke out on Thursday, the Reverend Thomas Alexander, the minister of Cairncastle, was visiting his sister at Crumlin. On Friday 8 June he returned home on a car, along with his sister, a servant and five gallons of whiskey, without being once stopped on the way. They travelled deliberately by the back roads. In the distance they could see Templepatrick in flames, and when they reached Ballynure, people were carrying furniture out of their houses to save it from the soldiers. Alexander did not reach Cairncastle until the early hours of Saturday morning. On Sunday he preached to his flock as usual.

Alexander was arrested several weeks after the Rising. Bob Major of Belfast, a fugitive from the Battle of Antrim, took refuge at Cairncastle and was hidden for a time in the houses of

Squire Shaw of Ballygalley, the Reverend John Lawson (the senior minister of Cairncastle, who was now infirm) and Alexander. As Agnew hints in his memorandum, Shaw really set up a kind of escape network for fugitives during the summer and autumn. Arrangements were made that a boat should come into Ballygalley Bay and take Major away. Alexander, with Shaw and some Larne fishermen, put off from the shore to watch for the rescue boat at the appointed time and place. However, unknown to them, it had already been taken by a revenue cutter, and even when it appeared, travelling in the cutter's wake, they followed it unsuspectingly, despite Shaw's pleas for caution, until it was too late to turn back.

They were hailed by the commander of the cruiser. 'Come on, gentlemen. When you have come so far don't turn back.' He made them come aboard, treating them with great courtesy, but telling them that they must consider themselves as prisoners, since they were attempting to escape from the country. He took them in to Carrickfergus, where the fishermen were released and allowed to return home. Shaw was confined for a week in Carrickfergus market house, and Alexander for a fortnight. Both seem to have escaped any further proceedings. Alexander continued to be minister of Cairncastle, leaving the General Synod with some of his congregation in 1829, at the time of the second Nonsubscription controversy, though they held on to the meeting house. He recounted his 1798 adventures to the local historian R.M. Young in November 1841.

Major was detained but later escaped, and a strange story is told of his subsequent wanderings, one which has a ring of truth. From Cairncastle, where he was again in hiding, he moved to Gallagh at Glenarm, and was sheltered there by James Hunter, whose house was burned down by the soldiers. Both men then succeeded in escaping to Norway, once more being taken off by a boat which came into Ballygalley Bay. Hunter eventually returned to Gallagh when the hue and cry had died down, and he and his sons emigrated to America. Major made his way to Prussia where he settled and married.

James Burns alleged that in or about 1837 a Prussian ship sailed in to Belfast Lough, where John McCammon, one of the Islandmagee pilots, picked her up to complete the journey into Belfast. The captain gave orders to his crew in German and then took McCammon down to his cabin and began to ask him a great many questions in perfect English about the country and people. At length he revealed that he was Major. He asked particularly after an illegitimate child, a girl who had been taken and reared by Tom Millikin of Ballynure. He also asked about William McClelland of Islandmagee, who was, by that time, a very prosperous and respectable entrepreneur.[120]

Although the insurgent cause in County Antrim was lost on the very first day, the county would remain disturbed for a long time to come. In the Ballymena area, for example, a gang of desperadoes led by Thomas Archer, who had distinguished himself in the attack on the market house, continued for many months to terrorise the neighbourhood. Archer was eventually betrayed and captured in the Star Bog beyond Galgorm in 1800. He was tried and hanged in the town, and his body was exhibited on Harryville Moat.

From the point of view of the military, however, the insurrection in County Antrim ended on Saturday 9 June. In County Down it was just beginning.

IV

THE
HEARTS
of
DOWN

While, from afar, we heard the cannon play,
Like distant thunder on a shiny day
JOHN DRYDEN, 'VERSES TO THE DUCHESS OF YORK'

Down is a milder county than Antrim, both in terms of climate and of landscape. The gentle green hills and fertile fields of the northern part of the county contrast with the dark splendour of Antrim's uplands and coastal scenery, and whereas Antrim's volcanic basalt is among the youngest of the earth's rocks, lava which had burst through the substratum of limestone and cooled on its surface, Down's Silurian measures are among the most ancient. Though only fifty miles from north to south, and less from east to west, Down has a coastline of two hundred miles, because of the three large inlets of Belfast, Strangford and Carlingford Loughs. Strangford, which got its name from the Vikings who raided it in the early Christian centuries, separates the Ards Peninsula from the rest of the county. At its mouth, with the villages of Portaferry and Strangford on either side, the lough becomes very narrow. Twice a day four hundred million tons of sea water pour back and forth through the entrance, creating strong currents and at times a fearsome whirlpool called the Routen Wheel. When the wind is in the east and the tide ebbing, the bar is a dangerous place, and continues to take its toll even of the experienced.

On the sea side of the Ards, the old rock platforms shelve far out into the Irish Sea forming low flat reefs known locally as 'pladdies'. Men who go down to the sea in ships have long since learned to treat the Down coast with respect. Modern coastal shipping gives it a wide berth, leaving it entirely to local fishermen, but in the days when vessels were more at the mercy of wind and waves, shipwreck was common. The reefs have evocative names – the Manxman, Burial Island, the Pillion, the Mill Pladdy and the Big Bow Meel. Two have a particularly bad reputation, Skullmartin, a mile out from Ballywalter, which shows its teeth only at low tide, and the South Rock, opposite Kearney, which is covered at all states of the tide. In 1783 the Irish parliament voted funds to build a lighthouse on the rock and its white tower still keeps a lonely vigil above the waves. Here, on one occasion, Henry Joy McCracken's mother was shipwrecked on her way home from Liverpool, and waded ashore with two hundred gold guineas sewn into her pockets.

All of the Ards is low and exposed to the wind, though the north-east corner around Donaghadee has a lighter rainfall than other parts of Ulster. In the eighteenth century there was a sharper contrast between the Upper and Lower Ards, and there were many peat mosses which helped to set apart 'islands' of habitation and settlement. In the spring and early summer the banks above the sandy beaches of the Ards, especially on the seaward side, flamed with a profusion of wild flowers – sea campion, thrift, squill and birdsfoot trefoil. The village of Cloghy had acquired a reputation for smuggling (contraband was carried across the peninsula to the Strangford shore) and the still secluded village of Kearney, which looked outward to the South Rock and other treacherous reefs, had predictably once been the haunt of wreckers; but other coastal villages such as Ballywalter and Ballyhalbert, old Anglo-Norman footholds, were populated mostly by hard-working fishermen and their families.

On the other side of the lough, the main part of the county was a fertile territory of small whitewashed farmsteads nestling among gentle hills and clusters of sheltering trees. The population of north Down and the Ards was largely Presbyterian, but in the west of the county Episcopalians predominated, reflecting the patterns of seventeenth-century plantation, and in the centre and south, where the land began to rise towards the majestic peaks of the Mountains of Mourne, the population was predominantly Catholic.

In April 1797 the French frigate *Amitié* sailed secretly from Brest with a large consignment of guns for the United Irishmen of County Down. The rendezvous was to be made off the Down coast, but a south-easterly gale blew up (the one most dreaded by local fishermen) and the *Amitié* was wrecked off Sheepland harbour, near Ardglass. All but one of her crew of 104 perished. The lone survivor was the helmsman, who struggled to reach the village of Sheepland, where the people looked after him, and sheltered him from the authorities. He stayed in Sheepland for a long time, and legend holds that every day he climbed the path to the headland and spent hours gazing pensively out to sea. Only a cluster of ruined cottages now marks the location of the village, but the path is still known as the 'Steerman's Path'.[1]

Very early on the morning of 7 June 1798, before sunrise, David Bailie Warden, a young schoolmaster and probationer for the Presbyterian ministry, climbed Scrabo Hill, a sandstone spur which rises abruptly out of the landscape just west of the town of Newtownards in County Down, expecting to find the United Irishmen assembling on its summit. Not a single man appeared, and far below, Warden could see lights ablaze in the windows of the market house, which was being used as a barracks. Clearly the garrison had been put on the alert.[2] The joint treachery of Mageean and Hughes had enabled the military authorities to identify the most vulnerable targets and position forces accordingly. It had also enabled them to take the prudent step of arresting the chosen commander-in-chief of the County Down insurgents, just two days before the Rising.

With his little farm, set in idyllic surroundings, his books, a private income and a growing family – one son in the Royal Navy – the Reverend William Steel Dickson might have seemed an unlikely candidate for the post of rebel general. But Steel Dickson was not the man whom the poet Horace extolled – happy to tend his ancestral acres and stay out of public business – and soon both his fields and his manse would be left unattended.

Dickson was in origin a County Antrim man, born near Carnmoney on Christmas Day, 1744.[3] He received his early education from the Reverend Robert White, the minister of Templepatrick, and he studied for a while at Glasgow University, where he sat at the feet of the great Adam Smith. Attracted at first to the law, he allowed himself to be persuaded by his old mentor to become a candidate for the ministry and after the necessary 'trials' he was licensed to preach the Gospel by the Templepatrick presbytery in 1767. In the eighteenth century licentiates usually became schoolmasters or tutors to well-to-do families while they waited for ordination, and often this allowed them to form useful connections. Dickson records that his frequent excursions as a supply preacher gave him 'access to many families of rank and respectability in the counties of Down and Antrim', among them the family of Alexander Stewart, the grandfather of Lord Castlereagh. In 1771 Dickson was ordained minister of the Nonsubscribing congregation of Ballyhalbert, where he met and married Isabella McMinn, a young lady of 'genteel family brought up in affluence and liberally educated'. The couple were to produce six children.[4] During his pastorate at Ballyhalbert a new meeting house was built a mile and a half farther inland at Glastry, which is still in use, with Dickson's name and the date incised in its stones.

When the British engaged in war with American colonists in 1775, Dickson roundly castigated it as 'unnatural, impolitic and unprincipled'. He did not disguise his opinions either from his flock or the world at large, and the minister of Ballyhalbert was soon being attacked on all sides as a traitor and 'trumpeter of sedition'.[5] Like many another of the same cast of mind, he responded to such criticism with even greater provocation. When the Volunteer movement arose, Dickson threw himself into it with great fervour, and even published a sermon on the propriety of learning the use of arms in times of public danger. In the spring of 1780 he resigned the charge of Ballyhalbert and was installed as minister of Portaferry, where he was to remain until the insurrection. He had a stipend which came to about one hundred pounds, and soon after his installation he opened an academy for boys which brought in another hundred pounds.

This, together with other income and his small farm, enabled him to live more comfortably than the majority of his brethren.

Dickson was an erudite and cultivated man, not without a strain of vanity, strongly anti-Calvinist in his religious outlook, and an innovator in spheres other than politics. He was, for example, an early advocate of the use of music in Presbyterian services, a subject which was bitterly contested in Scotland and Ireland for a long time afterwards. In 1783 the University of Glasgow conferred the degree of Doctor of Divinity on him, but the lure of politics was irresistible. In the elections of 1783 and 1790 he rendered considerable service to the Stewarts, spending up to forty hours in the saddle rounding up freeholders to cast their votes for them. He was proud of the part he had played in launching Castlereagh on his parliamentary career, but the young politician was later to express his gratitude by saying that Dickson's popularity in 1790 proved that he was 'a very dangerous man to have at liberty'.[6]

When the Society of United Irishmen was formed in Belfast in 1791 Dickson espoused their cause at once, taking the oath that December. A passionate advocate of Catholic emancipation, he took a leading part in the last of the great radical conventions at Dungannon in 1793, and preached to the delegates on the text of Joseph's advice to his brethren Genesis 45:24: 'See that ye fall not out by the way.'[7]

Dickson's efforts over the next five years to keep the Presbyterians from falling out by the way brought him sharply to the attention of the government. They also unsettled his congregation, and won him the implacable enmity of the local landlord, Colonel Edward Trotter Savage of Portaferry House, surveyor of excise in the town. Savage was instrumental in having five or six of Dickson's flock arrested in 1796 on the word of a weaver named Carr. Carr was transferred to Dublin in the hope that he might provide enough evidence to convict the minister, but this he was unable to do. On the evening of Christmas Day, 1796, after conducting divine service, Dickson set out on horseback for the capital and Savage at once conveyed his suspicions to Lord Londonderry, who passed them on to the government:

> By a letter received from Mr Savage of Portaferry I understand Doctor Dickson, the dissenting minister, who is supposed to be the leading man among the disaffected in the neighbourhood of Portaferry; and to be very deep in the confidence and plans of those who have invited the French to make an attack on Ireland; on Sunday last was apprized, as it is believed, that the French Fleet was to be off Cork; and that evening, after preaching, set off for Dublin. There is every reason to surmise that this journey can be with no good intention; as the country is circumstanced and the ground of suspicion so strong against him from his being known one of the most violent and seditious characters in the country – I think it would be highly prudent and expedient to have him hunted out in Dublin and if possible taken up and detained as a suspicious personage.[8]

Nevertheless, Dickson remained at liberty, and at some point between then and June 1798 he was invited to become adjutant-general of the Army of the Republic in County Down.

By the spring of 1798 all Dickson's activities were being closely watched, and particular suspicion had been aroused by his visits to Scotland, where, it was thought, he had established contact of some kind with subversive elements. In the account of his tribulations which he published in later years he goes into meticulous detail about the reasons for his frenetic travelling about north Down at the end of May and the beginning of June. On 28 May he was at the fair in Killinchy and did some business there; and in the days following he paid visits to the Reverend William Sinclair, the Presbyterian minister in Newtownards, Squire Robert Rollo Reid of Ballygowan (one of his old pupils), Nicholas Mageean, David Shaw, a Saintfield cotton manufacturer who provided him with 'some excellent cold beef and a tumbler of punch', John Coulter of Cotton, and James McKeown, whose child he baptised. He was much concerned to purchase a suitable horse, a quest which took him to Saintfield, Belfast, Downpatrick and Ballynahinch. On Monday

4 June he took the waters at the Spa and once again made his way to Ballynahinch, little guessing that it was the last moment of liberty he would enjoy for almost four years.[9]

On reaching Ballynahinch, Dickson went straight to an inn, and had scarcely sat down when he was told that a gentleman wished to speak with him in the street. It was Captain Daniel Magennis of the Castlewellan Yeomanry, who seemed embarrassed and begged him to walk a little way out of the town. He explained that there had been a meeting of yeomanry that day in Clough and that he had received a letter from Lord Annesley, commander of the Castlewellan Yeomanry, ordering him to detain Dickson and await further orders. He had no warrant for arrest, only Annesley's letter, and he suggested that Dickson might take horse and come with him. Dickson refused point-blank. Magennis could, if he liked, go back to his room and examine his papers and belongings; or he could post sentries on the inn and allow him to retire for the night. The officer declined both suggestions, saying that he supposed his arrest was 'only a whim of his Lordship' and that he would be set free in the morning. Eventually, however, the officer agreed to leave a sergeant at the inn. The sergeant at once made himself comfortable and settled down to sleep, without giving himself or Dickson the least trouble.

At noon on Wednesday 6 June, Colonel Bainbridge arrived and ordered Dickson's transfer to Lisburn, and then, without seeing him, went on to Montalto to wait on the Dowager Lady Moira. Dickson sent a messenger after him to request that, as the weather was very hot and his health delicate, he might be allowed to ride or travel in a chaise. Bainbridge was choleric. 'A chaise be damned!' was his reply. 'Let him walk, or take a seat on the car which goes to town with the old guns.' With stiff-necked Presbyterian pride, the minister chose to walk, and towards four o'clock in the afternoon he set out with a guard of fourteen soldiers and a cart laden with old cannon, on a rough and hilly road of eight miles, under a scorching sun and enveloped in clouds of dust. It was eight o'clock before they reached Blaris and Dickson was faint with exhaustion. Refreshed by some wine and water, however, and 'with a change of flannels next his skin', he waited on General Goldie.

As a Lowland Scot, Goldie was well accustomed to the ways of Presbyterian ministers. He was therefore more forthcoming than most English officers would have been. He received Dickson with 'all the politeness of a soldier and a gentleman' and seeing how tired he was, apologised for being unable to offer him a bed in his own lodgings. He would not keep him in confinement at Blaris, where conditions were bad, but proposed to send him to Belfast with a discreet sergeant and two dragoons. He was certain that General Nugent would release him at once, as there was no charge against him, only the suspicion aroused by his visit to Scotland in the spring.

When Dickson arrived at Nugent's headquarters in Belfast, however, he received a rude shock. The general at once ordered that he be taken to the black hole and questioned there. The first person he saw was Robert Hunter, a Belfast shipbroker who had been brought in a few minutes earlier and was being interrogated. Dickson's arrival was hardly noticed, but after a while soldiers of the Monaghan Militia became aware of his extreme fatigue and made room for him on the wooden platform which served them for chairs, table and bed. As soon as Hunter's interrogation had ended, Dickson was brought forward and asked a few perfunctory questions.

True to form, he asked for refreshment and demanded to know where he was to spend the night. He received a curt answer, but by great good fortune he recognised the captain of the guard as Robert Wallace of the Belfast Yeomanry, with whom he was acquainted. Wallace instructed that whatever the prisoners wanted should be brought for them during the night. A soldier offered Dickson and Hunter part of the platform to sleep on, and they lay down in the dust, with Dickson's saddlebags for pillows. The stench of the horse barracks was nauseating, and there was no distraction but the endless stream of military oaths and obscenities.

It was two o'clock next day before they were removed to the Donegall Arms, which was being used as the temporary provost prison. Dickson, with four others, was put into a room sixteen feet by ten, without furniture of any kind. The air was suffocating, as the weather continued very hot, and the yard outside was piled high with horse manure. The boards were cleaner than in the black hole, but the prisoners had to sit up and be counted every two hours, when the sentries were changed.[10]

The campaign in County Down was thus left leaderless before it had properly begun. Dickson's account is a kind of code, written with a curious respect for the facts: it does not lie, but neither does it tell the whole truth. All the people he names, with the possible exception of James McKeown, were high-ranking United Irish officers, and what Dickson was really discussing with them was his battle plan. According to the deposition of Richard Frazer of Ravarra, Dickson had been approached at Killinchy in May to see if he would act 'in a public capacity', and had replied that he was willing to do anything he could to serve or be useful to his country. Frazer thought Dickson understood this to mean 'filling an office under the system of United Irishmen'.[11]

On 3 June the Down men received an express message from County Antrim, which told them that the Antrim colonels 'were averse to action', but that the Defenders in the county numbered five thousand, all ready to take up arms. It asked if Down had been put in a state of readiness and the reply was 'yes'. On Tuesday 5 June, David Bailie Warden called on Nicholas Mageean near Saintfield, and after asking him for any news, Mageean lent him a horse to ride to Ballynahinch. There Warden 'happened accidentally to see Dr Dickson'. He conversed with him for about ten minutes, 'having a little before that time entered the Presbytery of Bangor'.

The next day Warden returned to Saintfield about 5 p.m., and meeting Mageean on the road, learned that John Hughes of Belfast had sent a special messenger to County Down to invite them to rise, adding that by noon on Thursday County

Antrim would be in arms and that the town of Antrim would be attacked. At the same time Mageean asked Warden to take command of one of the battalions, probably north Down, but Warden at that point refused. As Warden already knew of the resignation of the Antrim adjutant-general, and the consequent disorganisation of the county, Mageean's news gave him hopes that affairs had been better managed and that all might yet go well. He changed his mind about taking command, and acting on orders, he arranged for an attack on Newtownards.

The place of rendezvous at dawn on 7 June was to be Scrabo Hill. The inexplicable failure of the Newtownards men to appear was a severe disappointment to young Warden. There was little more that could be done that day, but on Friday he managed to contact 'the only representative of the Down High Command to have survived the arrests'. While they were debating what to do, a message came 'like a flash of lightning' that the men of Saintfield and Killinchy were already 'up'. Promising them every support, Warden at once set off on horseback to raise the towns of Bangor and Donaghadee, and all the adjacent areas of north Down. There was a noticeable reluctance everywhere, but eventually he succeeded in gathering together about three hundred men, and led them to an assembly in the old Movilla burying ground on the eastern side of Newtownards.[12]

Despite this initial hesitation, the mobilisation of north and east Down, when it took place, proved formidable. In the words of one observer, 'rebels came from the eastern part of the county as a plague of locusts came in Egypt'. And all accounts agree on one point, that though many of the insurgents came from the Saintfield–Ballynahinch direction, by far the greatest number of those subsequently involved were from the Ards, north Down and the Strangford Lough shore.[13] North Down rose in revolt on Saturday 9 June, and by that evening the Crown forces had already received a serious setback.

SAINTFIELD

It would be an error to assume that all the Dissenting ministers of Ulster at the end of the eighteenth century were radicals by definition, naturally inclined to subversion and sedition. The revolt of the American colonies, and the kind of politics which challenged the abuse of power by vested interests in Church and State, struck resonances in the meeting house, but the majority of ministers in the General Synod of Ulster, the main body of Presbyterians, and in those other Presbyterian bodies – the Reformed and Seceding Churches – were conservative in outlook and adhered to the scriptural tenet that rebellion was the sin of witchcraft. For every minister like Dickson, there were a score who simply devoted themselves to the spiritual needs of their flocks throughout the crisis. Nevertheless, Dickson was not alone, and there were in County Down a handful of very prominent clerical radicals – the Reverend Samuel Barber of Rathfriland,[14] the Reverend James Porter of Greyabbey,[15] the Reverend Arthur MacMahon of Holywood, who eventually became an officer of the Irish Legion in the service of the French Republic,[16] and the Reverend Thomas Ledlie Birch of Saintfield. All these ministers belonged to the General Synod. One who did not was the Reverend William Staveley of Knockbracken, near Belfast. He belonged to the Reformed Church, generally called Covenanters, and he was the minister who had attended William Orr at his execution.

Exactly a year before the Rising, the authorities received information that a large quantity of pikes and other arms was concealed in the Knockbracken meeting house. As a consequence, on Sunday 25 June 1797, while Staveley was conducting divine service, his congregation were distracted by the sight of Colonel Lucius Barber and a troop of cavalry on the meeting house green. Learning that their intention was to arrest him, Staveley ended the service, closed the Bible and, leaving the pulpit, surrendered himself to the military. He spent the next two months in prison, though there appears to have been no substance to the charge. Staveley always denied that he was a United Irishman. Nevertheless, he showed great courage, so soon after his release, in standing by Orr, whose farm marched with the Antrim property of his wife, and in expressing the Presbyterian sense of outrage at the verdict of the trial. The arms charge was to come back to plague him in June 1798 and he was once more imprisoned.[17]

The one Presbyterian minister who took a very active part in the Rising was Birch, whose congregation was First Saintfield. His church, situated in the main street, had a large and flourishing congregation, which included some of Birch's well-to-do relatives. The village lay some twelve miles south of Belfast and was the creation of Nicholas Price, the son of a Cromwellian settler of Welsh origins, who had originally purchased the land. Price opened a road through it from Belfast to Downpatrick, encouraged linen manufacture there, erected a barracks for a troop of horse and restored the parish church. He also gave the village its name, a literal translation of the older Irish name of the townland, Tonaghneave.[18]

While still a student at Glasgow, Birch had become an enthusiastic supporter of the American colonists, and in 1784 he drafted an address which the Yankee Club of Stewartstown sent to George Washington, expressing joy that America had thrown off the yoke of slavery. Washington returned polite thanks and the exchange was duly published in the *Belfast Mercury*.[19] Birch was in fact a prominent Freemason, like his idol, and the Yankee Club of Stewartstown was really a Masonic lodge. When the Volunteers were raised, Birch was appointed chaplain to the Saintfield Light Infantry. Like Steel Dickson, he actively supported Robert Stewart against the interest of the Hill family (though they too were Masons) in the County Down election of 1783, and an election squib made fun of him as 'Blubbering Birch', a soubriquet which his enemies were not to forget. But his service to the Stewarts was not forgotten either, and one day he was to owe his life to it.[20]

Birch had established a reputation as a radical (he called his manse in Saintfield Liberty Hall) and on 16 January 1792 he founded a society of United Irishmen in the village, the first in County Down of which there is any record. Their resolutions on Christmas Eve 1792 appeared in the *Northern Star*, calling for reform of parliament and Catholic emancipation. One read 'we look upon our brethren the Roman Catholics as men deprived of their just rights'. On Christmas Day Birch's congregation decided that all government 'ought by right to originate from the people' and that its end was the happiness of the governed. The congregation also proposed, for the defence of their families and properties, to acquire military expertise and thereby add 'upwards of 500 brave fellows' to the national guard of Ireland. It was no idle boast when Birch assured Wolfe Tone that he had completely converted his flock.[21]

There were, however, a few dissentients after the United Irish movement became illegal in 1794, and in 1796 they withdrew from the congregation and joined the Seceders. Birch poured the vials of his wrath on them in a pamphlet he called *Physicians Languishing Under Disease*. The contemporary Squire Nicholas Price was not pleased. He was making a reputation as the scourge of all suspected rebels in this part of Down, and he now determined to rid Saintfield of its radical pastor. His opportunity came in 1797 when eleven of Birch's congregation were arrested on a charge of attacking the house of Hugh McKee, a mile and a half to the west of the town. The McKees were loyalists who openly conveyed to the authorities such information as they could gather on the activities of the United Irishmen in the neighbourhood and they were very unpopular.

The accused were men of some standing in the local community; one of them was David Shaw. Tried at Down assizes, they were all acquitted, chiefly because of the withering attack which their counsel, John Philpot Curran, was able to mount against the sub-sheriff, the Reverend John Cleland. Birch attended the trial, and was arrested in the courtroom, arraigned on a charge of high treason. This was a capital offence, but it was soon reduced to a charge of misdemeanour, and the minister was released on bail until the next assizes, where he was eventually acquitted, the judge expressing indignation at the 'base malicious conduct' of his accuser, a farmer whose land adjoined Birch's.

On the eve of the Rebellion, Birch was before the assizes again, indicted this time by a certain Joseph Harper. The accusation was that he had offered Harper fifty pounds not to prosecute United Irishmen, and that he had assaulted Harper's son. The charge was dropped, however, for a reason which could scarcely bring comfort to any of the parties involved. On the Tuesday evening preceding the assize, Harper was shot dead on the road from Belfast to Saintfield. The date was 6 April. On 25 April Birch was secretly elected chaplain to the United army in County Down.[22]

All the indications are that Birch took the field with his men when the Rising began in Down on Saturday 9 June. During that morning contingents of United men from Killinchy and elsewhere converged on Saintfield, from which the military had withdrawn on the previous evening. The insurgents began to assemble at the Cow Green, and eventually moved on to Oughley Hill, two and a half miles north of the town. In the course of the day they took control of most of the surrounding district. Their first objective was to exact revenge from the unfortunate McKees. Ever since the incident in 1797, the family had been in constant expectation of a renewed attack and had provided themselves with muskets, ammunition and a large supply of powder. The farmer had also barricaded his house, and when the assault came, he defended it with great courage and resolution.

The United men attacked in two waves, the first led by James

McKibben, a Saintfield surgeon, and the second by James Shaw, who was wearing a green jacket with yellow facings. Both attacks were repulsed, with some casualties. At last one of the attackers – an eyewitness said it was a fiddler named Orr who lived between Saintfield and Killyleagh – brought up a ladder and managed to climb on to the roof, where he succeeded in setting the house on fire. There was no possibility of escape for the McKees, and the entire family perished in the flames. It was the only atrocity recorded as being committed by the rebels in County Down. Twelve men were hanged for the murders in 1799, but only one of them was from the Saintfield area.[23]

News of the attack on the McKees' farm may have been a factor which helped to persuade Colonel Granville Anson Chetwynd-Stapylton to leave Comber on Saturday morning with a mixed force of regulars and yeomanry and move on Saintfield, where the rebels were rumoured to be gathering in considerable strength. The Chetwynds of Ingestre in Staffordshire were an ancient and blue-blooded family which since the seventeenth century had produced a line of distinguished politicians and divines, and one celebrated antiquary. In 1717 Walter Chetwynd, a namesake of the antiquary, and the MP for Staffordshire, was created Viscount Chetwynd of Bearhaven, County Cork, in the peerage of Ireland. The third viscount, who died in 1770, disinherited his eldest son, and appointed as his heirs, his two grandsons, both of whom were called William Chetwynd. The boys were educated together at Cambridge and both went into the army. The son of the disinherited lord was wounded at Bunker's Hill during the American war, and died in the West Indies in 1779, after the taking of St Lucia. The other William was the son of the Reverend John Chetwynd, the incumbent of a Church of Ireland living in Cork.[24] On the morning of 9 June 1798, he was riding from Comber to Saintfield with the regiment commanded by his cousin, Colonel Chetwynd-Stapylton.

The colonel, riding at the head of the column, was the

fourth and youngest son of the disinherited viscount. Christened Granville Anson Chetwynd, he had in 1783 married the daughter of the last of the male line of the Staplytons of Yorkshire and assumed the name of Stapylton by royal decree. In 1793 Stapylton was recommended by the city of York to raise a regiment of regulars, which the government afterwards changed to a fencible corps for home service. He was appointed colonel of the regiment and two years later he took it to Ireland, where it remained until 1802.[25] During the fateful June of 1798 the York Fencibles were quartered in Comber in County Down.

His force consisted of 270 of the Yorks, supported by the Newtownards Yeomanry Cavalry and Infantry, and two six-pounder fieldpieces, together with a number of enthusiastic civilian volunteers, including no less than three Episcopalian clergy. The slow approach of the party to Saintfield was reported by insurgent pickets in the early afternoon, and an ambush was hastily prepared at the back of the town, some distance along the road to Comber at a point where strong ditches, banks and hedges provided good cover. The present road from Belfast to Downpatrick follows the eastern side of the Price demesne, and crosses the town at the lower end of the main street in which is situated the First Presbyterian Church. But in 1798 the only road from Belfast was one which entered the town at the western end. The Comber road left the main street at right angles, just west of the church, and ran north as far as the entrance to the demesne, before turning away to the north-east.

This is drumlin country, distinguished by the physical features of what geographers call the 'basket of eggs' formation. The drumlins are little rounded hills occurring in clusters, the moraines deposited by the retreating glaciers of the last Ice Age. At their bases lie ponds, marshy hollows called 'kettles', land which is very difficult to drain. To the left of the road, beyond the demesne gates, there was a partially wooded green slope, rising from deep ditches. Below the road, to the right, the ground fell away to a swampy hollow thick with trees and undergrowth. It was known as Doran's Wood, and the site is now occupied by Saintfield Secondary School. The main body of insurgents, mostly pikemen, concealed themselves in the demesne woods on the higher ground, while musketeers lined the ditches from the estate entrance to the point where the road is now crossed by the new Belfast route. A reserve body of pikemen took up position in Doran's Wood.

Near this intersection of roads there stood in 1798 an isolated farmhouse, the home of Jack Sheppard. Here Stapylton halted his force and cautiously sent forward two mounted scouts. Astonishingly, they returned to report that they had seen nothing suspicious, and the march was resumed. As the advance guard of yeoman cavalry entered the trap, the rebel musketmen rose from the ditches and opened fire, killing the rector of Comber, the Reverend Robert Mortimer, in the first burst. The yeomanry fell back on the main body, causing great confusion. The pikemen then rushed down from the demesne woods, led by Richard Frazer and one McKinstry, and attacked the baggage waggons at the rear of the column. McKinstry was killed almost at once, but Sergeant Lewick of the York Fencibles and several of his men were separated from the waggons and driven down into the marshy ground below the road where they were pursued and taken prisoner. 'When they came up to us,' Lewick remembered, 'they told us to lay down our arms or we should all be dead men instantly. They took us to a house and took all our arms from us. They then took us toward their camp . . . and said we should be well treated until such time as they heard of the army using any of their prisoners ill, then we should suffer the same fate.' This promise can hardly have given Lewick and his men much comfort.

Stapylton's problem in the first stages of the attack was to get his men off the road and deploy them in the open fields on his right, leaving room to bring his two six-pounder guns into action. The hand-to-hand fighting was severe and the regular troops were unused to close encounter with the murderous pikes. One of the fencibles, paradoxically a Frenchman who had seen action on the Continent, was later to tell the Reverend Samuel Edgar, the Seceding minister of Ballynahinch and a cousin of the murdered farmer Hugh McKee, that for danger and desperation the skirmish exceeded anything he had before experienced. 'The soldiers were driven into disorder, and every man had to fight his way in the best manner he could in opposition to the charged pike and other weapons, to which he had not been accustomed.' In the confusion Captain William Chetwynd, trying with great gallantry to rally and steady the men in the first rush, was shot dead by a rebel marksman. The marksman is known. He was Daniel Millin, a farmer from Tonaghmore, and he regretted his action to his dying day.

Ensign Michael Sparks, who seems to have been a relative and perhaps a brother of one of the other officers killed, wrote:

> The ground the rebels had chosen was the most advantageous that could be imagined, so much so, that I could not, during a great part of the Action, bring either of my two Guns to bear on the right, and was obliged to remain idle, exposed to an heavy fire for some minutes. At length a strong column of rebels advanced on our left, attempting to turn our flank and surround us. I waited until they came so close that I must make sure work, and then poured on them a heavy fire of Canister shot, which soon put that column to flight with dreadful slaughter. At that instant their party on the right made a desperate attack on our ranks where I was with the guns, and also on our baggage, and then it was that D[ea]r James and Lieut. Unite fell.

Sparks killed one pikeman with his sword and thought himself lucky to escape with a slight wound to his hand and a graze on his forehead.

When finally Stapylton got his men out of the narrow road, and his guns in action, the contest became more equal, grapeshot and canister creating many casualties in the rebel ranks. With his artillery and a well-armed force, he was confident that he could rout the insurgents, at least temporarily. But he was heavily outnumbered and his chief fear was that he might be encircled and forced to surrender, an anxiety enhanced when, at the critical moment, the reserve pikemen issued from Doran's Wood. In the circumstances Stapylton thought it best to bring off his wounded and retreat rapidly towards Comber. This he succeeded in doing in good order.[26]

His casualties were heavy. They included his cousin and two other officers, Lieutenant William Hawe Unite[27] and Ensign James Sparks. In addition, he had lost 5 sergeants, 2 drummers, 42 other ranks and 4 of the volunteers. The wounded, some of whom had been carried to Sheppard's farmhouse, were collected and brought away with the retreating column. (Michael Sparks says that the surgeon had run away.) Most of the dead were left lying on the field and the insurgents soon stripped them of their arms and uniforms. The corpse of the Reverend Robert Mortimer was left leaning against a gate.

Over the following two days the bodies were collected by the townspeople, and reverently buried in the hollow at a spot which has ever since been called York Island. Here in the 1950s local people found two skeletons and a sword and a bayonet of the York Fencibles. The insurgent dead were buried nearby, at the lower end of the Presbyterian churchyard, the graves unmarked, except for two stones later raised for Killinchy men, both over forty, who died that day. The inscriptions are now scarcely legible.

In the quiet parish church of Comber there is a memorial with this inscription:

In Memory of
Captain WILLIAM CHETWYND
Lieutenant WILLIAM HAWE UNITE
and Ensign JAMES SPARKS
late of the York Fencible
Infantry
who fell
bravely fighting for their
King and Glorious Constitution
In an engagement near Saintfield
With the rebels

On the 9th day of June, 1798
Their brother officers
Impressed with the deepest
sorrow
and with the highest sense
of their courage and manly virtues
have erected
This Monument.

PIKE SUNDAY

The news of the engagement at Saintfield put heart into the Ards men. On Pike Sunday, Warden's insurgent levies, armed with guns and pikes, moved into Newtownards in two columns and attacked the small garrison there. Corporal William Sparks of the York Fencibles recorded that about three o'clock that afternoon he saw a large body of armed men march down North Street. They were led by Samuel Rankin of Newtownards, who was armed with a broad troop sword, and William Davidson of Greenwell Street, who carried a pike. Sparks watched the rebels 'form a line before the market house and commence an attack on His Majesty's forces stationed there'. In a short time the rebels 'were dispersed by the fire of the King's troops'. Several of the attackers were killed, among them the two Maxwell brothers from Ballywalter, whose graves are still to be seen in the old Whitechurch graveyard near their home.[28]

Repulsed in this half-hearted and costly assault, which resulted in a good many desertions, the insurgents withdrew to Movilla churchyard for further deliberation. They decided to march to Conlig to await reinforcements, and there they were joined by a contingent from Bangor, a very welcome sight, for the Bangor men had brought with them six three-pounder swivel guns, taken from a ship in the harbour. With these reinforcements they returned to Newtownards, only to find that the garrison of York Fencibles had been withdrawn and that they were unopposed. They then marched through the town and took post on Scrabo to watch the course of events. Their ranks now contained some of the men who had fought at Saintfield, and during the rest of Sunday, large contingents came in from

Killinchy and Killyleagh. A quantity of ammunition was found in the market house, left behind by the fencibles, and this was a further boost to morale.[29]

The other scene of action in the Ards that day was in Portaferry, almost at the end of the peninsula. There, a determined attempt was made to overcome the garrison and occupy the town, part of a plan by the Ards men to cross the lough and raise the standard of rebellion in Lecale. As yet nothing had been heard of the Defenders, and it was hoped that when they were encouraged to take up arms, a huge mixed force would advance on Downpatrick, the county town.

There was no garrison of regulars to help defend the market house in Portaferry, which stood in the small square at the foot of the main street, and the burden of the defence fell entirely on the loyal Portaferry Yeomanry, commanded by Captain Matthews of Innishargie House. The attacking force of rebels had no artillery and were armed for the most part with pikes, pitchforks and a few rusty muskets, while the loyalists were well armed and well supplied with ammunition. It happened that a revenue cutter, commanded by Captain Hopkins, was lying alongside the quay, and later, during the action, was able to provide supporting fire, its guns raking the attackers along the line of Ferry Street.[30] Matthews was an experienced soldier, and he had prior warning of the proposed attack. Aware of what had occurred at Antrim, Ballymena and Randalstown a few days earlier, he took the precaution of blocking the two open archways of the market house's lower storey to reduce the danger of being smoked out. He also sent a messenger very early in the morning, about 6 a.m., to ask Colonel Stapylton for reinforcements.

The messenger was one McChesney, and not finding Stapylton at Comber, he made his way back towards Portaferry, but was stopped between Newtownards and Greyabbey by a large body of armed men, among whom he recognised the Reverend James Porter. He was told to read out the letter he had with him, but was too agitated to do so. Porter then took it from him, reluctantly, and read out the contents. At Porter's subsequent court martial another witness swore that he had seen him on Saturday with a great many armed men. Asked who would be their officers, Porter had replied that he did not know, but that 'there would be officers in plenty when they would go with the rest of the men to Conlig and Scrabo'. Other witnesses, however, swore that Porter was innocent of any of these actions. All that had happened was that some of the Greyabbey men, resolving to join the main force, had taken off their hats and asked Porter for his blessing and that he had said 'Oh! God bless you'. Then the party, under the command of John McMaster, had marched off to Conlig. Porter had not gone with them.[31]

At Portaferry events followed more or less the same pattern as at Newtownards. The insurgents assembled at a crossroads half a mile to the north-east of the town and entered it along Church Street. They were repulsed with heavy casualties. When six or seven of them had been killed and many more wounded, the whole body retired northwards and established a rebel camp at Innishargie, just a mile to the north-east of Kircubbin, and a central point in the peninsula. Once again, as at Newtownards, the garrison was immediately withdrawn after a successful defence, but this time, for reasons which are not clear, the insurgents did not reoccupy the town. The garrison of yeomanry crossed the lough to Strangford as part of General Nugent's policy of calling in all his outposts in Down to concentrate on holding Belfast, since it seemed likely that the entire countryside would be overrun by the United Irish army.

Among those active in the engagement at Portaferry were the Reverend Robert Gowdy of Dunover, and Archibald Warwick, a young probationer for the ministry. Both were later to be hanged for their part in the Rebellion. Gowdy was charged with having been in touch with Henry Munro at the camp near Saintfield and with bringing back a message to Andrew Orr of Cunningburn. An excise officer named William Harvey, who was taken prisoner by the rebels, later made a sworn statement that he had seen Warwick on horseback on Monday 11 June, with pistols in his pocket, and again on the following day at Innishargie, where Warwick reprobated one Dalzell 'for leading his men too hastily, for that he would have them all slaughtered'. He further testified that the persons in command at the Innishargie camp were Dalzell, Dorrian and McMullan. All three must have later succeeded in escaping to the Isle of Man, because in the following August, General Nugent was moved to complain that the Manx authorities had liberated twenty-seven prisoners who had taken refuge there, including McMullan, Dorrian and Dalzell. Nugent had sent a yeomanry officer and six privates to the island specifically to identify them.[32]

THE FLIGHT TO PORTPATRICK

On Thursday 7 June the Dowager Countess of Roden had been asked if she would like some of the troops stationed at Bryansford village to guard her residence, Tollymore Park. A devout lady, still recovering from the deep religious melancholy occasioned by her husband's death during the previous summer, she had arrived home on 23 May, the day the Rebellion broke out in the South, in the company of her daughter Louisa, and Margaret and Prudence Hutchinson, sisters of the Earl of Donoughmore. Tollymore, in the shadow of the Mournes, might have seemed vulnerable, but the countess declined the offer of military protection. An hour later, however, she received an express message from her eldest daughter, Harriot, which caused her to change her mind. Harriot was the wife of Lord Massereene's brother, the Hon. Chichester Skeffington, and her message was that a rising had taken place at Larne. They hoped it 'would soon be got under', but in the meantime she thought her mother should leave at once for Belfast, for which purpose she was sending horses to meet her at Saintfield, and an order from General Nugent that six of the dragoons guarding Bryansford should accompany her.

'The account was most alarming,' wrote Lady Roden, though she was well aware that Harriot Skeffington was as much in need of her mother's moral support as she was concerned about her safety, for she was worried about her husband 'Chitty', in the thick of things with his troop of yeoman cavalry. The countess and her friends waited until daybreak and then set out in two chaises. The little party consisted of the Hutchinsons, Louisa, three children, two maids and a footman. At Clough they were joined by Captain Wolseley, who gave them his protection for most of the way and took his leave of them two miles outside Belfast, 'as there were troops from thence into the town'. (On his return by the same road he narrowly escaped capture by the insurgents.) Lady Roden was thankful to reach Belfast in safety, without seeing anything alarming on the way. She was lucky, for, as she herself recorded, Saintfield was in rebel hands next day.

They got to Belfast about ten o'clock, to find Harriot distraught. She had not seen her husband for two days and nights, during which he had been in the Battle of Antrim. Later Lady Roden thought that when Colonel Lumley made his brave but ill-advised charge and part of the 22nd Dragoons were cut off, Chitty's coolness had saved the yeoman cavalry. They heard that he was safe, but could hardly believe it, not seeing him return. The troop did return to Belfast a few hours later, having been delayed by the duty of conveying prisoners. They entered the town to the cheers of the citizenry, though Lady Roden's 'doubt of the sincerity of these testimonies of joy damped the luxuriant feel one might have had'. All the friends Harriot could have turned to for comfort in the previous forty-eight hours had already fled to Scotland and she had been very glad to see her mother. The ladies debated what they should do. Chitty was against their leaving, but then they heard that the general had sent Lady Nugent to Scotland and 'every hour brought news of increased disturbances'. That day and the next were passed in the most agitated state.

By Saturday Chitty had changed his mind. He now thought they should go at once, fearing that if a large force descended on the town, the boats would be seized. There was in the harbour a small coal boat, the *Liberty*, with the happily named Captain Cargo. Skeffington saw them safely on board it at nightfall, and soon afterwards Harriot 'had the misery of hearing the trumpet sound to arms'. The *Liberty* edged itself awkwardly into Belfast's twisting channel, and ran aground almost at once, the fault of the pilot, so the captain alleged, but Lady Roden would not have been surprised if the grounding had been deliberate. They lost the tide and stayed on the sandbank until Sunday, when the ladies watched the York Fencibles flying over the Long Bridge. The ship was refloated and ran aground again; at least this meant that people were continually arriving from the town with the latest news. The pilot did not come aboard until barely time for the tide, and by then half the crew had left. All this appeared highly suspicious to Lady Roden, 'but as there was no mending our situation, it was needless to express my fears'. Enough panic was being spread by the 'cruel and false' rumours brought from the town.

It was Monday before they were able to sail, but the crossing was swift and they landed at Portpatrick between three and four o'clock that afternoon. The ship was very crowded, with fifty-three women and children in the hold, but Lady Roden did not hear a single cry of complaint, except from the children, who were tired and overexcited. Harriot had thoughtfully brought with her some mattresses. The captain, 'one of the best-hearted creatures in the world', showed them such kindness, 'as one could only have expected from a much higher style of education'.

At Portpatrick the scene was one of frenzied activity. The town was packed with military waiting to embark for Ireland, and refugees fleeing from it, so that they had no hope of a bed of any kind. They ate their dinner in a dirty bedroom at the inn, but meanwhile the regulating officer, Captain Carmichael, found rooms for them in the manse of the Presbyterian minister, Mr McKenzie. Mrs McKenzie would not accept anything for their accommodation, 'and it was impossible to trespass upon people who had so humanely received us', so Lady Roden resolved to leave Portpatrick as soon as she could. Not only were there no lodgings to be hired, but the proximity to Ireland meant that they were continually receiving reports of the most dreadful kind. Most of them were false, but they were having the worst possible effect on Harriot.

The family therefore moved on to Stranraer, where they took refuge with the Miss Campbells, friends of James Arbuckle of Donaghadee, who was married to another of Lady Roden's daughters, Sophia, and here too they encountered the Reverend William Bristow and his family. On Saturday 16 June they reached Dumfries via Newton Douglas, and stayed the week-end in 'gloomy and disagreeable' lodgings there. At three o'clock on Monday 18 June they came to Longtown, where their friends Sir James and Lady Graham lived. The Grahams, failing to persuade Lady Roden to make an extended stay with them at their residence, found her 'a little dwelling at the end of the town, with a pretty garden', and she remained in Longtown until September, when Sophia and James Arbuckle came to visit her and arrange for her to come home via Donaghadee. It was not until 21 September that she returned to Tollymore. 'Whoever writes the history of this eventful unhappy summer,' she confided to her diary, 'will particularly describe the astonishing mercies that have been granted to the defenders of religion and the laws in this distracted country.'[33]

Donaghadee lies nine miles to the north-east of Newtownards. Its garrison was one of those early called in by Nugent, leaving the loyal inhabitants stripped of any military protection. Donaghadee had been of strategic importance since the seventeenth century, as the Irish end of the short sea route to Portpatrick in Scotland. Its capture was therefore high on the insurgents' list of priorities, and was duly accomplished without bloodshed. Some of the loyalists kept an anxious vigil for three nights, but in the end they desired only to make themselves as inconspicuous as possible.

To complicate matters, a sizeable body of refugees, mostly those in comfortable circumstances, headed for Donaghadee in order to cross into Scotland. Writing from Stranraer on Monday 11 June, Edward Hull told Lord Downshire that he had em-barked on the packet on Thursday night with his mother and sister. 'Our time was short, and we could bring nothing whatever but our clothes.' On the same evening about thirty other loyalists embarked with their families, having had 'to fight their way out'. In fact there does not seem to have been any confrontation, although the insurgents had taken control of the town as soon as the regular troops left. Everyone else in Donaghadee had at least to pretend that they were on the rebel side. 'Mr Nevin was dragged out of bed and a pike presented to him, either to make use of, or to submit to being put to death.' Hull eventually got a place for his mother and sister to stay in Cairnryan.[34]

The most important person in Donaghadee was James Arbuckle, the collector of customs, who really controlled the port. Arbuckle, who had a keen sense of his status, had the good fortune to be in Dublin on business when the Rebellion broke out in the North. News reached him that his house was in the hands of the rebels. 'All my furniture, books, plate, wines, etc., etc., gone to the mischief.' He wrote to a friend in Scotland that his wife Sophia was 'half dead with terror', and that he intended to take her to Wales via Holyhead. He had recently ordered a new chaise, and he was thankful that it had not yet been sent over to Ireland, 'for except *it*, and between 50 and 60 guineas in my pocket, some shirts and stockings, and two black coats, I do not think I have ought else I can call indisputably my own'. However, he suddenly had the consoling recollection that he had a legacy of five hundred pounds safely lodged in a bank at Newcastle.[35]

Arbuckle did not return to Donaghadee until 5 July, when he efficiently organised a public-relations exercise in south-west Scotland to ensure that merchants knew traffic was proceeding normally. He was surprised to find that his property had suffered very little damage:

> The rascals behaved well towards me; they never even entered my house. They sent to borrow a spy-glass and very handsomely returned it uninjured. They forced a foot-boy of ours, a lad of about seventeen or eighteen, to trail the puissant pike. Yet I cannot give them a great deal of credit for all this abstinence from plunder, for if the defeat of the rebel powers had not been

effected at Ballynahinch they would, in the course of a few days, have proceeded to a general participation of the property of loyalists.[36]

In Glasgow the eminent chemist Joseph Black was diverted from his work on latent heat by concern about his relations. His brother George had arrived in Scotland after a hasty exodus from Belfast, and his nephew (also called George) was supplying eagerly awaited details of the progress of the Rebellion and its suppression. He wrote to his brother:

> I received your letter this morning, and one from George, and both of them gave me relief, yours on account of your arrival with your fellow-travellers in Scotland, and your finding better accommodation than might have been expected, and George's on account of its containing better news of very successful actions of the King's Troops, although he says the reinforcements from Scotland had not yet arrived (prevented, I suppose, by westerly winds). The action he mentions is one in which a party of rebels posted on Scraba [sic] hill were beaten and dispersed, but of this one there were only reports, no official accounts yet published; he says also that your cottage in the country remained untouched by either party.

'It is difficult for me at this distance to give you good advice with respect to your further proceedings,' Black goes on. 'If you are both to remove far from home, and hope soon to return and enjoy your delightful retreat at Strandmills [Stranmillis], the place where you are at present, or Irvine or Ayr, are most likely to suit you for a temporary residence.' Soon Black was writing to thank his nephew for regularly sending him the *Belfast News-Letter* with the latest news.[37]

While refugees were streaming out of Ulster, John Brown, a former sovereign of Belfast, ran into danger through his efforts to get home. A prominent Volunteer and Freemason, Brown had been very active in raising the four Belfast Yeomanry companies at the time of the threatened French invasion. He was in Cheltenham when the revolt in the North began, and he at once attempted to return home by Liverpool, but with the good weather and light breezes the passage was interminably slow. He recorded:

> After five days at sea, the vessel, the *Linen Hall*, was boarded by the rebels in Donaghadee Sound, and after searching and finding no arms or anything they thought valuable, they left us. Unfortunately two of the steerage passengers got ashore at Donaghadee in the boat, and told who I was. In about half an hour we were again boarded by two boats, being still without an air of wind in the Sound, who demanded me, as the late Sovereign of Belfast and a Captain of Yeomanry. I was, with Mrs Brown, who was determined to go with me, then taken to Donaghadee, and instantly ordered to be sent to the Rebel Camp about twelve miles distant at Ballynahinch, where I was to be try'd by mock Court Martial, and I was told by a man who seemed to command them that I would have no chance of escaping as I was so well known.

It was on Tuesday 12 June that Brown was brought ashore as a prisoner. 'The humanity of a Mrs Smith, to whose house we were brought,' wrote Brown, 'prevented my going that night, and she promised to have a chaise ready for me next morning.' But on that day General Nugent had marched against the rebels at Ballynahinch and defeated them:

> This defeat saved my life. The news arrived at Donaghadee, and also that the troops were marching in there about 10 o'clock, when every man fled and my two sentinels also. I then procured a small boat with a pair of oars, and with Mrs Brown and an old man rowed to Belfast Lough, where the *Fons* Frigate, [commanded by] Lord Ranelagh, lay, and after being twice pursued by boats from the shore we, in about 4 hours, got safe aboard the Frigate and his Lordship, who had the evening before heard of our misfortune, very politely gave us his boat to land us at Carrickfergus and that evening I got here [Belfast].[38]

'YOUR FATHER
IS ALIVE AND WELL'

In Belfast, once the insurrection had begun, the imprisoned Steel Dickson found that his situation had become more dangerous. The sentries at the Donegall Arms were increased, and the dragoons of the 22nd, incensed by news of their casualties at Antrim, swore that they would not leave one of the prisoners alive. One soldier seized a musket from a sentry and levelled it at their heads, but the provost sergeant took it from him and dragged the soldier away, reporting the incident to the commanding officer. It was not repeated.

The authorities now resorted to the device of placing informers among the prisoners in order to gather the evidence necessary for their trials. Foremost among them was Hughes, on whose information Dickson had been arrested on 5 June, but he played his part well. Dickson 'not only prayed with him, and for him . . . but was quite delighted with the wonderful comfort which devotional exercises seemed to give him'. Some of the other prisoners, however, had suspected Hughes from the first. Mageean also visited Dickson on various pretexts, and no obstacle was put in the way of his visits.

It was soon apparent that John Pollock, the Crown solicitor in Belfast, was desperately trying to get evidence for Dickson's conviction. On the very night of Dickson's arrival he came to see him, and, according to Dickson, he was blind drunk at the time. The minister was roused 'at a late hour' by a voice bellowing for 'the d—d infernal traitor . . . the scoundrel Dickson'. Looking up, Dickson saw a figure, 'not very gainly or dignified, with the appearance of a gentleman under each arm, lighted towards me by a sentinel. He seemed rather unsteady in his gait . . . His language to me, during the few minutes he was allowed to stay, I shall not repeat. His two supporters promptly turned him round and carried him off, raging as he was, and swearing that he would hang the traitor next day.'

A second interview, in a house away from the prison, was more decorous, but present this time was the menacing figure of the Reverend John Cleland, who had collected dossiers of evidence on the County Down rebels. Dickson says that Pollock tried to overawe him into some kind of admission, but in vain. More threats were issued a few days later, Dickson representing himself as coolly answering his interrogator until the latter almost choked in a paroxysm of rage. 'You are d—d confident. By —, I have enough information against you, sufficient to hang *twenty* men.'

And the truth was that Pollock had such information. He produced his trump card. 'Pray, do you know a Nicholas Mageean, sir? I suppose you never met him at any committees, or other seditious meetings?' Dickson replied, 'with all the countenance I could command', that he did know a Mageean, but had never been at any meeting, seditious or otherwise, in his company; whereupon Pollock 'threw open a large book, which lay before him, in which the corners of many leaves were turned down' and named specific places and days. Dickson prevaricated. It was true that he had been in Killinchy and Saintfield on the days mentioned, and had sent Mageean a message about a horse. At the word 'horse' Pollock seemed again in danger of apoplexy, but he recovered. 'Ay, ay. A charger for a *General*, I suppose. Now, pray sir, will you presume to say that you did not receive your commission, as a Rebel General, at Killinchy, in the presence of Mageean?'

Dickson's answer was curious. 'Whether I did or did not receive such a commission, it could not be in the presence of Mageean, as he was not in Killinchy that day, or within several miles of it. He was at home, sowing barley.' (This information had been whispered to Dickson in the prison by a countryman who was a neighbour of Mageean's.)[39] The book which

Pollock had before him was Cleland's dossier and it included a statement by Mageean that on Thursday 31 May, just one week before the Rising, the colonels of County Down had met in Saintfield. They are all named, and the first name on the list is that of the Reverend James Porter. At this meeting 'they generally resolved to act', and this resolve was carried to Dr Dickson by Nicholas Mageean. Thereupon Dickson sent Mageean to Belfast with a letter to Hughes and Simms with the decision of the meeting, and stating that he and the doctor would wait from ten o'clock in the morning until six o'clock in the evening at Mountpottinger for the decision of the Antrim meeting. But Hughes said that they could not get the decision of the Antrim colonels as they were meeting that very day in Ballymena. Their decision would be conveyed to Dickson via Mageean on Saturday 2 June.

That Saturday Mageean went to Belfast to see Hughes and Robert Hunter, from whom he learned that Simms had resigned as adjutant-general for Antrim, and only two of the twenty-three colonels who met were resolved for action. The others would not act on any plan but the invasion of the French, or success by the insurgents above Dublin. They were to meet again on Tuesday to elect a new adjutant-general in place of Simms. Dr Dickson, as 'Adjutant-General of Co. Down', told Mageean that he proposed to take up his headquarters at Ballynahinch on Monday 12 June, and to make that place the rendezvous for the forces of the county. In the face of this evidence, Dickson's life was saved only by Mageean's steadfast refusal to appear in court.[40]

On the day after the attack on Portaferry, Steel Dickson's wife applied to Captain Matthews for protection for herself and her children. He told her that he could not secure her protection against 'a set of ruffians', but he wrote out for her a passport to Donaghadee, from which she could reach Scotland. Mrs Dickson then prepared two common wheel-cars to transport the family and its possessions. Such was the prevailing terror that her servant refused to drive one of the cars, and no man in the district could be persuaded, for any money, to take his place. The Dicksons' second son, John, who was only seventeen, now took charge of the family and they reached Donaghadee safely, though they were frequently stopped by bands of insurgents along the way.

For some unexplained reason, either to keep an eye on the property or more likely to try to establish some contact with his father, Isabella Dickson sent the boy back to Portaferry, reckoning that he would be safe because of his youth. He was stopped almost at once on the road by men who commandeered the wheel-car and took him, first to the camp at Innishargie, and then to Newtownards. Despite his father's principles, this was not to the boy's liking and he escaped, making his way on foot back to Portaferry. There, innocently relating his adventures, he was arrested, confined for two days and then taken to Downpatrick. Steel Dickson says that his son was arrested by Colonel Savage, his sworn enemy, who also tried to incite the military to burn down his house.

At Downpatrick John Dickson began to share some of the experiences that had already befallen his father. He was left for a fortnight in the jail yard, with only straw for bedding and his greatcoat for a blanket, and for some days the only food he had was given to him by the soldiers from their own rations. He was then brought before Lord Annesley and a number of magistrates and officers and closely interrogated. He answered all their questions concerning himself 'with the simplicity of a child and the coolness of a man', but on being asked who were the leaders of the insurgents who took him to Innishargie, he refused to answer. He was then told 'Hark ye, my lad, you need not be afraid to tell all you know of the business – you cannot hurt your father – he was hanged in Belfast yesterday.'

Fortunately Stapylton was one of the officers present. Isabella Dickson had in the meantime written to him a circumstantial account of the boy's being stopped by insurgents after leaving Donaghadee, and Stapylton intervened to protest that he was telling the truth. Then, turning to John, he said, 'Don't be alarmed, my child – you have nothing to fear. Your father is alive and well.' Stapylton had young Dickson sent home to Portaferry, on his own parole, in order to procure securities for his future good behaviour. The boy did so, and returned to Downpatrick next day, when he was set free.

The Dicksons' property did not escape, however. A cow and a dozen sheep were slaughtered to feed the yeomen and the crew of the revenue cutter in Strangford Lough. Several of Dickson's horses were also taken, but he recorded that a cow and a horse were later returned to his daughter by 'two very poor yeomen'. The manse was not ransacked, though it was left locked and uninhabited for a week 'while fire and pillage were raging all round'.[41]

AT THE CREEVY ROCKS

After the engagement at Saintfield on Saturday 9 June, the insurgents set up their main camp at the Creevy Rocks, a mile or so to the south of the town on the road to Ballynahinch. One unsympathetic observer described it as 'a motley crowd of men and boys, women and children'.[42] From this base they sent out emissaries to every part of east Down and the Ards to rouse the country to arms. In this they were at least partly successful, with a certain amount of intimidation, and during Sunday their numbers were considerably augmented.

On that day, Pike Sunday, according to well-established tradition, Birch preached to the rebel host gathered on the rocks, taking his text from Ezekiel, 9:1: 'Cause them that have charge over the city to draw near, even every man with his destroying weapon in his hand.' There is a record, which may be spurious, that he then addressed the hushed and expectant audience with these words:

> Men of Down are gathered here today, being the Sabbath of the Lord God, to pray and fight for the liberty of this kingdom of Ireland. We have grasped the pike and musket and fight for the right against might; to drive the bloodhounds of King George the German King beyond the seas. This is Ireland, we are Irish, and we shall be free.[43]

The problem is that at Birch's court martial, though many witnesses were prepared to say that they saw him at the Creevy Rocks that day, none mentions his preaching a sermon, and the record of the trial runs to several thousand words. The only source for the actual text of the sermon appears to be a document in the collection of the twentieth-century antiquarian,

Colin Johnston Robb, who was an authority on County Down in 1798. Robb lived in the house built at Magheratimpany by his great-grandfather, James Robb, who was a yeomanry officer at the Battle of Ballynahinch. This James Robb had a brother John, who fought on the rebel side, and tradition says that they met during the action. Colin Johnston Robb had the epaulette from his ancestor's uniform, and a jug that he drank from, after being wounded at Ballynahinch.[44]

Among the new arrivals at Creevy Rocks was Henry Munro, a young man of some standing in the Down United Irish structure, who had served his time in the linen trade in Lisburn. As a seller of linen webs, he was obliged to travel about the country a good deal, and, as in McCracken's case, this provided an excellent cover for clandestine political activity. Unlike most of the rebel leaders, Munro was a member of the Church of Ireland and he had an interesting lineage, for he was a direct descendant of Major-General Robert Munro who, sent over from Scotland with an army to curb the Irish rebellion of 1641, was defeated by Owen Roe O'Neill at Benburb in 1646. Born in 1758, the linen draper was an enthusiastic Volunteer and a Freemason. He had become a United Irishman in 1795, influenced it is said by having to witness the flogging of a fellow Mason called Hood, a member of Munro's own lodge.

Munro's sister-in-law was later to declare that when he went to the Creevy Rocks he had acted 'more from impulse than reflection'. Just before the outbreak of the Rising he had left his home in Lisburn, but not with the smallest intention of joining the rebels. Whatever the truth of this, he was a person of such authority that he was instantly elected to leadership. James Hope says that Munro appeared unexpectedly at Creevy Rocks, 'and was appointed by acclamation to the chief command'. He at once attempted to construct some semblance of military discipline, and organised the drilling and weapon-training of the men. (A month later one Richard Vincent was hanged for 'drilling men at Creevy Rocks', and another man called James

Cochrane deposed that after being drilled all day by Munro he managed to escape in Saintfield.)[45]

The Reverend Samuel Edgar noticed as he passed through Ballynahinch at about 10 a.m. on Saturday that virtually no one was working. The people of Ballynahinch and its neighbourhood were assembling in little close groups. 'Work seemed to have been given over, and consultations, apparently secret and unusual, occupied its place.' During the day a party of Castlewellan Yeomanry brought in a prisoner under some suspicion or charge of disaffection. There was a scuffle in the main street, and the prisoner was rescued by the townspeople, but in the course of the fracas a shopkeeper called Richard Cordner, who tried to intervene, was shot and killed. The military left the town without their prisoner, but the incident boded ill. Scores of people fled their houses 'in terrifying apprehensions that the military were on the road to burn the town'.

Before he reached his manse, Edgar met one of his neighbours, whom he afterwards learned was a United Irish captain, just leaving home to join the people in arms. The man stopped to speak, and ask the minister for his advice. Edgar, like most of the Seceders, had avoided anything to do with the United Irishmen and their politics, and he advised his neighbour to stay at home. 'I told him he would do well not to go, as I feared the cause he had espoused was not good . . . "So I think", was the reply; but he hastily rejoined, "I have embarked on the business and must go."' A short time later Edgar met a poor girl, 'warm in the cause', who had been helping to raise some gunpowder that had been buried in the earth for safety, but 'on trying its power, it exploded, and scorched dreadfully her arms and face'.

Edgar remembered:

> The countryside was all in motion. Some hesitated what side to join. Some decided to join neither, but were much perplexed in devising means of safety from the soldiers and the people. Goods and furniture were carried to places of concealment.

Some left the neighbourhood, and the better to cover their departure from a scene of disturbance, and to escape in safety, summoned the people, as they themselves retreated from the theatre of action, to turn out and repair to the camp.

As he neared his home Edgar was suddenly alarmed to see a lone horseman in full uniform and carrying a sabre, on a height only a hundred paces in front of him and directly in his path. 'The sight was not a little appalling to one unarmed', but he found that the yeoman was as much afraid of their meeting as he was himself. He told Edgar that he had joined a yeomanry corps, taken the oath of allegiance, and firmly determined to keep it, was going to join the King's forces at Blaris.

Everywhere as he passed, Edgar saw signs of dreadful preparation:

Some were busy sharpening their pikes and preparing for battle; others, armed with these frightful weapons, were meeting me and crossing my path on their way to the camp. One stated the number in the camp to be 17,000. None asked what I was, or whither I was going. I had an accidental salutation from a respectable woman, as I passed the door of her house. Her husband, immaculate in character, except as connected with the political frenzy that cost him his life, had gone to the camp in the rank of commander. She wore the *déshabillé* of mourning; her speech was fraught with gloomy forebodings; her eyes were swollen with tears. Next morning however she was gay; her eyes sparkled; her language was sprightly, and her prospects were bright, owing to news from the place of encampment.[46]

The inhabitants of Ballynahinch were right to be apprehensive of a military response to the humiliation of the Castlewellan Yeomanry. It came swiftly, at four o'clock on Sunday morning, with the arrival of a force of eight hundred men under the command of the assistant quartermaster-general, Lieutenant-Colonel George Stewart – a mixed force consisting of Argyle Fencible Infantry from Blaris camp, along with cavalry and artillery from Lisburn and Hillsborough. Stewart occupied the town, and such insurgents as there were in it immediately fled, but about two o'clock that afternoon Stewart received orders from Nugent to march to Downpatrick nine miles away, and secure the county town. He left a small holding party.[47]

On Monday morning Munro sent his adjutant, James Townsend, a probationer minister from Newtownards, with a rebel contingent to take possession of Ballynahinch. The garrison left by Stewart appears to have offered no opposition and Townsend occupied the town and Windmill Hill, a high point to the east of it. Later during the morning Munro followed with the rest of the insurgent host from Creevy Rocks and established his main camp on Ednavady Hill in the Montalto estate of Francis Rawdon Hastings, Earl of Moira, just to the south-west of the town. From this camp, also, messengers were sent out to recruit in all directions, but the response was generally disappointing. There had been assemblies of men at Ballywillwill, seven miles to the south, and at Rathfriland, but neither contingent came to Ednavady. Some men from the Rathfriland area did reach Ednavady, however, because one of them was William Brunty, the uncle of Charlotte, Emily and Anne Brontë.

From the anonymous surge of humanity at Ballynahinch, a few other faces can be identified. Among the officers was Andrew Clokey of the Spa, who had become a friend of Wolfe Tone's when the latter stayed at Montalto. He survived to a contented old age, and was affectionately remembered in the locality as 'Clokey, the last of the rebels'. It became a familiar saying. Andrew Brice, the carpenter at Lord Moira's residence, later deposed that at two o'clock on Thursday 12 June he was abducted and forced to make copies of Munro's proclamation that henceforth no rents would be paid, 'as such rent is confiscated to the use of the National Liberty War'. He was scolded for writing 'Morris' in mistake for 'Munro'. And the Public Record Office of Northern Ireland preserves a scribbled letter from young John Patton to his father at Ballybogilbo, Greyabbey.

SAINTFIELD JUNE

Dear Father,

I am afraid you will be troubled about me, but I hope you need not. With God's [help] I hope there is no danger. We marched to Conlig and then to Scrabo, and from these [also?] without meeting any enemy. Our army is about 5,000 commanded by General Munro. A part of the men went to B'nahinch today, and the soldiers ran before ours got near them. We are well treated here, and the men in good heart. There was 48 yeomen and soldiers killed here Saturday, and 9 of the other. I intend to be home as soon as possible.

Yrs

John Patton[48]

EDNAVADY HILL

Nugent had now to decide when it might be safe to take the field himself. Reinforcements had been promised and were arriving from Britain, but they were often the wrong regiments for the task. Cavalry units were coming in at Carrickfergus from Portpatrick, but he needed more infantry, and the situation was still so critical in the South that hardly a soldier could be spared.[49] But he had held Belfast quiet for almost a week, and all the reports from Antrim were good. Some intelligence from Down was trickling through to Belfast from servants and others who had fled to the town from the Saintfield and Ballynahinch area. He learned where the rebels were massing and had established their main camp; that they had rounded up all the horses belonging to the refugees; and that they had some swivel guns – the cannon taken from the ships in Bangor harbour.[50]

James McKey of the Belfast Yeoman Cavalry wrote to Lord Downshire on 11 June that General Nugent was waiting only for additional force to begin the offensive against Munro. General Knox was daily expected to reach Belfast with a great body of troops from County Tyrone, which had remained undisturbed. McKey approved of Nugent's strategy. The rebels were flushed with what they had done, and at being allowed to remain so long in a body without being attacked. Sending out a few troops against such numbers was only sacrificing fine fellows and answering no purpose but adding to their enthusiasm. This was an obvious reference to the ambush at Saintfield, and McKey was indignant at the thought of the Reverend Robert Mortimer's death. 'My heart was like to burst with grief today at seeing Mrs Mortimer and her nine children, who these murderers were the means of robbing of a husband, a Father, and their only support.'[51]

By the morning of Tuesday 12 June, Nugent, reassured by all the reports from County Antrim and by the tranquillity of Belfast, judged that the right moment had come. At 9 a.m. a long column of troops, guns and ammunition waggons began to wind its way out of Belfast and across the Long Bridge into County Down. It consisted of the Monaghan Militia, the Fifeshire Fencibles (Durham's regiment), sixty dragoons of the 22nd, and, under Barber's command, a detachment of the Royal Artillery with half a dozen six-pounder guns and two howitzers. 'Such a sight as I never saw,' wrote one observer, 'an Army whose line of march extended upward of three miles, Horse, Foot and artillery, with Howitzers, Pioneers, miners, sappers, entrenching tools, etc., etc.'[52]

The Long Bridge was one of the distinguishing features of Belfast, a phenomenon which every visitor felt impelled to mention. Its construction in 1682, from County Down red sandstone, had been the engineering marvel of its time, for it consisted of no less than twenty-one arches, only two of which actually spanned the river. The rest were built across the marshy flats of silt and sleech which were so troublesome a feature of Belfast's estuarine location. For more than a century it had provided Belfast's principal link with County Down. King William's cannon had creaked over it on their way to the Battle of the Boyne and had damaged the stonework. One of its massive blocks, they say, is still to be found in the urban maze of east Belfast. On the morning of 12 June the bridge and its approaches were guarded by sentries of the Belfast Yeomanry. The last sentry passed by the army was Dr William Bruce, minister of First (New Light) Congregation, Belfast, and principal of the Belfast Academy.[53]

Nugent's intelligence was good, and his plan was to find and engage the main rebel force, after Colonel Stewart and the Argyles had been brought back from Downpatrick to take up a position which would cut them off from any possible help from south Down. Before leaving Belfast, he ordered Stapylton with the York Fencibles, one hundred of the Monaghan Militia, forty dragoons and a field gun to take post at Comber to cut off the retreat of the rebels to the Ards. Stapylton had already reported that he had 'destroyed a great number of them endeavouring to escape that way'. On Monday, Nugent had also moved Goldie from Blaris camp, with part of the Breadalbane Fencibles as a corps of reserve, 'with orders to prevent the inhabitants of Belfast from rising in the absence of the troops'. They were backed up by the Belfast Yeoman Cavalry.

The progress of the main column after leaving Belfast was slow, and Nugent was wary of ambush. The day was very hot, and the Monaghans sweated under their heavy accoutrements. The waggons were continually held up by the necessity of dealing with broken bridges and culverts, but soon the line of advance could be traced by the smoke of burning farmsteads. It was afternoon by the time Nugent reached Saintfield, only to find that the town was totally deserted and that the camp at Creevy Rocks nearby had been abandoned. He halted only long enough to collect this intelligence and then pressed on towards Ballynahinch.[54]

James Thomson was a lad of twelve in 1798. His uncle was a gardener at Montalto, and his father's home at Spamount, near Ballynahinch, was one of those to whom Munro's message came. Nearly thirty years later, when Thomson had achieved note as a mathematician at Glasgow, he set down his vivid recollections of the hours which followed. The imperative request for provisions 'gave employment to the females of the family, and such others as could be procured to assist, in preparing oaten cakes and boiling large portions of salted beef and bacon'. These preparations were complete by one o'clock on Tuesday, and three of the women 'were appointed to carry to the camp the articles already mentioned, with butter and several other items'. At his urgent request young Thomson was allowed to accompany them, it being thought that his youth would protect him from the danger of detention or harm. His article provides one of the few, and undoubtedly the fullest, eyewitness accounts of the insurgent camp:

> When we arrived there were on the ground a considerable number of females, chiefly servants, or the daughters or wives of cottiers or small farmers. These were almost all employed in the same business as ourselves; though it is said that two or three of them remained on the field during the battle, submitting to their share of its labours and dangers and performing as valiant deeds as the men. Nothing could surpass the delicacy and kindness with which these female visitors were received and conducted through the camp. When those of our party entered the field they were immediately lightened of their burdens and escorted along with them to a particular part of the ground where the provisions were placed under the care of persons appointed to receive and distribute them: and two or three young men offered their services to conduct us through the field.
>
> Everything was explained with minuteness: pikes of different constructions were pointed out and their uses explained; the cannon and ammunition were shown; the tremendous effects glanced at, which they were calculated to produce. The leaders were also pointed out – the more distinguished and greater favourites amongst them – with pride and exultation, and their dresses and ornaments explained . . . The eye was presented with a mixed and motley multitude; some walking about; others stretched listlessly on the green turf along the field; a considerable number sheltering themselves from the scorching rays of a burning sun under the shade of the trees with which the field was skirted . . .

There are, in all this, many touches which are instantly recognisable to anyone born in Ulster. A kind of Sabbath sobriety broods over the scene. This is the familiar church outing, blessed by a sunny summer day. The occasion was more important than the installation of a new minister, or a meeting of the kirk session, but demanded the same attention to the decencies of rural society. The business of the meeting was to sever Ireland from the dominion of Britain, to give her a

separate existence and a name among the nations, to abolish
tithes and taxes and give liberty and equality to all, 'in a word,
to make Ireland at least as happy as the United States and the
French Republic were considered [to be]'. So the men put on
their best clothes, as they would for a funeral or a church
service, and the women baked the cakes and brought the clean
shirts, for this was the way that things were done.

'They wore no uniforms; yet they represented a tolerably
decent appearance, being dressed no doubt in their "Sunday
clothes".' The only thing in which they all concurred was the
wearing of green: almost every individual having a knot of
ribbons of that colour, sometimes intermixed with yellow, in
his hat. The leaders also wore green and yellow belts, and both
leaders and men sported a variety of tokens of affection given
to them by the women, 'whose hearts beat as high in patriotic
ardour as those of their husbands, their sweethearts, or their
brothers'. The most common of these decorations were: the
harp, entwined with shamrock or bays, but without the crown;
the British lion and unicorn 'in a falling position'; and the cap
of liberty, with corresponding inscriptions such as 'LIBERTY OR
DEATH', 'A DOWNFALL TO TYRANTS' and 'FREEDOM TO
IRELAND'.

The weapons were as diverse as the dress:

> By far the majority had pikes – truly formidable instruments in
> a close fight – with wooden shafts, seven or eight feet long, and
> sharpened heads of steel, generally 10 or 12 inches in length,
> some of them with a sort of hook, thought likely to be of use
> in dragging horsemen from their seats, or in cutting the bridles
> of their horses. Others wore old swords, and some had merely
> pitchforks. Those of the higher class were armed with guns. The
> army was composed chiefly of persons in youth or middle life;
> with not a few, however, on the precincts of old age, or on the
> borders between boyhood and youth. Their leaders were
> everywhere moving through the field, speaking familiarly and
> kindly to the men, and cheering their courage.

The visitors had finished their tour of the camp and were just about to leave when there was a sudden commotion, and all eyes were directed to the road from Downpatrick, where a detachment of soldiers could be seen approaching at a distance of about three miles. In an instant the whole camp was in motion, and 'a degree of trepidation and alarm pervaded the undisciplined mass'. Thomson and his female relatives lost no time in quitting the field, and his impression was that there were many present who would dearly have liked to accompany them. They arrived home to find his family considerably agitated, and following the troop movements with a small telescope from the hill beside the house.

As the Thomson family continued their lookout from the hill their attention was now turned in another direction, as they began to see the first signs of the ominous smoke and flames marking Nugent's progress from Belfast. The news rapidly reached Ballynahinch, where the respectable inhabitants now expected that their homes would soon share the same fate, and they began at once to remove and conceal provisions, along with all their most valuable possessions. 'In this way beds and wearing apparel, barrels of meal, flitches of beef and bacon and casks of butter were deposited in meadows and cornfields, in the bottoms of ditches, in gardens, under rubbish, or whatever places appeared least likely to excite suspicion.' Thomson watched the lease of a farm, with money and other documents, being concealed under a large stone in the middle of a field, and he later heard of someone hiding a hundred guineas in a magpie's nest in a high tree.[55]

Stewart's mixed force of Argyles and Downpatrick Yeomanry had reached the environs of Ballynahinch two hours before Nugent's column came in sight. These were the soldiers who had first been seen from Ednavady camp. When Nugent did arrive, the Argyles fired their cannon three times to signal that they were in position. Approaching the town from the Belfast road, Nugent had run into Munro's rear-guard, posted at Bell's Bridge, and then encountered the strong force holding Windmill Hill. He threw out a screen of infantry and prepared to wait for Stewart to join him in an assault on the hill. But Munro's pikemen were in such numbers there that he was apprehensive of their turning his right flank (as they indeed unsuccessfully attempted) and therefore he formed the Fifeshire Fencibles *en potence* with the militia (that is, at right angles to them) to protect his flank. Then he sent orders to Stewart to form on the left of the militia and drive in the rebel post.

Munro saw that he would be encircled, and ordered the immediate evacuation of the hill and the town. Samuel McCance, who commanded the pikemen, obeyed the order with the utmost reluctance. The insurgent force withdrew through the town to Lord Moira's demesne. One straggler, a man named Hugh McCulloch, was captured on the hill, and summarily hanged from the sail of the windmill. Nugent made Windmill Hill his command post. Barber's artillery now began to shell the town and Ednavady Hill beyond. The bombardment continued until darkness fell.[56]

There was some irony in the fact that Munro had decided to establish his main camp in the Montalto estate, for its owner was a liberal peer who had made repeated exertions on behalf of his country, and was a friend of Wolfe Tone. In March and November 1797 the Earl of Moira had moved in the British House of Lords that 'an humble address should be presented to the King, praying him to interpose his personal interference for the allaying of the alarming discontents then subsisting in Ireland'. Moira told his fellow peers:

> Before God and my country, I speak of what I myself have seen in Ireland, the most absurd, as well as the most disgusting, tyranny that any nation ever groaned under. I have seen troops sent, full of this prejudice – that every inhabitant of that kingdom is a rebel to the British government; the most wanton insults, the most grievous oppressions practised upon men of all ranks and conditions, in a part of the country as free of disturbance as the city of London.[57]

Moira had begun improving his estate in 1770, when it was

described as one of the most elegant in the country, with more than one hundred thousand trees of various kinds growing on it. There were good gardens, with many kinds of fruit trees, a pinery and a grapery, and the demesne was adorned with shrubberies, temples, statues, ponds and walks. One visitor remarked that Lord Moira employed a French chef and ate off silver plate, but was shocked to find that the dinner table was lit by tallow, and not wax, candles. This was the site which was now occupied by Munro's Army of the Republic, intent on righting the country's wrongs.[58]

The artillery bombardment of the Montalto woods had a bad effect on morale. As the hot cannon balls scythed through the trees and brushwood, large parties of men simply disappeared in the gathering dark and presumably made their way home through the countryside, or sought refuge on the inhospitable slopes of Slieve Croob, a few miles to the south. One eye-witness to the night on Ednavady Hill, the anonymous source whose 'personal narrative' is printed by William McComb in his account of Ballynahinch, had joined the insurrection on the first day, along with his elder brother, and had been in some of the action at Newtownards. Passing through Saintfield on the way to Ballynahinch, he had watched the dead soldiers being buried; the country people who had fallen had already been interred. 'To see a number of my fellow-men thrown on a car like dead dogs and cast carelessly into a large pit' filled his mind with gloomy reflections. 'I had before this only thought of the glories of war, but its horrors had never been taken into consideration.' He now found himself at Montalto, and during the night he was reunited with his brother, who said to him: 'You see we are deserted by all our friends. We must all die early in the morning. If I be killed first, search my pockets and take what money you can find, and endeavour to save your life by flight. If you reach home alive tell my wife how I fell.' (He had been married for only a month).[59]

In the town, after the troops had occupied it, the night was given over to plundering and looting. Many of the Monaghans got drunk and houses were being set on fire. Charles Teeling's assertion that Henry Munro was too chivalrous to sanction a night attack on the town while his enemies were thus occupied, and that seven hundred or more of the Catholic Defenders at Ednavady at once defected in disgust, makes Munro appear too romantic and naive. There was, however, some rift between Defenders and Presbyterians over strategy. The whole question of why south Down contributed so little to the insurrection, and why the enterprise was so effectively sealed off from what was happening in Louth and farther south is a puzzling one for historians. In the Newry area the Defenders did assemble with the intention of marching north to join Munro at Ballynahinch, but events moved too quickly for them and they dispersed. Whatever the truth, Munro decided on a dawn attack in the early hours of Wednesday morning. The troops in the town were now completely out of hand, and he might have had a considerable advantage if he had attacked in the darkness, a few hours earlier.

There had been, however, a steady defection of the rebel army during the hours of darkness. James Hope later maintained that the entire Killinchy division left Ednavady during the night, and that the brunt of the subsequent fighting in the town was borne by the men of north Down. Certainly one of the leaders of the attacking force was James Scott of Bangor, the man who had seized the guns from a ship in Bangor harbour and taken them to Newtownards.[60]

Edgar records that most of the insurgents who took part in the action were from Bangor, Holywood, Donaghadee, the Ards, Killinchy (despite Hope's evidence), Killyleagh and Castlereagh, with some young commanders from Belfast. It is perhaps significant that this tally of localities is so specific, as if to exonerate his own people. Comparatively speaking, he adds, very few of the inhabitants of the neighbourhood were concerned. It is difficult to know if this is true. Munro's second adjutant, Dr Valentine Swail, was from Ballynahinch. It was he who advised Munro to attack the army during the night, while the Monaghans were busy drinking and plundering the town. This might easily have been accomplished by a party crossing the river at the Mill Bridge (as they later attempted to do in daylight), while another detachment could have crossed to the north, above the town. Munro rejected this advice, and in Edgar's opinion most fortunately, for 'had it been adopted there would have been a most frightful loss of life'.

Following the battle, Swail hid successfully on the Montalto demesne for several weeks. His family knew where he was concealed, but dared not go near his hiding place, though a faithful old servant, Shulah Durnin, managed to supply him with food and necessities. Eventually Swail obtained the government's permission to remove himself and his family to America, and local people did not forget Shulah Durnin's heroic constancy.[61]

Nugent correctly surmised that the main rebel attack would come in the morning, and that the insurgents would issue from the demesne entrance gate and advance up Bridge Street (which is now Dromore Street). The bulk of his cavalry he held in reserve on the northern outskirts of the town, in the vicinity of his battle station at the windmill. The main body of his infantry was stationed in the town, under the command of Colonel Leslie. Barber, commanding the artillery, had at his disposal the six-pounder and howitzer guns. Nugent placed two of the six-pounders in Bridge Street to command the approach.

He had placed strong detachments to the right and left of his position in order to cover the road to Downpatrick on the south-east, and the road to Hillsborough to the north-west. His object was to leave the rebels only one line of retreat, into the mountains in their rear. Munro's plan was to advance a strong force from his right flank, through the demesne grounds and eastward to cross the river at Mill Bridge on the road from Ballynahinch to Clough, and then north across the Mill Fields to attack Nugent's headquarters on Windmill Hill. To forestall this, Nugent sent Stewart with the Argyle Fencibles, part of the 22nd Dragoons, and three companies of yeomanry, supported by a six-pounder and a howitzer, to enfilade the rebels' right flank. Stewart made his way down the Mill Fields and up Crabtree Hill towards the old Magheradroll church-yard, from which position he was able to fire into Montalto grounds.

The battle began at 3 a.m. with the resumption of the artillery bombardment.[62] McComb's witness was one of those Munro ordered into the town. He says that initially they refused to obey the order,

> and three parties were then sent before us, but before reaching the town they all found means to flinch, and we were obliged to go up in the face of a party of the Monaghan Militia, who did not fail to salute us with a brisk fire. We ran up like bloodhounds, and the Monaghans fled into the town, where they kept up a kind of broken fire, which we returned, although only about twenty of us were armed.[63]

The fighting in the streets of Ballynahinch that morning was probably the heaviest of the entire insurrection. The Monaghans were driven back through the town by the sheer ferocity of the rebel attack, and the adjutant, Captain Henry Evatt, was killed. Another officer, Lieutenant Hillis, was wounded, and the insurgents succeeded in capturing both of the field guns. Meanwhile, Munro had sent a fresh detachment over the bridge, and turning eastward they got into Church Street near the parish church. Here they joined up with the main attacking party and managed to drive the army back as far as Market Square. Although their ammunition was exhausted and they came under heavy musket fire, and canister and grapeshot, which took a terrible toll, they pressed on with pike and bayonet, pushing the military into Meeting House Street (now Windmill Street) and towards Nugent's base.

Nugent at once ordered a cavalry charge, and when this failed to dislodge the insurgents, he began to fear that they might take Windmill Hill itself, and ordered a general retreat from the town. And now occurred the ultimate irony, as lack of military knowledge robbed the insurgents of their hard-won advantage. The inexperienced United men mistook the bugles calling retreat for a signal that government reinforcements had arrived, and, as at Antrim, both forces began to retreat simultaneously, the army to the east, and Munro's insurgents to the west. The army was quicker to appreciate the altered situation, and Barber at once returned to the attack.[64]

While this was going on there was also heavy fighting at the Mill Bridge, on Munro's right flank. Munro's attack had turned into a defensive operation, and the military, having artillery support, had the advantage.[65] The sequel is recounted in Nugent's report to Lake:

> Lieutenant-Colonel Stewart now advanced within two hundred yards of the main body of the rebels where they made three different attempts with their musquetry, supported by a very great number of Pikemen, to dislodge him, but were completely beat back by the steadiness and firmness of the Argyle Fencibles and Yeomanry, covered by the Howitzer and the gun served with grape shot, which killed a great number of the Rebels, many of whom they carried off, notwithstanding our heavy fire.
>
> To favour Lieutenant Col. Stewart's Attack I detached the Monaghan Militia with two Field Pieces, some yeomanry infantry, a few of the 22nd Light Dragoons, through the Town, to enter Lord Moira's Demesne, to attack the Rebels in front; at the same time I ordered a strong party of Cavalry to watch their motions on the right – by these movements together with a cannonade in front on their right flank the Rebels began to retreat, and it soon became general, for they fled in all directions – parties of Dragoons were sent out, and killed great numbers in their Retreat, whilst Lieut. Col. Stewart took possession of their strong Post on the Hill where he found their eight guns with a great quantity of ammunition, their Colours, Cars, Provisions, &c, &c – a very considerable number of the Rebels were concealed in the Plantation near Lord Moira's House, who were killed there.

Nugent added a grim postscript. 'The Troops having been fired upon from the Houses in the Town of Ballynahinch, it was set on fire and a considerable part of it consumed.'[66] He was no doubt putting an operational gloss on the excesses of the Monaghans the previous night. He halted for two hours to collect his scattered and battle-elated troops, and then briskly ordered the march back to Belfast.

The defeat of the rebels on Ednavady Hill coincided with their retreat in the town. The cavalry was now ordered to pursue all those fleeing from Ballynahinch, and many of the fugitives were cut down in the next hour or so. Nugent claimed to have killed three hundred in the fighting and a further two hundred in the pursuit, but these numbers are almost certainly exaggerated. Local people thought that perhaps one hundred of the insurgents were killed and a large number wounded, while the army lost about forty, who were at once carried off in tumbrils. Nugent said that he lost one captain and five rank and file, and that one lieutenant and sixteen others were wounded. Several of the yeoman infantry were killed or wounded.[67]

Sixty-three houses in the town were burned down, but sixty-nine were left standing, including the houses of worship. Damage from all causes was set at about twenty thousand pounds. The town was deserted by its inhabitants, but during the next two days men with white bands round their hats came in from the countryside, calling themselves 'Supplementary Yeomanry'. Many of them were armed with rusty guns and bayonets, and 'what little the devouring flames had spared, this banditti in great measure carried away'. The town was still in this forlorn state when Nugent's brother-in-law Cortlandt Skinner rode through it some days later at the head of his troop of Belfast Yeoman Cavalry. Skinner was a magistrate, and he 'very humanely appointed a guard of twelve men of the most respectable of the people, to whom he committed the care of the town'. After that the pillage in some measure ceased.[68]

It was in these cavalry sweeps after the battle that most of the casualties, and the worst of the atrocities, occurred, and the stories rapidly passed into folklore. The behaviour of the 22nd

Dragoons, carried away by the exhilaration of battle, was particularly inhuman. In the townland of Ballykine, about a mile and a quarter from Ballynahinch, there was for long an isolated grave, standing higher than the level of the surrounding field and marked by a stone at its head. In 1861, when the owner of the field was seventy-six, he recalled that as a boy he had helped his father to bury a poor man killed at that spot. A crazed dragoon had arrived at their farmhouse, swearing that he would have twenty lives that day before he slept, in revenge for his brother Billy, killed at Saintfield. He tried to shoot the farmer, who, with a child under each arm, pleaded for his life. The gun did not go off, and while he was reloading, his attention was distracted by a man running away across the field. The dragoon at once pursued him, striking at him with his sword, and then, when the man stumbled and fell, running him through.

The terrorised family did not dare venture out again until nightfall, when the farmer and his son buried the man, first cutting all the silver buttons from his coat. These were later sold in Belfast for two pounds. As is not uncommon in such stories, it is recorded that an exhumation in the nineteenth century confirmed the facts. Part of the grave was opened, and the skull was removed. Then the entire grave was dug up. A hat was found in a good state of preservation, with three cuts in the crown and more in the side, and a fine bottle-green coat with all the buttons missing. The hat ended up in the office of D.S. Ker, the MP for Ballynahinch.

The dragoon's lust for revenge did not abate. His murderous progress can be traced in a whole series of incidents, and he was reputed to have killed as many as fifteen people within half a mile of the same spot. He shot dead two brothers who, taking advantage of the fine weather, were swimming in Ballykine Lough. His next victim was a poor simpleton who was herding cattle. He overtook one William Fee in a field, and with a cut of his sabre almost severed his hand at the wrist, but at this point another soldier arrived and dragged him away. Fee hid in the field, and later managed to attract the attention of a boy, whom he begged piteously to bring him a drink of milk. The boy brought it to him, at the risk of his own life, and watched horrified as the blood dripped into the bowl of milk. Next morning the man had disappeared.

This gave rise to another familiar kind of story which may, or may not, be authentic. Thirty years later the boy, now grown, saw a man whom he thought he recognised, leaning over the half-door in Weighhouse Lane in Belfast. The scar on his wrist was plainly visible. 'Do you know me?' he asked. 'No,' said the man. 'Well, I was the boy who gave you the bowl of milk on the day that your wrist was wounded.' Fee was overjoyed, and took him into his house.

Nugent had told his cavalrymen when he ordered the sweep, 'Now boys, be merciful', but the dragoons were in no mood to obey. The afternoon of the rout witnessed 'a fearful and indiscriminate slaughter'. Passing the house of a farmer in Ballylone, the thirsty dragoons stopped to ask for milk. Basins of milk and cream were carried out to them, and one of the soldiers drew attention to the fact that the farmer had a bandage round his hand. 'He is a rebel,' the dragoon said. 'Look at the cloth round his hand; he has been wounded in the battle.' Thereupon the trooper shot the farmer dead. As it happened, the family were all loyalists. Before they left, the soldiers examined the hand, and found that the bandage merely covered a bad boil. They rounded on their comrade, calling him a murderer, and there was a report that he was later court-martialled in Belfast, though this seems unlikely. Elsewhere there were reports of dragoons entering houses and hacking cheeses with their bloody sabres. Often they took the farmer's horses, and exacted five or ten pounds for their return. In some instances they tried to take prisoners away from the yeomen in order to dispatch them on the spot. It was an afternoon of fearful carnage.[69]

The worst of the atrocities committed that afternoon, however, the one at least which has lingered longest in popular memory, was laid to the account of the yeomanry. Three fugitives from Ednavady were overtaken by a party of the Hillsborough Yeoman Cavalry as they fled along the road towards Lisburn. A young woman called Elizabeth Gray, with her brother George and her fiancé, Willie Boal, were about to cross the county road when they were apparently seen by a vedette posted at the nearby crossroads. The scene of the encounter was a marshy hollow at Ballycreen, about two miles from Ballynahinch. Betsy Gray (to give her the name by which she is best remembered) had gone ahead of the men and was taken first. When George Gray and Boal went to her aid they were instantly shot down. Then a cavalryman called Jack Gill struck off the girl's gloved hand with his sabre, and Thomas Nelson 'of the parish of Annahilt, aided by James Little of the same place' shot her through the head.[70]

The nearby farm belonged then, and for a century later, to a family called Armstrong. Young Matthew Armstrong found the mutilated bodies, and with the help of two neighbours carried them to a hollow on his property, and buried them there in a single grave, 'leaving those faithful Hearts of Down sleeping the sleep that knows no waking'. Almost at once, legend began to weave its tendrils round this brutal killing. Little's wife was afterwards seen wearing the girl's earrings and green petticoat. Feuds were created which lasted down to the twentieth century.

The story ran that Elizabeth Gray was a young woman of extraordinary beauty, who had led the insurgents at Ballynahinch, mounted on a white horse and carrying a green flag, or, alternatively a sword, which in her flight to Ballycreen she concealed in the thatch of a farmhouse, where it was later found and reverently preserved. She became Ulster's own Joan of Arc. The ballad-makers were not slow to add to her apotheosis.[71]

> Now woe be on thee, Anahilt,
> And woe be on the day,
> When brother, lover, both were slain,
> And with them, Bessie Gray.[72]

Mary Balfour, the daughter of the incumbent of the parish of
Limavady, County Derry, and a somewhat neglected poet who
was strongly sympathetic to the United Irishmen, devoted some
grave and tender lines to Betsy in a collection of her poems
published early in the nineteenth century:

> The star of evening slowly rose,
>   Through shades of twilight gleaming,
> It shone to witness Erin's woes,
>   Her children's life-blood streaming:
> 'Twas then, sweet star, thy pensive ray,
>   Fell on the cold unconscious clay,
> That wraps the breast of Bessie Gray,
>   In softened lustre beaming.

In 1886 Wesley Greenhill Lyttle, a journalist and popular
entertainer who regaled rural audiences with *Robin's Readings* –
monologues in the Scottish dialect of County Down – published a novel, *Betsy Gray, or The Hearts of Down*, in which fact and
fiction were recklessly mingled. Lyttle was then the editor of
the *North Down Herald and Bangor Gazette*, a strongly Liberal
newspaper, and it was in its columns that his novel first
appeared, in weekly serial instalments. The short episodic
chapters weakened the story's construction, and the dialogue
and much else were invented by Lyttle (infants are cheerfully
soothed with the patent medicines of the late nineteenth
century), but he was a Newtownards man, and his knowledge
of local folk memory was extensive. The basic facts relating to
Betsy Gray were not challenged by local people at the time and
the book achieved enormous popularity, finding a treasured
place in many a country cottage. Though by then most of the
rural population of north Down were unionists loyal to the
Crown, they deeply admired the stand which their ancestors
had made to redress flagrant wrongs.[73]

Lyttle had called for a monument to be raised at 'the lonely
grave in the vale of Ballycreen' but this was the time when the
Home Rule controversy was at its height, and nothing was done

until 1896, when an American who claimed to be a grand-
nephew of Betsy Gray was given permission by the Armstrong
family to erect 'a stone of native granite, a polished oblong
block with margined sides, resting on a chamfered plinth with
peaked terminal', surrounded by wrought iron railings. Inscrib-
ed on one side of it were the names of the three victims, and
the date of their deaths.[74]

Flowers were now regularly laid at the grave, which became
a favourite place of pilgrimage for Catholic families on Sunday
afternoons, much to the irritation of local Protestants. In 1898,
when nationalist ceremonies were being planned all over
Ireland to mark the centenary of the Rising, word got round
that there would be such a ceremony at Ballycreen. On the eve
of the meeting, a party of local loyalists smashed the stone to
pieces with sledgehammers. 'They meant no disrespect to
Betsy's memory,' one witness recalled in old age, '. . . the local
Protestants were inflamed because it was being organised by
Roman Catholics and other Home Rulers. They did not like
these people claiming Betsy.'[75] On the appointed day, when
the first parties of Home Rulers arrived from Belfast in horse-
drawn carriages, the reins of the horses were cut and the
carriages overturned, and the disturbances were deplored in
hand-wringing editorials by the local press.

Thereafter there was a tug-of-war for Betsy's memory
between the two religions, and among various families claiming relationship. With interest at this level of intensity, it is surprising that Betsy Gray's origins and family background should
still be a matter of doubt. Lyttle based his story on the traditional
view that she was a girl from the Six Road Ends at Gransha in
north Down. Mary Ann McCracken, normally a reliable source,
says, however, that she hailed from Killinchy, and this view was
accepted by McComb and others. A third claim was put forward for Tullyniskey, near Waringsford in the parish of Garvaghy. The balance of probability suggests that Lyttle was right,
and that she was the daughter of Hans Gray, a widowed farmer
of Gransha who died in 1807.[76]

'IT WILL BE A GLORIOUS DAY'

After the army left Belfast on its way to Ballynahinch, the town was very quiet, but the atmosphere was one of apprehension and vigilance. The military left on guard remained on the alert for any sign of insurgency, and the Belfast Yeoman Cavalry were especially on their mettle. James McKey wrote to Lord Downshire:

> Now it is 4 o'clock and the anxiety of the Troops left to guard the town is very great. Many think they hear the cannon. Our Troop are here with about Five Hundred Infantry. All the shops and houses are shut, and no-one is allowed to stir out. Everything has the most Tremendous appearance. I am clear in my own mind, it will be a glorious day. I only regret I could not partake of the glory, as I would doubly enjoy it, knowing every fa[rmer] in that country. I have got Half an hour to refresh myself and I write this drinking. God send our army victorious.[77]

Garrison orders issued by Nugent on the eve of his march on Ballynahinch, and recorded in the orderly book of the Belfast Yeoman Cavalry, give some idea of their responsibilities:

> Detail the guard tomorrow as usual. Field Officer for the day . . . Lieutenant-Colonel Durham, Fifeshire Fencibles. Major-General Nugent has appointed Captain Light, of the Fifeshire Fencibles, to be Commissary for the garrison of Belfast.
>
> The gentlemen of the Belfast Yeomanry cavalry, who serve without pay, are to receive rations for their horses the day they are on picquet. The ration is 14lbs of hay and 10lbs oats. The cavalry picquet is to be mounted entirely by the Yeoman Cavalry.

The General Court Martial is adjourned until tomorrow at twelve o'clock.

Twenty of the Orangemen to mount guard as last night.

The York Fencibles and the Newtownards and Comber Yeomanry, mounted and dismounted, are to do their proportion of duty tomorrow.[78]

The password that night was 'Stapleton'[sic], but on Thursday 14 June it was 'Victory'. Late on Wednesday evening Nugent's force had returned to Belfast in triumph. 'I am just now interrupted by loud huzzas and acclamations of victory', wrote Humphrey Galbraith to Lord Downshire. 'The whole victorious army is returned with the Green Colours, cannon and prisoners, three skurvy-looking rascals, two with pikes and one with a gun and bayonet, they'll be hanged tomorrow.'[79]

A day or two later, Mrs McTier wrote to her brother, remarking incidentally that she believed Lord O'Neill was still alive. 'Perhaps never much hurt, though the lady who took him from off the street in Antrim and sat up with him the first night gave me a full account. A supplementary corps of yeomanry did duty yesterday by guarding the town, among whom were Dr Bruce [her minister], Mr Vance [minister of Second Belfast], J. Kennedy, etc., etc.' Before the troops had left, a great number of respectable people had been taken up, though she hoped it was only to make them secure. She continued to have a high opinion of General Nugent, for she thought she could discern a good head and a benevolent heart in the regulations, and this fact had helped her to decide to stand her ground, when so many ladies had taken flight from Belfast 'at this new and awful period'.

She reported that on Sunday afternoon

eight soldiers, a woman and a child were sent to me, and by Major Fox on horseback, desired to make their quarters good. I opened the door myself and they immediately rushed into the parlour. I told the sergeant my situation. He pressed me to bed them, which I offered to do if he insisted on it, but that I and my family must leave the house. He behaved well the instant they were well treated. I gave them good ale, though they prayed for water, being just off their march from Newtown, where they had been fighting all day. I [pitie]d them much. Two were wounded. They took a shilling apiece, and we parted with civility on all sides.

Ever since then her doors had been locked, and all packed ready for flight if absolutely necessary. However, it would take great fear, which she had not felt yet, to make her stir from home.[80] On Friday 15 June General Nugent wrote to Knox:

We have taken Munro of Lisburn who commanded at Ballynahinch the other day, as well as many others of their Leaders. The Rebels are so disheartened by their Defeat that they sent to me last night to lay down their Arms, etc., on a promise of Pardon which I have offered, excepting their leaders. For the present the Rebellion here is entirely crushed, but there is the best positive Information that a General Rising is still in Agitation.[81]

For people alive at the time, the crisis was by no means over; in some ways it seemed to be just beginning. Nugent went on to say that the rebels could not, however, be very formidable without arms, and would have to wait for the arrival of the French to have any prospect of success. (In fact the third and final stage of the 1798 Rebellion began only in August, in the west of Ireland, when the French did arrive.) In one form or another the spectre of insurrection was to haunt the north of Ireland until 1805 at least.

For the moment the country remained in a very disturbed state. There was a brief reign of terror while the military had a free hand to hunt down and capture as many of the rebels as possible, and punish the guilty and innocent alike by the burning of houses and furniture, and the driving off of cattle and horses. There was some evidence also of a desire to take revenge on those in a higher station of society, the gentry and magistrates whose attitude to the Rebellion had been ambiguous at best, but who had prudently stayed aloof from the action. On 20 June Colonel John Joseph Atherton, from his base at Newtownards, reported to Nugent:

> I have had tolerable success today in apprehending the persons mentioned in the memorandum...We have burned Johnstone's house at Crawford's-Bourn-Mills, at Bangor, destroyed the furniture of Pat Agnew, James Francis and Gibbison, and Campbell's, not yet finished at Ballyholme; burned the house of Johnston at the Demesnes near Bangor; the houses of Jas. Richardson and John Scott at Ballymaconnell-Mills; burned the house of McConnell, miller, and James Martin, a Captain and a friend of McCullock's, hanged at Ballynahinch. Groomsport, reserved. Cotton the same...We hope you will think we have done tolerably well. Tomorrow we go to Portaferry, or rather its neighbourhood. Ought we not to punish the gentlemen of the country who have never assisted the well-disposed people, yeomanry, &c? For my own part a gentleman of any kind, but more particularly a magistrate, who deserts his post at such a period, ought to be – I will not say what. Mr Echlin, of Echlinville; Rev. Hutcheson of Donaghadee; Mr Arbuckle, Collector of Donaghadee, an official man; Mr Ker, Portavoe; Mr Ward of Bangor is now, and only now, to be found.
>
> List of inactive magistrates, or rather friends to the United Irishmen – Sir John Blackwood, John Crawford, of Crawford's-Bourn; John Kennedy, Cultra, &c. But among others, the Rev. H. Montgomery of Rosemount, who is no friend to Government, or its measures, and whom I strongly suspect. I have got his bailiff.[82]

The zeal of Colonel Atherton may have been exceptional, and Nugent strove continuously to exercise moderation and restraint, but there was plenty of evidence that the military in general shared Atherton's opinion. Goldie's aide-de-camp, William Newall, wrote at the end of the month: 'we are much employed in the Examination and trial of prisoners – our Guard-houses, gaols, etc., are quite full and many more are daily brought in. Numbers of them are people of property and they are the people we wish to get hold off [sic] and to punish – we will hang many of them in the course of this and next week.' A few days earlier he had written that they were still taking up people of property for being concerned in the Rebellion, ' many that were not at all suspected. It's wonderful to see what a business it has been, and of five years' standing at least.'[83]

For the most part, though, the hammer of justice fell on the men of no property, on the poor and unprivileged, who had been carried away by grievance and political enthusiasm. Martial law allowed prisoners to be tried as soon as they were taken, and scores were summarily executed, often on doubtful evidence. Many of their names were hardly known, and it would be difficult, even now, to compile a comprehensive list of all those who were hanged. Accounts of executions after summary courts martial appear in many parochial histories; sometimes, where the circumstances were specially dramatic or poignant, they have etched themselves deeply on folk consciousness – like the execution of young Willie Nelson, who stole the horses at Redhall, and was hanged on a sycamore tree near his mother's house, or of Archibald Warwick, hanged at Kircubbin in a thunderstorm, four months after the end of the Rebellion.[84]

V

THE
HANGING
DAY

I'll hae to swear ** forc'd me out
Better he swing than I,
                Some hangin' day.

JAMES ORR, *DONEGORE HILL*

THE BELFAST MOUNTAINS

For the McCracken family in Belfast it had been a week of anguish. Pike Sunday was remembered as a day of gloom and anxiety, everyone talking about the débâcle at Antrim. Friday's *Belfast News-Letter* had carried the first details of the action and the casualties, not completely accurate, but, given the circumstances, a swift and highly creditable piece of reporting.[1] No word reached home of Henry or his brother. Two or three days later, however, a message came, by clandestine channels, from Rose Ann's brother, Jim McGladdery. Hearing it, Mary and Rose Ann decided to set out on foot to look for their menfolk. The difficulties and dangers involved might have deterred the most resolute man; on the other hand, their sex lulled suspicion.[2]

Belfast lay under the strictest curfew, passes were required of all those leaving the town, and a search for fugitives was continuously going on. However, the women succeeded in reaching Whitehouse, a village four or five miles from Belfast on the lough shore, and there they found McGladdery concealed in a gardener's lodge. The gardener was one Cunningham, whose employer, a banker, was conveniently away in England. They now learned the welcome news that William McCracken was safe, having returned to Belfast disguised as a countryman, with a basket of eggs on his arm. Mary pleaded with her sister-in-law to return home but she refused, so after dark McGladdery led them up the slopes of the Cave Hill to a remote cottage where they spent the night.

They spent the whole of the next day on the Belfast hills, high up on the plateau, where the going was rough and boggy. In the back room of a lonely cottage they found eight fugitives, one of them a schoolmaster, earnestly discussing what they should do. Mary strongly advised them to separate and return to their homes. They told her that 'there was something in view' but, in the event of its not taking place, they would certainly follow her advice. Three of the men then agreed to escort Mary and Rose Ann farther into the hills to a place where they thought Henry Joy McCracken might be found. After 'a brisk walk' of two hours or so they came to the summit of the black Bohill, and there Mary found her brother, scanning the horizon with James Hope and five other men.

McCracken was astonished to see his sister, and his whole face lit up with joy. They sat together for a long time, 'talking over their adventures and escapes', far into the summer night. Then McCracken took the women to another cottage, where 'we were received in darkness, the woman not daring to light a candle or make the fire blaze'. He left them, promising to return at seven in the morning. They spent a few very uncomfortable hours huddled on a chair and a stool, and Mary thought the night long. Worse was to follow, for at seven o'clock there was no sign of Harry. They became very uneasy when 'Leith, a thoughtless fellow', arrived, accompanied by the schoolmaster, and they had not met him on the way. But McCracken came at last, having waited for the others until after nine o'clock. They then began the walk home, accompanied for part of the way by McCracken, who was anxious to make contact with McGladdery. 'Even then they had hopes of another movement.'

Establishing McCracken's whereabouts meant that the family was able to send him money, clothes and other small comforts by various intermediaries. On 18 June he acknowledged the safe receipt of several guineas and clothes, which included 'a flannel waistcoat with no sleeves'. It was the first complete change of clothes he had had since the battle. 'I will endeavour to arrange matters,' he wrote, 'so that anything I want will come regularly to me. At present I cannot, as my lodging is in the open air, which with great abundance of exercise keeps me in good health and high spirits, altho' my companions are not so numerous now as they were lately. *These are the times that try men's souls.*' The quotation from Paine was significant, for Paine continued: 'The summer soldier and the sunshine patriot will, in this crisis, shrink from the service of their country; but he that stands it *now*, deserves the love and thanks of man and woman.'[3] Not surprisingly, the letter goes on to dilate on the treachery he has experienced, for 'the rich always betray the poor'. In Antrim

> little or nothing was lost by the people until the brave men who fought the battle had retreated . . . but after the villains who were entrusted with the direction of the lower part of the County gave up, hostages and all, without any cause, private emolument excepted, murder then began and cruelties have continued ever since. It is unfortunate that a few wicked men could destroy a county after having been purchased with blood, for it was a fact which I am sure you never knew that on Friday the 8th June all the county was in the hands of the people, Antrim, Belfast and Carrickfergus excepted.[4]

Shortly after receiving this letter, Mary Ann went to see Harry again. This time the rendezvous was the cottage of a poor labourer, David Bodle (or Boal) on Cave Hill. In the meantime she had managed to obtain a forged pass for him, and arranged for the captain of a foreign vessel to take him on board at a secluded part of the lough shore. There is no record of these arrangements, but it may be assumed that Captain McCracken's seafaring connections played some part in them. The plan was that Henry should ultimately find refuge in America. When all the preparations were complete, and the final farewells had been made, his mother sent him her own copy of Edward Young's *Night Thoughts*.

On 7 July he came down from Cave Hill and spent the night in a safe house at Greencastle. Next morning he put on workman's clothes, and carrying a bag of carpenter's tools in his hand, he began to walk towards Carrickfergus with two companions, Gavin Watt and John Queeny. On the outskirts of the town they had the bad luck to pass four yeomen. One of them, a man called Niblock, suddenly recognised McCracken, from whom he had once bought muslins, and the three men were instantly arrested. However, it soon became clear that the yeomen might be prepared to negotiate. They halted on the way, and one of the yeomen laid down his musket. Gavin Watt at once removed the priming and shouted to McCracken to run away. But McCracken either thought the risk too great, or would not abandon his companions. Instead he offered the yeomen a bill for thirty pounds which he had in his pocket. The party then adjourned to a public house to talk it over. One of the yeomen did not agree with his companions, however. He made some excuse to slip away for a moment, and returned with an officer.

It was on Sunday 8 July, her twenty-eighth birthday, that Mary Ann heard the news of her brother's arrest. She and her father, who was now seventy-eight, at once set off for Carrickfergus. With great difficulty they obtained permission to speak to him in his cell, and only with an officer present. McCracken had no illusions about his fate, and urged Mary to make no appeals on his behalf. Before she left, she noticed that he had scratched on the wall of his cell a line from one of the poems his mother had sent him: 'A friend's worth all the hazard we can run.' Captain McCracken and his daughter stayed the night in Carrickfergus, and next morning they tried to see Harry again. This time they were only allowed to speak to him through a window. He handed his sister his ring to give to his mother. It was the one Thomas Richardson had made for him, engraved with a shamrock and the words 'Remember Orr'.[5]

MᴄCracken was brought to Belfast on 16 July. Mary Ann and her eldest sister Margaret were able to catch a glimpse of him standing in the hot sun in Castle Place, under a heavy military escort, but they were not allowed to speak to him. Mary wrote:

> We hastened to Colonel Durham, who lived in Castle Place, we knocked at the door, and, just as it was opened, the colonel, who was out, came up: and when we earnestly requested that he would give an order for admission to see our brother, who was to be tried next day, he replied that 'If your father and mother, sister and brother, and all the friends we had in the world, were in similar circumstances, he would give no such order.' He had by this time entered his hall door, which he shut against us with great violence.

They returned home in despair, but learning that some of the officers were dining that evening at the Exchange, they hurried there and sent a message in to Colonel Barber. He instantly dispatched a young officer to accompany them to the barracks, and 'when we apologised to this gentleman for giving him so much trouble, he said he did not consider it any trouble and would be glad to serve us', and when they reached the barracks, he 'stood at a distance from the door of the cell, that we might have an opportunity of conversing at our ease with my brother'.

The court martial was fixed for noon on 17 July. McCracken was anxious that his cousins Eleanor Holmes and Mary Tomb should give evidence that they had warned him to leave Belfast on the eve of the Rising. If there was no other evidence against him, he thought this might be useful. At six o'clock next morning, therefore, Mary had to take a carriage to Lisburn to fetch Mary Tomb, who was staying with friends. On reaching Belfast again, they went straight to the Exchange, where the trial had already begun. Mary was immediately struck by the serenity of her brother's expression. She thought she had never seen him look more healthy or at ease with himself 'as at that moment, when he was perfectly aware of his approaching fate'.

Before calling the prosecution witnesses, John Pollock took Captain McCracken aside, and told him that he had enough evidence to hang his son, but would spare his life if he could be persuaded to say in whose place he had acted as commander-in-chief. Pollock called Harry over and made the same offer to him. McCracken said, 'I will do anything which my father knows is right for me to do.' 'Harry, my dear,' said his father, 'I know nothing of the business, but you know best what you ought to do.' At this McCracken said, 'Farewell, Father', and walked back to the table.[6]

At this stage he did not know what witnesses would be brought against him. One of his own workmen, William Thompson, an English calico printer, had refused to testify. He was given two hundred lashes and would have died of his treatment had Mary Ann not nursed him back to health. There was a rumour that Samuel Orr, who had defected at Slemish, would appear, but he also refused. Instead Pollock called on the evidence of two men McCracken had never seen in his life. One Minniss swore that McCracken had come to his house and forced him to join the insurgents at Antrim, where he had seen him take an active part in the fighting. Another man, James Beck, testified that he also had seen McCracken at Antrim, and identified him by a mark on his neck, which was only visible when his neckerchief was removed.

This evidence was probably perjured. Hope later alleged that both men had been taken to the barracks to have McCracken pointed out to them, and that the guard had drawn their attention to the distinctive mark on his neck. But, as McCracken himself admitted, the truth would have served the same purpose.

The day was very hot and McCracken was busily taking notes. He told his sister that he was thirsty, and asked her if she could bring him an orange, or some wine and water. She hurried home to Rosemary Lane, and on the way met William Thompson's wife, who offered to swear that she had seen McCracken in Belfast on 7 June. Both McCracken and his attorney, Thomas Stewart, rejected this offer. The cousins Eleanor Holmes and Mary Tomb were then called. Mrs Tomb wept during Pollock's hectoring cross-examination, but did not lose her head, and he failed to trap her into some damaging admission.

The authorities, aware of the general sympathy for McCracken, were patently anxious that the trial should be seen to be fair. Both Mary Ann and the prisoner were allowed to address the court on the evidence, and afterwards McCracken whispered to his sister that she must be prepared for his conviction. Once again, Mary slipped away home to bring the news to her mother, who insisted on going to General Nugent's house to beg that the sentence might be commuted to banishment, but Nugent refused to see her. When Mary returned to the Exchange it was to find that sentence of death had already been passed, and McCracken was being hurried away to the barracks. She followed him there and asked Fox, the town major, for permission to speak to him. Fox told her to wait, but she rushed after him and heard him tell McCracken, 'You are ordered for immediate execution', as he opened the cell door.

She saw the look of astonishment on her brother's face – he had assumed that he would be allowed some time after the trial – and then her knees gave way and he leapt forward to catch her in his arms. But she did not faint then:

> I did not lose consciousness for a single instant, but felt a strange sort of composure and self-possession; and in this frame of mind I continued during the whole day. I knew it was incumbent on me to avoid disturbing the last moments of my brother's life, and I endeavoured to render them worthy of his whole career. We conversed as calmly as we had ever done.

He asked her to write to Thomas Russell to 'inform him of my death, and tell him I have done my duty'. She asked him if there was anything else, and he said 'No', but she was conscious that there was something troubling his thoughts which he could not bring himself to say to her. He said he would like to see his minister, the Reverend Sinclair Kelburn, and a message was sent to the manse. Kelburn had been in poor health since his release from Kilmainham and he was confined to bed, but he insisted on rising and going to the barracks. It was a very long time before he appeared, and Mary suggested that they might send for Dr Dickson, who was a prisoner under the same roof. McCracken would have preferred to talk to Kelburn, but he agreed, and Dickson was sent to him. The two men walked to the far end of the room, and Mary saw Dickson take out his pocketbook and write something in it. Soon afterwards, Kelburn arrived. He at once burst into tears, murmuring brokenly, 'Oh, Harry, you did not know how much I loved you.' Struggling to regain his composure, he turned to Major Fox and said, 'I hope, Major, you will take care of the arms I sent you; the gun was a fowling-piece of my father's, for which I have a great regard, and I would be sorry to lose it.' Then Kelburn asked them to kneel in prayer.

Mary wrote:

> During the early part of the day, Harry and I had conversed with tranquillity on the subject of his death. We had been brought up in a firm conviction of an all-wise and over-ruling Providence, and the duty of entire resignation to the Divine will. I remarked that his death was as much a dispensation of Providence as if it had happened in the course of nature, to which he assented.

When both ministers had gone, she asked for a pair of scissors to cut off a lock of his hair, and after some understandable hesitation they were brought to her. She cut off some of the hair which curled about his neck, and folding it in a paper put it in her dress, but just then Fox entered the room and demanded that she give it up, saying that 'too much use had been made of such things'. Mary refused. She would give it up only at her own death, she said. McCracken said, 'Oh, Mary, give it to him; of what value is it?', and to spare her brother further distress, she obeyed. It was, however, returned to her, and it is preserved, still bright and golden, in the Madden papers in Trinity College Dublin.

At 5 p.m. he was taken for execution on an improvised gallows in High Street in front of the market house, in which he had conducted his Sunday school – the ground had been given to the town by his great-great-grandfather, George Martin.[7] Mary wrote:

> I took his arm and we walked together to the place of execution, where I was told it was the General's orders that I should leave him. I peremptorily refused. Harry begged I would go. Clasping my hands around him (I did not weep till then), I said I could bear anything but leaving him. Three times he kissed me and entreated I would go; and looking round to recognise some friend to put me in charge of, he beckoned to a Mr Boyd, and said 'He will take charge of you' . . . and fearing any farther refusal would disturb the last moments of my dearest brother, I suffered myself to be led away.[8]

Mary was told that, after she left, Fox made one last try to persuade her brother to give information. McCracken asked Fox what reason he had to think he was a villain, but, since they were to part, he would shake hands with him. She also learned that when he ascended the scaffold, he tried to address the people, but the noise the horses made was so great he could not be heard. And then 'a few minutes put him beyond the power of oppression'. Nugent allowed the body to be given to her, on condition it was interred before dark.[9] But first Mary sent for Dr MacDonnell, Russell's friend, whose graduation thesis had been on 'the resuscitation of the apparently drowned'. MacDonnell was a Glensman from north Antrim, the associate of many of the Belfast United Irishmen, but he did not share their politics.[10] He did not come, but sent his brother, 'a skilful surgeon', in his place. His efforts were unsuccessful. Mary stayed by the body while many mourners crowded in to pay their last respects.

When the funeral cortège set out for St George's churchyard, a short distance away, Mary realised that she was the only member of the family to follow the coffin. A kind-hearted man took her arm in his, and at that her brother John, who hated the whole business, ran after her and stayed by her side. She did not faint until she heard the first shovelful of earth fall on the coffin, and it was John who brought her home.

William McCracken moved with his family to Castle Street and continued the textile business, though it was said he never really recovered from the sorrow of Henry's death. He died suddenly in 1814, a fortnight after the death of his mother.

By the lights of the time, and given the restraints he was under, Nugent's releasing of McCracken's body was an attempt at humanity. That so many ordinary people filed past it, weeping, in the room where it was laid, showed the gesture was not without its dangers. Above all, he had instructed that the head was not to be severed and publicly displayed. As the little funeral cortège made its way to St George's, it had to pass the blackened heads of James Dickey, John Storey, Hugh Grimes and Henry Byers, set on spikes above the market house. They had been placed there for a purpose – to impress on the citizens of Belfast that this was the penalty for disaffection and treason, and the same pattern was followed in other centres throughout the province. In that hot summer, the town authorities in Belfast issued a warning about the consumption of uncooked fruit because of the swarms of flies.[11]

James Dickey had evaded capture until 25 June, when he was overtaken by a party of the Sutherland Fencibles 'in the neighbourhood of Divis Mountain'. There is a story that he had himself built up in a turf clamp, and was half dead from starvation when an attorney of his acquaintance happened to pass by on the road. Dickey attracted his attention, and the man, whose name was John Dillon, gave him money and went to fetch him food. Instead, he betrayed Dickey to the military. Dickey was tried in Belfast on 26 June, and met his end with the utmost composure. 'The prisoner seemed insensible of his unhappy situation. He said he would not give the court much trouble; what was true he would acknowledge and what were lies he would contradict.' He was sentenced to death and hanged, though not before he delivered a vatic pronouncement that boded no good for the future. The Presbyterians, he said, had been completely deceived by their Catholic allies, and if the Rebellion had succeeded, they would have had to fight them next. The Reverend Sinclair Kelburn was with him at the end.

So was Colonel Durham, but not in a spiritual capacity. According to Durham, Dickey was endeavouring to win as much time as possible from the field officer of the day, perhaps in the hope that his friends might rescue him. Seeing this, General Nugent desired Durham to go and have the execution performed, and not to let the crowd get larger. Durham pushed his way through the throng and told Dickey the sentence must be carried out. Dickey asked for porter to drink. 'I could not allow it, but I sent a Drummer for a glass of water.' While they waited, Dickey told him that a gentleman in Randalstown owed him two pounds. He asked Durham to get it from him and give it to a certain girl he named. 'When you are hanged,' said Durham. Lawyer to the last, Dickey pointed out that the man would not pay. 'I will give you a bill upon him,' he said. 'I gave him the fold-down of a letter I had in my pocket. He sat down in the street, and wrote me as clear a bill as any man could write, and was hanged in five minutes.'

Durham was much impressed by Dickey's coolness, as he saw it. When the attorney had observed Durham looking at a cut in his trousers, he had said, 'One of your dragoons gave me that at Antrim . . . if my men [had] stuck to me as yours did that day to you I would have beat you.'[12]

Byers was unlucky in having his sentence left to the whim of his landlord. He was a young man who had been one of Munro's officers at Ballynahinch and he was married to the daughter of one of Squire Price's servants at Saintfield House. He was tried by court martial at Belfast on a charge of driving to Saintfield some of Mr Price's bullocks, and also for riding one of his horses upon expresses.

The court, not desiring to put him to death, transmitted the decision to Mr Price's house, and left the sentence to his option.

Mr Price posted to Belfast, and had Byers ordered immediately for execution, and upon his being brought forward to the guard-house door, clapped him upon the shoulders, and pointing to the gallows and the heads above it upon the market house spire, told him to take heart and go boldly for he should soon have plenty of his neighbours for Company.[13]

On 14 June Richard Caldwell and John Gunning, under assumed names, managed to make their way to Cushendall, and next day they persuaded a boatman to take them across to Scotland. He landed them on the Mull of Kintyre that evening and they headed inland, but a week later they were both arrested by the Reverend Alexander Campbell, the minister of Kilcalmonell. Brought back from Portpatrick on HM cutter *Princess Elizabeth*, they were tried by court martial at Coleraine and sentenced to be hanged. Caldwell's head was to be severed and placed on a spike at the market house. His father went to Dublin, however, and through influence obtained an interview with the newly appointed lord lieutenant Lord Cornwallis, whose guiding principle was magnanimity in victory. The sentence was reduced to 'transportation' to America, and later Lord Henry Murray had Gunning's sentence commuted to penal transportation to Botany Bay.[14]

Eventually the entire Caldwell family moved to America and prospered there. Richard sailed from Derry on 1 September 1798, and the other members of his family from Belfast in May 1799, after chartering a brig for the purpose. They made their new home at Salisbury Mills, New York, and a few years later Richard was said to have the handsomest farm in the county.

Most of the north Antrim leaders were fortunate. John Nevin eluded capture at first, and was later smuggled through Coleraine in a barrel. He sailed from Magilligan to America, where he 'traded with the Indians' and died in 1806. Two other men involved, Peter and William Lyle of the Orble, also emigrated to America, and in the next generation the sons of both were officers in the civil war. In north Antrim, Murray's men burned the village of Kilmoyle, in mistake for the

Kilmoyle where Nevin lived, and the townland was long known as 'burnt Kilmail'. When the Lyle farm was similarly burned, the smell of the burning meal spread over the whole countryside.[15]

When all was lost at Ballynahinch, Munro and William Kean, formerly a clerk in the office of the *Northern Star*, made for the desolate slopes of Slieve Croob. There they were concealed in a pig house on the farm of William Holmes in the townland of Clintynagullion. Holmes betrayed them almost at once. They were arrested and brought first to Dromore and put in the custody of a local landowner, Mr Crane Brush, who then escorted them to Lisburn. Kean subsequently escaped, but Munro was tried by court martial on 16 June and sentenced to death. A gallows had been erected in Castle Street, and he was brought out to it about four o'clock in the afternoon. He asked to be allowed to go into the house of the rector, the Reverend Snowden Cupples, to receive the sacrament, and this was granted. Munro had behaved with great dignity during the trial and had impressed the army officers present. His last words were 'Tell my country I have deserved better of her.' His head was placed on the Lisburn market house.[16]

The Reverend Thomas Ledlie Birch was tried at Lisburn immediately after Munro on 18, 19 and 20 June, and one observer contrasted his 'long and blubbering defence' unfavourably with the fortitude shown by Munro.

He had been arrested on 16 June by a troop of the 24th Light Dragoons, and brought to face a court martial in Lisburn on a charge of treason and rebellion. His brother, Dr George Birch, was a respected physician in Newtownards, a friend of Lord Castlereagh and a captain of the Newtownards Yeomanry. Both his sons, however, had fought on the rebel side at Ballynahinch. The records of the trial make no reference to the minister having been in arms and the court found that the evidence against him was not sufficiently strong and he was acquitted of the charge against him. There can be no doubt that he owed his life to his brother's influence with the Stewarts, for George

Birch had already told him before the trial that if he agreed to go into exile he would be saved. Ledlie Birch therefore addressed the court with these words:

> Gentlemen, I may have done wrong, but it was in error. I love my king and country and shall ever pray for their happiness. I have the most perfect confidence in the justice and humanity of this court, and most cheerfully resign my honour and life to its disposal, and sensible that I cannot be any longer happy or useful in this country, I shall, when ordered by General Goldie or any other person authorised to order me, quit his Majesty's Dominions, never to return without subjecting myself to such punishment as is inflicted on persons returning from transportation without leave, and retire to America or some other country not at war with his Majesty.

For his own safety, Birch was not released from custody, a wise precaution since, on the following day, a party of yeomen approached the guardhouse with the intention of taking him out to hang him, but they were prevented by the dragoons who formed up in the street outside. Two days later he was taken to Belfast and put on board the prison tender in the lough. Conditions there were unpleasant, especially in the summer heat, but not intolerable, and he had the company of Steel Dickson, William Sinclair, and David Bailie Warden among others. He was not released until 16 August when he was allowed to sail to New York from Belfast, on board the *Harmony* of New Bedford.[17]

The Reverend James Porter had no one to plead on his behalf, and was indeed not expecting to be arrested.[18] Whatever his earlier affiliations, he seems to have played little or no part in the Rebellion. His son, James Porter, who became attorney-general of Louisiana, has left an account of the days which followed, recalled from the memories of childhood:

> My father, conscious of having committed no offence, did not attempt to fly. He remained with his family. To his, and my mother's, great surprise, and to her dreadful consternation, he

was arrested a few days later and placed with many others . . . in the market house of Newtownards, then converted into a prison. My mother . . . said from the moment of his arrest that she was certain the hatred of Lord Londonderry would cost her husband his life. The first official notice he had of his offence was in the written charges preferred against him, and on which the young officer who handed it to him, with an air of perfect nonchalance, and humming a loyal tune as he turned on his heel and left him, told him he must prepare for trial.

On the following day (30 June) Porter was conducted before a court martial consisting of the officer commanding the dragoons at Newtownards, two captains and four subalterns. 'To his dismay he perceived that the Earl of Londonderry had taken his seat among them and he found, as the trial proceeded, how potent was his influence and how fearfully it was brought to bear upon him.' Porter denied absolutely having intercepted a King's messenger, and declared his innocence, but he was found guilty, and told that he would be executed in sight of his own meeting house at Greyabbey three days later. He received the sentence calmly. 'A stranger could not have discovered from his countenance or language that anything extraordinary had happened to him. But the event overwhelmed my mother with grief.'

However, Mrs Porter was determined to do everything humanly possible to save her husband's life. With her seven children, the youngest in her arms, she walked to Mount Stewart, 'waited upon Lady Londonderry, represented to her her wretched condition, and implored her interference'. The countess and her daughter, Lady Elizabeth, who was soon to die of consumption, were much affected by her plight, and Lady Londonderry at once agreed to write a letter to General Nugent. Mrs Porter's hopes were raised, but before she left the room, Lord Londonderry entered it and asked the purpose of her visit. He then directed his wife to add a postscript to the letter, and, handing it to Mrs Porter, told her she might make what use of it she pleased.

Lady Londonderry had written:

The wife of Mr Porter, the dissenting minister of Greyabbey, solicits me in a state of absolute despair to address you on behalf of her husband, who is accused of being a leader in the rebellion. She asserts that he never was engaged in the transaction at any time and that his being found amongst them was accidental. How this may be I cannot presume to say. I only know that Mr Porter is a man of sense and acquirements, whose interest it could hardly be to overturn the government by which he was protected. Perhaps, however, you are better informed, but the great humanity of your character which is considered to be equal to your fairness, spirit and ability, exposes you to importunity and perhaps to impertinence which I would rather risk at this moment than await an opportunity of giving a mind like yours occasion to make inquiry. I hope therefore to be sanguine in asking at the urgent request of this most wretched woman whether the sentence may be changed to transportation or any other penalty but life, a life important to the wife and seven children. At best my ignorance of the extent of his delinquency will, I trust, induce you to excuse my presumption.

If the document is genuine, Londonderry had obliged her to add the postscript: 'L. does not allow me to interfere in Mr. Porter's case. I cannot therefore, and beg not to be mentioned. I only send the letter to gratify the humour.' Mrs Porter told her son that nothing in her life ever filled her with so much horror as his lordship's smile as he handed her the letter with the postscript added.

She did not give up, even then, and at once set out in a carriage for Belfast, again accompanied by all her children, in the hope of speaking to Nugent directly. 'I was then twelve years of age,' wrote James Porter. 'I remember the rain fell in torrents. We were well drenched, and I recollect the effect produced on me by the heads of the condemned rebels which were stuck up in Belfast.' His mother was sent away from Nugent's door, with the declaration that there was no answer for her.

On the morning of the day which terminated my father's life

(2 July 1798) he got into a carriage at the hour of 11 o'clock and was conducted under a guard of cavalry from Newtownards to Greyabbey. A temporary gallows was erected on a small hill which overlooked the meeting-house where he had officiated as pastor for ten years. My mother rode with him to the place of execution. During the ride the conversation turned on her future course in life. He directed her to send his sons to America as soon as they were of age to leave her, and told her that he had had too many evidences in his life of God's providence to doubt that she and her daughters would be protected and provided for. Arrived at the fatal spot, my mother kissed him for the last time. When she returned to the manse, the children were all at the door, waiting for her arrival. She did not sit down. In an hour after, the body she had left in health and strength and all the pride of manly beauty was delivered to her a corpse. She had it carried into the room, and I remember that until the next morning no solicitation or entreaty could tear her from its side. Nor would she sit down. She stood and looked on it with her hands clasped. Not a tear fell, not a word escaped her lips.[19]

EPILOGUE

In her diary Lady Nugent did not disguise the relief which she and the general felt on leaving Ireland in 1801,

> having witnessed . . . all the horrors of a civil war, during which my dear husband had the command in the North; so that he was not only obliged to meet the poor, infatuated, misguided people in the open field, but, after defeating them there, had also the distressing task of holding courts martial, and signing the death warrants of very many, which was indeed heart-breaking to us both.[1]

Soon afterwards, Nugent was appointed lieutenant-governor of Jamaica, and later on, like General Lake, he was to hold senior command in India. He was made commander-in-chief there in 1811, and he was a field marshal when he died in 1849 at the age of ninety-two.[2]

The storm of insurrection which swept over Ireland in the summer of 1798 had three distinct phases, apart in geography and, to some extent, in time. The first and most serious rebellion, which came closest to success, was that which burst out in the south-east on 23 May, and effectively ended with the capture of the main rebel stronghold at Vinegar Hill on 21 June, though desultory action continued until mid-July. It had been raging for two weeks when the northern rising began on 7 June, long enough for stories of atrocities against Protestants at Scullabogue and Wexford to reach Antrim and Down and have a profound effect. It was August when the French came, landing in the far west at Killala, County Mayo, remote from the two centres of insurrection. General Jean Humbert and his 1,100 troops marched inland, joined by several thousand men of

Connacht and country folk who thought of the Rebellion as a religious crusade. They routed a much superior force, mainly of militia and yeomanry, at Castlebar, and held out until 8 September, when Humbert was obliged to surrender to Lake at Ballinamuck.

The first news of the rebellion in May had taken Wolfe Tone completely by surprise, and he was astonished that Ulster had not led the way. When another French expedition sailed from Brest a few days later, Tone was among the three thousand soldiers it transported. It was intercepted and engaged by a British squadron off County Donegal and all the French ships were captured. Tone was instantly recognised among the prisoners and sent to Dublin for trial by court martial. Condemned, he asked to be shot rather than hanged, and when this was denied to him, he committed suicide in his prison cell.

Longevity, however, was granted to some of the principal actors in the drama of June 1798, and a few were still recounting their adventures in the seventh decade of the nineteenth century. James Burns, who loaded and fired the rebel cannon in the main street of Antrim, died in Larne workhouse in 1864. When he was in his ninety-second year, he related to the Reverend Classon Porter some fascinating details about the turn out and those who were involved in it.[3] Ezekiel Vance, the saddler who fought on the other side, lived to a contented old age in his native town of Antrim, and his descendants maintained the heroic tradition. On 15 July 1916, Lieutenant Ezekiel Vance died of wounds in the German field hospital at Candrey, part of Ulster's sacrifice on the Somme.[4]

Colonel William Lumley did not, as many accounts state, die of the wound he received during his impetuous charge. He lived to fight many another day, holding command in Egypt, South Africa and South America, before taking a distinguished part in Wellington's campaign in the Peninsula. Knighted in 1815, and made a general in 1837, he died at Grosvenor Square in 1850.[5]

Mrs Martha McTier was ninety-five when she died in the

year of Queen Victoria's accession. She had outlived her husband, Samuel McTier, by more than forty years. Two years earlier, the officers who compiled the Ordnance Survey memoirs had discovered a woman living in Lisburn who was one hundred and seven. Margaret McCurry had been over thirty at the time of the French landing at Carrickfergus in 1760, and remembered it well; but she had more painful memories of 1798, when her husband was killed and their farm burned down, a catastrophe which ultimately forced her to 'beg her bread' through the streets of Lisburn.[6]

Mary Ann McCracken was ninety-six when she died in 1866. She devoted the rest of her long life to social reform, endeavouring to improve the lot of women, children and the poor. 'And now a better day has dawned,' she wrote, as the young Queen began her reign. '. . . In looking forty years back, and in thinking, too, of those who were gone, how delighted they would have been at the political changes that have taken place – which could not possibly in their day have been anticipated, by peaceful means . . .'[7] She was no doubt thinking especially of Catholic emancipation in 1829 and the Reform Act of 1832. When she was over seventy, she gave up much of her meagre leisure to corresponding with Dr Richard Madden, and providing him with materials which he used in his seven-volume hagiography of the United Irishmen. Her life of self-sacrifice and dedication to the needs of others have won her acclaim in her own right, and, in the words of her biographer, 'she bequeathed to her birth-place a legacy of unusual nobility and courage'. She lies buried near the Charitable Institution her father helped to found, and her tombstone bears the words: 'wept by her brother's scaffold'.[8]

A fortnight after her brother's execution, Steel Dickson had sent for her to come and see him on 'urgent business'. He revealed that Harry had an illegitimate daughter, a little girl called Maria, who was almost four. It has always been assumed that her mother was Mary Bodel, the daughter of the man in whose cottage on Cave Hill McCracken had often sheltered.

This child was 'left to our care', Mary wrote, and she was at once taken in to the McCracken family, despite John McCracken's initial protests. 'We have got an addition to the family since you were here,' he wrote to his son Frank, then in the Barbados. 'It is a little girl said to be a daughter of poor Harry's; it was brought very much against my inclinations.' The child's mother and family emigrated to America, assisted by Mary Ann. Maria grew up to be Mary's constant companion and a willing helper in all her philanthropic enterprises. In middle age she married the widower William McCleery, another of the radical circle, and it was in their home that Mary spent her last years.

Two centuries have elapsed since 1798, so that at first it seems incredible that Mary Ann McCracken should have lived long enough to be the subject of photography. But there is a splendidly clear photograph of her in old age, from which she looks out at us with shrewd Ulster eyes, and an expression that mingles endurance and willpower – as if to say, with Elizabeth Barrett Browning, 'Measure not the work, until the day is out and the labour done.'[9]

Robert McKerlie, the young Scottish ensign who served under Lord Henry Murray at Coleraine, also lived long enough to be photographed, and again the face gives us his character, and warns us that life is earnest – the Victorians did not smile for photographers. Two years after the Rebellion, he returned to Scotland and joined the newly raised regiment of the Dumfriesshire Militia, commanded by the Earl of Dalkeith. After the Peace of Amiens in 1802 he went to France with Lord Dalkeith, and kept an interesting journal of his impressions of the Napoleonic state. In 1804 he was appointed principal ordnance storekeeper at Edinburgh Castle.[10]

The indomitable James Hope continued to devote himself to the principles of reform by revolution, but he bore a charmed life. It seemed difficult ever to obtain enough evidence against him. He moved with his wife Rose to Dublin, where he took up work again as a weaver, but he continued to associate with the surviving United Irishmen, plotting another attempt to rouse the North on behalf of Emmet's rebellion in 1803. He was sent to Antrim in that summer, and Thomas Russell ('the man from God-knows-where')[11] undertook to call out the men of Down. Russell was hanged at Downpatrick in October 1803, but Hope escaped yet again. After the death of Pitt in 1806, and a change of government in Britain, Hope was able to return to his home in Antrim, and he lived there for the rest of his life. He died in 1847, at the age of eighty-three, and his headstone in Mallusk graveyard records that he was 'one of Nature's noblest works, an honest man'.[12]

Steel Dickson, along with Neilson, Simms and seventeen other state prisoners, was taken to Scotland and incarcerated in Fort George in the Moray Firth until 1802. He tried to resume his life as a minister at Portaferry, but the implacable hatred of Cleland drove him out of the Ards, and he accepted a call from the congregation at Keady, in County Armagh, at a greatly reduced stipend. In 1812 he published an account of his tribulations, complaining bitterly about the treatment he had received from his brethren in the Synod. When he became too old to carry on his pastoral duties, he was supported by the charity of friends, including Drennan and Francis McCracken, and when he died in 1824, he was buried not far from Mary Ann McCracken, but in a pauper's grave. The spot remained unmarked until 1909, when Francis Joseph Bigger erected a stone over it with an epitaph in Irish. It read: 'Do cum onora na h-Ereann' (sic), 'For the honour of Ireland'. A street in Portaferry is named after him.[13]

Those of his brethren who were obliged to transport themselves across the Atlantic, including Birch, fared well on the whole. They were adopted by American presbyteries, and one or two took an active part in politics. None had a more distinguished career than David Bailie Warden, though he did not persist in the ministry. Refused a certificate to preach, he wrote and published a withering attack on members of the Presbytery of Bangor, who, he alleged, had supported 'republican morality' to a man, only a few months previously, and had now turned their coats 'from motives of prudence'. Soon after his arrival in the United States he was offered the Chair of Natural Philosophy at Union College, New York, but he had already agreed to become principal of Columbia Academy at Kinderhook.

He became an American citizen in 1804, and before long he came back across the Atlantic as private secretary to General John Armstrong, the newly appointed United States minister in Paris. On the instructions of President Jefferson, Warden was designated to act as American consul *pro tempore* in 1808. When Armstrong was succeeded by Joel Barlow, Warden had to return to the United States on a sloop-of-war, but he was reinstated in his office by a vote of the senate. After Barlow's death, Warden was the acting American minister in France until Napoleon's return from Russia enabled William H. Crawford to present his credentials as the American ambassador. America was invited to send observers to the Congress of Vienna in 1815, and there Warden met Castlereagh again. It can hardly have given Castlereagh pleasure to come face to face, in such circumstances, with the son of one of his tenants, whom he had hunted round the shores of Strangford Lough seventeen years before, and it is said that Warden had the satisfaction of opposing him in discussion. (The chairs on which the delegates sat at Vienna are still to be seen at Mount Stewart.)

Warden's achievements were not confined to public service. He was the author of a three-volume history of his adopted country, among many other works, and he even found time, in the midst of his scholarly labours, to be elected a corresponding member of the Belfast Literary Society, and to contribute a couple of papers to its proceedings. After his retirement, he lived permanently in France and devoted himself to the study of French literature, eventually being elected a member of the Institut de France, a remarkable distinction for a foreigner. He died in Paris in 1845, and the State of New York acquired his books for its public library, where they are still to be found, 'surmounted by his portrait'.[14]

His adversary, Lord Castlereagh, did not live to be old. In 1822, when he was at the height of his fame, he suffered a mental breakdown, brought on by overwork and an exaggerated dread of scandal and possible blackmail. At an audience with George IV on 9 August he exhibited such alarming symptoms that the King alerted the Duke of Wellington, who wrote to Castlereagh's physician, Dr John Bankhead. He was persuaded to go into the country to rest and recuperate, and, as a precaution, all his razors were removed, but three days later he found a penknife and cut the carotid artery in his throat. He died in the arms of his doctor, who was one of the twenty-two children of the Presbyterian minister of Ballycarry in County Antrim.[15]

The lad who visited the rebel camp at Ednavady on Tuesday, 12 June, was a pupil of the Reverend Samuel Edgar, and intended to become a minister. Instead James Thomson became a professor of mathematics in Glasgow University. This was a considerable achievement, but it was surpassed by that of his son, the famous scientist Lord Kelvin, who helped to formulate the second law of thermodynamics, and gave mankind the submarine cable, among many other ingenious inventions.[16]

After the Battle of Ballynahinch, William Brunty succeeded in reaching his home near Rathfriland in safety. He was fortunate to escape punishment, but the experience helped to confirm the antipathy to rebels and revolution which his clever elder brother, the Reverend Patrick Brontë, frequently expressed throughout his life. William in later years opened a public house,[17] but Patrick's destiny led to St John's College, Cambridge, the bleak parsonage at Haworth and immortality.

The iniquity of oblivion, as Sir Thomas Browne observed, 'blindly scattereth her poppy, and deals with the memory of men without distinction to the merit of perpetuity'. The ever-curious de Latocnaye disappears again into the mist of time. In 1801 he published *A Frenchman's Walk through Sweden and Norway*. After that we hear nothing. At least he ended his Irish perambulation on a positive note. If the government could extirpate the seeds of sedition, he wrote, Ireland would become a happy and prosperous nation.[18]

And some there be, which have no memorial, who perished as though they had never been. After the Battle of Antrim, the dead were brought down from the town in blockwheel carts and buried on the shore close to where the Sixmilewater flows into Lough Neagh. The ground there was sandy and easily trenched. Ezekiel Vance saw the carts leaving the town and assumed at first that they were laden with pig carcases on their way from Derry to Belfast. On closer inspection he was horrified to see that the carts were piled high with human bodies, all of them naked. Peggy Gordon, the Amazon who had helped the soldiers to secure the guns at the castle wall, and who in later years would be employed to convey abandoned infants to the Foundling Hospital in Dublin, had been busy among the dead in the market house overnight. She afterwards appeared in a fine pair of boots, and one Richard Price wore a green coat which he took from Hay, the leader of the Ballyeaston men. It still showed the bullet hole made when Hay received his fatal wound.

From the window of his cottage on the edge of the demesne, Lord Massereene's agent, Samuel Skelton, watched the yeomanry burying parties, digging in the hot sun. The bodies were shot in, a cartload at a time. 'Where the devil did these rascals come from?' the officer asked the driver of one cart. A poor wretch raised a blood-streaked face from the cart and feebly answered: 'I come frae Ballyboley.' He was buried along with the rest.[19]

NOTES

Where the full title of a book, article or pamphlet is not given, the complete reference will be found in the bibliography.

ABBREVIATIONS

BM	Belfast Mercury
BMM	Belfast Monthly Magazine
BNL	Belfast News-Letter
DAB	Dictionary of American Biography
DNB	Dictionary of National Biography
HMC	Historical Manuscripts Commission
IS	Irish Sword
LHL	Linen Hall Library
NAI	National Archives (Ireland)
NS	Northern Star
OSM	Ordnance Survey Memoirs
PBNHPS	Proceedings and Reports of the Belfast Natural History and Philosophical Society
PRONI	Public Record Office of Northern Ireland
RGSU	Records of the General Synod of Ulster
SRO	Scottish Record Office
TCD	Trinity College Dublin
UJA	Ulster Journal of Archaeology
WHS	Wesley Historical Society (Irish Branch)

PROLOGUE

1 Rudyard Kipling, expressing a similar sentiment about Sussex. ('Sussex', *Rudyard Kipling: The Complete Verse*, London, 1990)

2 MS Registry of the Weather, LHL. For the background to the keeping of a daily record see John Killen, *A History of the Linen Hall Library*, pp. 32–3

I THE MURMURING SURGE

1 de Latocnaye, *A Frenchman's Walk through Ireland*: 'The rain in this country is terrible; it seems to penetrate to the bones, and would make you shiver with cold in the middle of summer', pp. 52–3; the swordstick adapted, p. 87

2 *Ibid.*, pp. 255–6

3 The Chevalier de Latocnaye is a somewhat elusive figure. His name is given by Gamble as Jacques Louis de Bougrenet, which seems likely to be correct. R.P. Kerwiler's *Répertoire général de bio-bibliographie bretonne*, vol. 5, lists a Jean Pierre de Bougrenet, author and historian, who was a captain of engineers '*sous les ordres du Prince de Condé*'. The 'Prince de Condé' would

appear to be Henri Marie Allard, a
leader of the resistance in the Vendée.
A Vicomte Henri Marie Anne de
Bougrenet de la Tocnaye was '*sous-intendant militaire à Tours*' in 1850.
Besides books on his travels, de
Latocnaye wrote a work on the causes
of the French Revolution.

4   For the distribution of the *Northern Star*
see Rebellion Papers, NAI,
620/15/8/1–12

5   For a brief outline of this sectarian war
in County Armagh, see A.T.Q.
Stewart, *The Narrow Ground*, pp.
128–37. For a comprehensive collection
of the relevant documents see D.W.
Miller, *Peep o' Day Boys and Defenders.*

6   de Latocnaye, pp. 260, 262, 267

7   *Ibid.*, p. 255

8   *Ibid.*, p. 225; Hyde, *Rise of Castlereagh*,
p. 169

9   Hyde, p. 169

10 Martha McTier–William Drennan,
29 November 1796 (Drennan MSS,
PRONI, D 591/640)

11 McDowell, *Ireland in the Age of
Imperialism and Revolution*, pp. 471–2

12 *Ibid.*, p. 472

13 *The Formation of the Orange Order*
(edited papers of Colonel William
Blacker and Colonel Robert Wallace),
p. 16; McDowell, *Ireland*, p. 466;
W.E.H. Lecky, *History of Ireland*, vol. 3,
p. 426, and, for the consequences,
pp. 426–45

14 McNeven, *Pieces of Irish History*, p. 178

15 McDowell, *Ireland*, p. 566; Hutchison,
Tyrone Precinct, p. 106; W.E.H. Lecky,
vol. 3, pp. 472–3

16 Hyde, p. 148

17 *Ibid.*, p. 151

18 Teeling, *Personal Narrative*, pp. 15–19;
Hyde, p. 152

19 Martha McTier–William Drennan, 16
September 1796 (Drennan MSS, PRONI,
D 591/629)

20 Teeling, pp. 27–30

21 Castlereagh–Pitt, 17 October 1796
(Hyde, pp. 160–1)

22 Hyde, pp. 165–6

23 W.E.H. Lecky, vol. 3, p. 475

24 de Latocnaye, pp. 209–10

25 McSkimmin, *Annals of Ulster*, pp. 56–7

26 W.E.H. Lecky, vol. 3, pp. 475–6

27 Hyde, p. 165

28 NS, 14 November 1797; *Formation of the
Orange Order*, pp. 136–9

29 de Latocnaye, p. 225

30 Accounts of the French expedition:
Tone, *Autobiography*, vol. 2, pp. 152–77;
W.E.H. Lecky, vol. 3, pp. 527–41;
Elliott, *Wolfe Tone*, pp. 324–33; Elliott,
Partners in Revolution, pp. 109–15 (map
p. 112); MacDermot, *Theobald Wolfe
Tone*, pp. 207–33

31 W.E.H. Lecky, vol. 3, p. 531

32 Tone, vol. 2, p. 173

33 Scobie, *An Old Highland Fencible Corps*,
p. 112

34 Tone, vol. 2, p. 175

35 W.E.H. Lecky, vol. 3, p. 540

II   A SILENCE IN THE HEAVENS

1   de Latocnaye, p. 229

2   W.E.H. Lecky, vol. 4, p. 29

3   *Ibid.*, p. 20

4   *Ibid.*, pp. 40–2

5   Lake–Pelham, 11, 17, 18, 29 May 1797;
4, 6, 9 June 1797; 2 July 1797 (Pelham
MSS, PRONI, T 765/5)

6   Martha McTier–William Drennan,
17 March 1797 (Drennan MSS, PRONI,
D 591/652)

7   Martha McTier–William Drennan, late
March 1797 (Drennan MSS, PRONI,
D 591/658A)

8   NS, 5 May 1797; Charles Dickson,
Revolt, p. 169

9   Cooke–Nugent, 22 July 1796 (Nugent
corres., McCance MSS, PRONI, D 272/73)

10 Lake–Pelham, 1 May 1797 (Pelham MSS,
PRONI, T 765/5/2)

11 Lake–Pelham, 11 May 1797 (Pelham
MSS, PRONI, T 765/5/32)

12 Lake–Pelham, 14 May 1797 (Pelham
MSS, PRONI, T 765/5/49)

13 Quoted in Scobie, pp. 125–6. There
was considerable ill feeling between the
Reays and the Monaghan Militia. See
William Simms–Thomas Russell, 22
February 1798, Sirr MSS (TCD, 868/2 fol.
225), describing a fight among the

soldiers – 'I do not think the quarrel between the two regiments is by any means little.'

14 Petition for mercy of William and Owen McKenna, Daniel Gillion (*sic*) and Peter McCavern (*sic*), the black hole, New Barrack, Belfast, to General Lake, 13 May 1797. (Pelham MSS, PRONI, T 765/5/57)

15 Lake–Pelham, 16 May 1797, 3 p.m., Blaris Huts (Pelham MSS, PRONI, T 765/5/7)

16 Lake–Pelham, 17 May 1797 (Pelham MSS, PRONI, T 765/5/75); William Drennan–Martha McTier, *c.* 22 May 1797 (Drennan MSS, PRONI, D 591/662); O'Byrne, *As I Roved Out*, pp. 406–8

17 Martha McTier–William Drennan, 19 May 1797 (Drennan MSS, PRONI, D 591/662); Charles Dickson, pp. 114–15

18 Charles Dickson, p. 115; Camden–Grenville, Fortescue MSS, HMC, vol. 3, p. 387

19 Accounts of the trial of William Orr: W.E.H. Lecky, vol. 4, pp. 103–16; Charles Dickson, pp. 177–82; McDowell, *Ireland*, pp. 542–3; Elliott, *Partners in Revolution*, pp. 129–30; Dr Alexander Haliday–Lord Charlemont, 6 October 1797 (Charlemont corres., HMC, vol. 2, pp. 306–7)

20 McSkimmin, p. 91 n.

21 Charles Dickson, pp. 166–8

22 Mary Ann McCracken–Henry Joy McCracken, 27 September 1797 (McCracken MSS, PRONI, T 1210/31)

23 William Drennan–Martha McTier, 29 September 1797 (Drennan MSS, PRONI, D 591/677)

24 Charles Dickson, pp. 179–80

25 Haliday–Charlemont, 6 October 1797, from Mount Stewart (Charlemont corres., HMC, vol. 2, p. 306)

26 'The Three Sisters', Young, *Ulster in '98*, pp. 71–2

27 *William Stavely*, Mid-Antrim Historical Group, no. 18, p. 25

28 Young, *Ulster in '98*, p. 89

29 'The Dying Declaration of William Orr of Farranshane' (PRONI, T 2627/4/92)

30 John Galt's Diary, 20 May 1798 (PRONI, D 561); Young, *Ulster in '98*, p. 89; McDowell, *Ireland*, p. 543; McNeill, *Mary Ann McCracken*, p. 179

31 'The Wake of William Orr', William Drennan, *Fugitive Pieces*, pp. 79–81

32 Camden–Duke of Portland, 23 April 1798, cited in W.E.H. Lecky, vol. 4, p. 237

33 Lord Dunfermline, *Lieutenant-General Sir Ralph Abercromby*, pp. 125–30; Pakenham, *The Year of Liberty*, p. 52

34 Dunfermline, p. 93; Pakenham, p. 50

35 Pakenham, pp. 54–5

36 Charles Dickson, p. 118

37 Henry Joy McCracken: Edna C. Fitzhenry, *Henry Joy McCracken*; McNeill, *Mary Ann McCracken*; Madden, *Antrim and Down in 1798*; Young, *Historical Notices of Old Belfast*

38 McNeill, pp. 21–36

39 Young, *Old Belfast*, p. 188

40 McNeill, p. 111

41 Henry Joy McCracken to his sisters, 10 January 1797 (McCracken MSS, PRONI, T 1210/4); 29 January 1797 (T 1210/5)

42 Henry Joy McCracken–Mary Ann McCracken (McCracken MSS, PRONI, T 1210/41)

43 Pakenham, pp. 93–4, 103, 107–8

44 W.E.H. Lecky, vol. 4, p. 413

45 Charles Dickson, pp. 204–5

46 Madden, *Antrim and Down in 1798*, pp. 92–3

47 *Ibid.*, pp. 98–9

48 Cleland MSS (PRONI, D 714/2/23)

49 Charles Dickson, pp. 164–5

50 *Ibid.*, pp. 165–6

51 McSkimmin, p. 105; Charles Dickson, p. 125

52 Madden, *Antrim and Down in 1798*, pp. 44–6

53 McSkimmin, p. 107

54 Young, *Old Belfast*, p. 183; Young, *Ulster in '98*, p. 90; Elliott, *Partners in Revolution*, p. 205; McSkimmin, p. 107

55 Hope's account, Madden, *Antrim and Down in 1798*, pp. 44–6; McSkimmin, p. 108

III THE BLUE HILLS OF ANTRIM

1 Tone, vol. 1, p. 214
2 McSkimmin, p. 109; Brian M. Walker, *Sentry Hill*, p. 16
3 McNeill, pp. 171–2; McSkimmin, pp. 109–10. For the words of 'The Swinish Multitude' see McNeill, p. 172. It was sung to the tune of 'The Lass of Richmond Hill', which, incidentally, is attributed to the United Irish informer, Leonard McNally. The word 'swine' is used affectionately in several United Irish songs, an allusion to Edmund Burke's 'Learning will be cast into the mire, and trodden down under the hoofs of the swinish multitude' (*Reflections on the Revolution in France*). See Zimmerman, *Songs of Irish Rebellion*, p. 126. The uniform which McCracken wore is in the Ulster Museum, Belfast.
4 Young, *Ulster in '98*, p. 30
5 Ibid., pp. 43–4; McSkimmin, p. 118; Charles Dickson, pp. 128–9
6 McSkimmin, pp. 118–19
7 Ibid., pp. 112–13
8 BMM, June 1809, p. 424; Fitzpatrick, *The Sham Squire*, pp. 349–50
9 James Orr, 'Donegore Hill' (*Poems on Various Subjects*, p. 33)
10 Ibid., p. 35
11 Ibid., p. 34
12 Young, *Ulster in '98*, p. 30
13 Durham, MS Autobiography (Dundas MSS, SRO, TD 80/70/Box 24/9)
14 Ibid.
15 DNB: *Lady Nugent's Journal*, pp. xlix–lii; BNL, 16 January 1797; Martha McTier to Drennan, 31 May 1798. She mentions that her mother is living next door to Colonel Durham 'who is very well thought of' (Drennan MSS, PRONI, D 591/716).
16 Durham, MS Autobiography (Dundas MSS, SRO, TD 80/70/Box 24/9)
17 *New Statistical Account of Scotland*, vol. 9, pp. 437–8; Admiral Sir Philip Durham, DNB.
18 Durham, MS Autobiography (Dundas MSS, SRO, TD 80/70/Box 24/9)
19 J. Mackay, *Burns*, pp. 494, 496, 555–62; M. Lindsay, *Burns Encyclopedia*, p. 303
20 General Goldie's passion for cards: on one occasion Goldie and his officers played all night at the house of Cunningham Greg, whom Lake regarded as one of the most suspect of the Belfast merchants. In 1799 Martha McTier wrote: 'General Goldie it's said is broke. While he was here Magee's family was surprised at a violent rapping at the door at midnight, and the appearance of two soldiers, who, however, only demanded half a dozen packs of cards for the General, which were procured with all haste.' (Martha McTier–William Drennan, 30 April [1799], Drennan MSS, PRONI, D 591/770). Magee was a printer and stationer in Belfast.
21 Purdon, *Memoirs of Service of the 64th Regiment*; William Newall–Patrick Heron, 9 June 1798 (Heron of Kirroughtree MSS, SRO, GD 307/16/3)
22 William Newall–Patrick Heron, 7 June 1798 (Heron of Kirroughtree MSS, SRO, GD 307/16/2)
23 'In speaking of this insurrection, it is very rarely called a rebellion, but commonly the "turn out", the call used at the time to those who appeared tardy to come forth to the ranks.' (McSkimmin, p. 112 n.)
24 Reverend Classon Porter, *Congregational Memoirs of the Old Congregation of Larne and Kilwaughter*, p. 2
25 Ibid., pp. 16–20, 21
26 Ibid., pp. 85–91
27 Dr George Casement–George Anson McCleverty, 20 July 1798 (Massereene/Foster MSS, PRONI, D 562/3038)
28 Young, *Ulster in '98*, p. 50
29 Porter, p. 85; Reid, *History of the Presbyterian Church in Ireland*, vol. 3, p. 392 n.
30 Porter, p. 89
31 McSkimmin, p. 111

32 Massereene/Foster MSS, (PRONI, D 562/3038)

33 Akenson, *Between Two Revolutions*, pp. 123–4

34 Akenson, pp. 132–3

35 OSM, vol. 10, p. 26

36 Akenson, p. 2

37 OSM, vol. 10, p. 37; Akenson, p. 128

38 Akenson, p. 2

39 James Orr, 'Donegore Hill', *Poems on Various Subjects*, pp. 33, 188–9; Akenson and Crawford, *James Orr, Bard of Ballycarry*, pp. 8, 39–42; McSkimmin, pp. 111–12

40 The Hon. Mrs McClintock, 'Redhall' in Avy Dowlin (ed.), *Ballycarry in Olden Days*, pp. 23–4; W.M. Knox, 'The Old Mill Glen', *Ballycarry in the Olden Days*, p. 27

41 Young, *Ulster in '98*. The butler's name was Murray; McSkimmin, p. 111

42 Professor Akenson has calculated that 180 Islandmagee men, at most, took part in the Rising (*Between Two Revolutions*, pp. 2, 180 n. 29).

43 Hill, *The Macdonnells of Antrim*, pp. 251, 370–1

44 Blair, *County Antrim Characters*, pp. 6–7; McConnell, *Fasti*, p. 187

45 Smith, 'Memories of '98', *UJA*, 2nd series, vol. 2, pp. 90–1

46 Memorandum by Edward Jones Agnew of Kilwaughter: 'What happened in the late rebellion as I saw it on the 7th and 8th June 1798' (McClelland transcription) in Charles Dickson, pp. 223–4

47 Agnew family tree made available by the Reverend Dr John Nelson; Merrick and Clarke, *Old Belfast Families*, pp. 150–1; Strain, *Belfast and its Charitable Society*, pp. 249–50; Young, *Ulster in '98*, p. 88

48 Agnew memorandum, pp. 223–4; Fr Devenny an informer, Young, *Ulster in '98*, p. 48. It was said that the information was passed to the authorities by his mother.

49 McSkimmin, pp. 114–16; Charles Dickson, pp. 129–30

50 McSkimmin, p. 116; Edward

51 McSkimmin, p. 117; Young, *Ulster in '98*, p. 7; Larkin, *Journal of the South Derry Historical Society*, vol. 1, no. 3, pp. 218–20

52 Smyth, *The Story of Antrim*, p. 29

53 McSkimmin, pp. 118–19

54 *Ibid.*

55 Accounts of the Battle of Antrim: Musgrave, *Memoirs of the Different Rebellions in Ireland*, pp. 547–54; McSkimmin, pp. 118–24; Charles Dickson, pp. 130–5; Smith, *Historical Gleanings*, pp. 20–6; Allen, *David Allens*, pp. 51–6; Young, *Ulster in '98*, pp. 1–13; Purdon, *Memoirs of Service in the 64th Regiment*, pp. 33–4; Madden, *Antrim and Down in 1798*, pp. 47–51

56 Hope's account in Madden, *Antrim and Down in 1798*, p. 47

57 Durham, MS Autobiography (Dundas MSS, SRO, TD 80/70/Box 24/9)

58 Burns's account in Young, *Ulster in '98*, p. 31

59 James Keen's Narrative (WHS). Burns said Campbell was 'as clever a man as ever stepped in black shoe leather'. ('Clever' was an Ulster colloquialism for 'fine-looking' or 'well set up'.)

60 Hudson–Charlemont, 27 July 1798 (Charlemont MSS, HMC, vol. 2, pp. 329–30). There was a suggestion that O'Neill was attempting to exert some influence over his own tenants, and that his assailant was one of them.

61 Durham, MS Autobiography (Dundas MSS, SRO, TD 80/70/Box 24/9)

62 Smith, 'Memories of '98', *UJA*, 2nd series, vol. 1, pp. 134–5

63 Durham, MS Autobiography (Dundas MSS, SRO, TD 80/70/Box 24/9)

64 A. Malcomson, *Earl of Massereene*, pp. 31, 121–2; Massereene/Foster MSS (PRONI, D 562)

65 Durham, MS Autobiography (Dundas MSS, SRO, TD 80/70/Box 24/9). For the private theatre built by Lord O'Neill

Hudson–Charlemont, 27 July 1798 (Charlemont corres., HMC, vol. 2., pp. 328–9); Slessor's Diary, 9 June 1798 (Alethea Hayter, *The Backbone*, p. 42)

and the visit of Mrs Siddons to Shane's Castle, see Allen, pp. 48–9, and Ellison, p. 95

66   Smith, 'Memories of '98', *UJA*, 2nd series, vol. 1, p. 141

67   Smith, 'Memories of '98', *UJA*, 2nd series, vol. 1, p. 138. A stone in Antrim churchyard has the inscription: 'Here lieth the body of William Eccles who departed this life, 7 June 1798, aged 46 years.'

68   James Keen's Narrative (WHS)

69   Smith, 'Memories of '98', *UJA*, 2nd series, vol. 1, p. 213

70   James Keen's Narrative (WHS)

71   Young, *Ulster in '98*, pp. 14–15

72   The main source for the account which follows is *Old Ballymena*, pp. 23–45

73   But see also Robert Swan's account in McCance MSS (PRONI, D 272/31): 'A number of men having got a tar barrel upon forks.'

74   *Old Ballymena*, p. 37; McDowell, *Ireland*, p. 639

75   W.J. Fitzpatrick, pp. 342–3 (Dr Patrick); McCance MSS PRONI, D 272/31 and D 272/7 (Robert Swan); *Old Ballymena*, p. 37 (Francis Dixon); Blair, pp. 28–30 (James Bones). A grandson of Bones married Marion Woodrow, who was the aunt of President Woodrow Wilson. As a young man, Wilson often stayed with his aunt and uncle at the Bones home in Rome, Georgia (Blair, p. 29).

76   McDowell, *Ireland*, p. 639. White was an ancestor of Sir George White VC, the defender of Ladysmith in 1899–1900, and his son, Captain Jack White, who formed the Irish Citizen Army in 1913.

77   Statement of Robert Swan's conduct on the 7, 8 and 9 June 1798 (McCance MSS, PRONI, D 272/31)

78   Adam Dickey's Narrative (W.J. Fitzpatrick, p. 343); Charles Dickson, p. 168 n. 11. Though McCleverty's wound was dismissed as superficial, he appears to have died from it.

79   Hudson–Charlemont, 18 July 1798

(Charlemont corres., HMC, vol. 2, p. 327)

80   Diary of the Reverend John Steinhauer, Gracehill.

81   *Old Ballymena*, pp. 37–9. Lord Edward Fitzgerald died from his wounds on 4 June.

82   Agnew's memorandum (Charles Dickson, p. 224)

83   Stewart–McNaghten, 10 June 1798 (McCance MSS, PRONI, D 272/32)

84   Deposition of Andrew Stewart (McCance MSS, PRONI, D 272/22)

85   Blair, p. 7

86   Casement–McCleverty, 20 July 1798 (Massereene/Foster MSS, PRONI, D 562/3038)

87   McDowell, *Ireland*, p. 638

88   Rebellion Papers, NAI, 620/2/8/8

89   T.H. Mullin, *Coleraine in Georgian Times*, pp. 158–9, 161

90   Caldwell MSS, PRONI, D 1518/1/1

91   T.H. Mullin, *Coleraine in Georgian Times*, pp. 158–60

92   *Ibid.*, p. 161

93   For McKerlie's memoirs, see McKerlie, *Two Sons of Galloway*, pp. 15–106

94   *Ibid.*, p. 20

95   John Galt's Diary, 14 June 1798 (PRONI, D 561)

96   Morton, 'The Royal Manx Fencibles in Ulster, 1796–1798', in *IS*, vol. 2, no. 6, pp. 150–1

97   McKerlie, pp. 53–5

98   John Galt's Diary, 14 June 1798 (PRONI, D 561)

99   Caldwell MSS (PRONI, D 1518/1/1)

100   Young, *Ulster in '98*, p. 30; *Old Ballymena*, p. 39; McSkimmin, p. 131

101   *Old Ballymena*, p. 39

102   *Ibid.*, p. 40; Adam Dickey's Narrative (W.J. Fitzpatrick, p. 341)

103   McSkimmin, p. 132

104   *Ibid.*, pp. 133–4; *Old Ballymena*, pp. 40–1

105   *Old Ballymena*, p. 43

106   Hudson–Charlemont, 26 June 1798 (Charlemont corres., HMC, vol. 2, p. 325)

107   Slessor's Diary, 9 June 1798 (Hayter, p. 42)

108 Hudson–Charlemont, 27 July 1798
     (Charlemont corres., HMC, vol. 2,
     p. 329)
109 Slessor's Diary, 9 June 1798 (Hayter,
     p. 42); Gracehill Diaries, 9 June 1798;
     Professor Finlay Holmes, 'The 1798
     Rebellion', in Mid-Antrim Part 2,
     p. 39; Shields, Narrative Singing,
     p. 108. Though hardly mentioned in
     the Presbyterian annals, Roddy
     McCorley is a major figure in
     nationalist martyrology because he
     became the subject of a famous song.
110 Old Ballymena, p. 44
111 Cooke, in a letter of 16 July 1798, says
     that 'Colonel Clavering's most
     unwarrantable proclamation fetters
     government extremely . . . how far
     would it compromise the faith of
     government were they to proceed
     against those who have availed
     themselves of the offer of pardon?'
     (Cooke–[Castlereagh?], 16 July 1798.
     McCance MSS, PRONI, D 272/4)
112 Old Ballymena, pp. 44–8
113 Young, Ulster in '98, pp. 15–16
114 Old Ballymena, p. 45; Young, Ulster in
     '98, pp. 33–4; 'Fogy' was a name for
     an invalid or garrison soldier – hence
     'Old Fogy'.
115 Young, Ulster in '98, pp. 47–8
116 Gracehill Diaries, 9 June 1798;
     Slessor's Diary, 9 June 1798 (Hayter,
     p. 42); Caldwell MSS, PRONI,
     D 1518/1/12; Young, Ulster in '98,
     pp. 20–1; UJA, 2nd series, vol. 1, pp.
     216–17
117 UJA, 2nd series, vol. 15, pp. 158–60
118 Moravian History Magazine, vol. 8
     (spring 1995), pp. 16–17
119 UJA, 2nd series, vol. 1, p. 210
120 Young, Ulster in '98, pp. 19–20.
     McClelland's subsequent career was
     remarkable. For a while after the
     defeat at Antrim he hid in a cave near
     his home at Portmuck, and when the
     hue and cry had died down, his family
     put it about that he had gone to
     America. In fact he became a very
     successful smuggler, organising large-
     scale operations centred on the

Netherlands. He eventually reappeared
at home, and endeavoured to prove his
loyalty by joining the yeomanry as a
lieutenant. Efficiency was his
watchword, and in the 1830s the
Ordnance Survey officers singled him
out as one of the most progressive
farmers in the area. He adopted the
most modern agricultural methods,
introducing machinery on his farm and
building limekilns to produce lime for
fertiliser. A pier was specially built in
1827 'for the purpose of shipping
limestone from the almost adjacent
quarries by Mr William McClelland',
but a neighbouring landowner was
able to prohibit the exportation of
limestone from that parish and the
dock filled up with shingle.
Nevertheless, McClelland's enterprise
was the beginning of the modern
cement industry at Magheramorne. He
died in 1859, by which time he was
well into his ninth decade. (Young,
Ulster in '98, p. 41; Akenson, pp. 20,
29, 60; OSM, vol. 10, pp. 80, 82, 84)

IV   THE HEARTS OF DOWN

1   Young, Old Belfast, p. 175; Ian Wilson,
     Shipwrecks of the Ulster Coast, p. 37. In
     1963 the Belfast Sub-Aqua Club located
     cannon at the site of the wreck, and a
     more thorough archaeological
     investigation began in 1995.
2   Narrative of the Principal Proceedings
     of the Republican Army of County of
     Down (NAI Rebellion Papers 620/4/41).
     The fact that this document purports to
     be the narrative of one William Fox, a
     schoolmaster, has misled several writers
     (see Pakenham, p. 225; Charles
     Dickson, p. 221; McCavery, Newtown,
     pp. 97, 99). However, it is clear from
     internal evidence that the writer is
     David Bailie Warden, and he is correctly
     identified by McDowell (Ireland, p. 640),
     citing Home Office papers 100/86,
     'Warden's Narrative', in the Public
     Record Office. I am grateful to Professor
     David Wilson for confirming that
     620/4/41 is in Warden's handwriting.

3   William Steel Dickson's life: Bailie,
      'William Steel Dickson' in *Irish
      Booklore*, vol. 2, no. 2, pp. 239–67;
      William Steel Dickson, *Narrative*; Reid,
      *History of the Presbyterian Church in
      Ireland*, vol. 3, pp. 397–8; DNB
4   William Steel Dickson, pp. 6–7
5   *Ibid.*, pp. 7–8
6   *Ibid.*, p. 20
7   NS, 20 February 1793
8   NAI, Rebellion Papers 620/28/5; Charles
      Dickson, p. 185
9   William Steel Dickson, pp. 33–4, 46–50
10   *Ibid.*, pp. 54–7
11   Charles Dickson, p. 186
12   Warden's Narrative (NAI 620/4/41)
13   Lyttle, *Betsy Gray*, reprint, Appendix,
      p. 176; McComb; *Guide to Belfast*,
      p. 138
14   Samuel Barber: W.D. Bailie, 'The Rev.
      Samuel Barber, 1738–1811', in
      Challenge and Conflict, pp. 72 ff; UJA, 2nd
      series, vol. 16 (1910), pp. 33–42.
      Significantly, Barber had been born in
      Killead, County Antrim, and licensed
      by the Presbytery of Templepatrick.
      While waiting for a congregation, he
      had preached as 'supply' in Broadisland,
      Ballyeaston, Larne and Ballycarry, all
      areas involved in the Rising. Ordained
      at Rathfriland in 1783, he took a
      prominent part in the Volunteer
      movement, as captain of the Rathfriland
      corps. As early as 1779 he had preached
      to his Volunteer brethren in a spirit far
      removed from the Sermon on the
      Mount, taking his text from the Book
      of Joel, 3:9 and 10: 'Prepare war, wake
      up the mighty men, let all men of war
      draw near; let them come up. Beat your
      plowshares into swords, and your
      pruninghooks into spears: let the weak
      say, I *am* strong.' The text of this
      sermon was interesting. 'Let the sounds
      of *Derry* and *Inniskillin*, the *Boyne* and
      Aughrim, rouse us to an imitation of
      worthy fathers. Let us hand down the
      dear-bought and invaluable inheritance
      to our children, as our fathers did to us,
      that our offspring may never become
      the property of a cruel master . . . Many

flourishing colonies, equal in extent and
fertility to kingdoms, have separated (I
fear) forever from the British
Government and leagued with our
enemies.'
      Barber managed to combine these
sentiments with ardent support for the
cause of the 'present generation of
Roman Catholics' who have behaved
'peaceably and quietly, though as a
religious society they have been
subjected to penal laws, shocking to
enumerate'. (Strong support for
Catholic emancipation was the
distinguishing characteristic of all the
radical ministers.) What part Barber
might have played in the Down
insurrection can only be guessed at: he
was arrested for treason on 3 June and
spent the next two years in prison. He
was then over sixty years of age. ([Joy],
Historical Collections, p. 474)

15   James Porter: Porter MSS, PRONI,
      D 3579; A.G. Lecky, *The Laggan and its
      Presbyterianism*, pp. 87–8; Young, *Ulster
      in '98*, pp. 57–60; Charles Dickson,
      pp. 189–92. Porter, who hailed
      originally from Donegal, had married in
      his youth one of the daughters of the
      family in County Down which
      employed him as a tutor. He was by all
      accounts a very intelligent and
      prepossessing man, who had a serious
      interest in natural philosophy and
      astronomy, and travelled about the
      country giving lectures, which were
      very popular, and conducting scientific
      experiments. After 1796 he was
      suspected of using these pursuits as a
      cover for swearing in United Irishmen.
      He gave some of his lectures at Mount
      Stewart and won the friendship and
      admiration of Lady Londonderry, but
      his authorship of a series of biting satires
      in the *Northern Star* ('Billy Bluff and
      Squire Firebrand') antagonised Lord
      Londonderry, who found himself
      caricatured in them as 'Lord
      Mountmumble'.
      Information was given to the
      authorities that Porter had become a

United Irishman in February or March 1796, 'sworn in a room in Belfast . . . Henry J. McCracken lay'd down the book, desired him to read the oath, which he did, and kissed the book. Neilson came into the room just after he was sworn.' Thereafter, Porter's name appears several times in Mageean's reports, and once as a candidate for the supreme command in County Down. But such evidence may be suspect. Porter seems to have taken no part in the Rising, apart from the reluctant interception of a military dispatch, the action which was to cost him his life. At his court martial he claimed that he first heard of the insurrection on Saturday, the day of the engagement at Saintfield, and 'was told it by Alec Byers who was killed'.

16 Arthur MacMahon: W.A. Maguire, 'Arthur MacMahon, United Irishman and French Soldier', *IS*, vol. 9, no. 36 (summer 1970), pp. 207–15. MacMahon, who was for two years minister at Holywood, County Down, has attracted less attention because from 1797 he was one of the most active of the United Irish agents in France. He eventually became an officer of the Irish Legion in the French service. He claimed to have suffered great persecution from the Londonderry family, forcing him to flee to Scotland and then to France, but the real reason was that he was one of the seven chosen 'colonels' of the United Irish army in Down, and a member of the Ulster committee, which advocated an immediate insurrection in 1797 without waiting for the French. Dr Maguire has patiently uncovered the truth about his career, which has given rise to many legends.

17 Ferguson, *Brief Biographical Sketches*, pp. 26–56

18 *Saintfield Heritage*, pp. 11–12

19 *BM*, 5 October 1784; McDowell, *Irish Public Opinion*, p. 49

20 McClelland, 'Thomas Ledlie Birch, United Irishman', *PBNHPS*, 2nd series,

vol. 7, pp. 24–35; *UJA*, 2nd series, vol. 14, p. 51

21 *NS*, 26 December 1792; Tone, vol. 1, p. 116

22 McClelland, 'Birch', pp. 29–30

23 Lyttle, reprint, Appendix, pp. 166–8

24 Chetwynd-Stapylton, *The Chetwynds of Ingestre*, pp. 250–2

25 *Ibid.*

26 Charles Dickson, pp. 140–3; Musgrave, p. 555. Others besides Frazer and McKinstry who took part in the attack were Dr James Jackson of Newtownards and William Adair, a Presbyterian student from near Comber (Charles Dickson, p. 142). Sparks's letter is printed in Young, *Old Belfast*.

27 Unite's unusual surname suggests that he might have been related to the family of silversmiths of that name. The best known of the dynasty, George Unite, was born in Yorkshire in 1798, and his three sons were also silversmiths. The family legend was that an ancestor had designed the gold coin which James VI and I had minted to celebrate the Union of the crowns of Scotland and England in 1603. The coin was called a 'unite', and the King was so pleased with it that he allowed the engraver to assume the name.

28 Warden's Narrative (NAI, 620/4/41). The Maxwell headstone was erected 'to the memory of Hugh and David Maxwell of Ballywalter . . . They fell in the attack on the town of Newtownards, the 10th of June 1798.' The graveyard also has the stone of James Kain, who was killed in the same attack. (see *Gravestone Inscriptions*, vol. 15, p. 134)

29 *Ibid.*

30 Charles Dickson, pp. 144–5

31 *Ibid.*, pp. 190–1

32 *Ibid.*, pp. 146–7

33 Lady Roden, Diary, 7 June–12 September 1798, pp. 14–25; Lady Roden also worried throughout the summer about her son, the Earl of Roden, who, as commander of the First Fencible Light Dragoons (nicknamed

'the Foxhunters') was involved from the outset of the Rebellion in some of the most savage fighting in the south of Ireland. (See Lady Roden's Diary, Appendix N, pp. 170–5, and Pakenham, pp. 114, 123, 309–10)

34   Edward Hull–Lord Downshire, 11 June 1798 (Downshire MSS, PRONI, D 607/F/224). Colonel Durham recorded that 'a few days after my return to Belfast [on 8 June] Lady Nugent and my wife and many ladies left the town, and crossed over to [Port] Pattrick'. Nugent was clearly anxious to ensure their absolute safety before taking the field against the rebels in Down. (Dundas MSS, SRO, TD 80/70/Box 24/9)

35   James Arbuckle–Patrick Heron, 12 June 1798. (Heron of Kirroughtree MSS, SRO, GD 307/16/17)

36   James Arbuckle–Patrick Heron, 11 July 1798 (Heron of Kirroughtree MSS, SRO, GD 307/16/19)

37   Joseph Black–George Black, 16 June 1798 (Black MSS, Edinburgh University Library, 874/v/99–100)

38   Millin, *Sidelights on Belfast History*, pp. 92–3

39   William Steel Dickson, pp. 46–50

40   Cleland MSS (PRONI, D 714/2/23)

41   William Steel Dickson, pp. 78–9

42   Charles Dickson, p. 148

43   McClelland, 'Birch', p. 31, quoting C.J. Robb in the *Sunday Press*, 1 May 1935. The source is not given.

44   Lyttle, reprint, Appendix, p. 170

45   Charles Dickson, pp. 199–201; Young, *Ulster in '98*, pp. 76–8; BNL, 17 July 1798

46   Reverend Samuel Edgar's Narrative (McComb, pp. 132–4)

47   *Ibid.*, pp. 133, 135

48   Charles Dickson, p. 148; Barker, *The Brontës*, pp. 4, 836 n. 16; Lyttle, reprint, Appendix, p. 171; McCance MSS, PRONI, D 272/73/31, and D 272/36, spelling corrected

49   Pakenham, pp. 223–4, 229

50   James McKey–Lord Downshire, 11 June 1798 (Downshire MSS, PRONI, D 607/F/222)

51   *Ibid.*

52   Humphrey Galbraith–Edward Hull, 13 June 1798 (Downshire MSS, PRONI, D 607/F/235)

53   O'Byrne, pp. 208–11; UJA, 2nd series, vol. 15 (1909) p. 168; *Belfast Literary Society*, p. 31. Dr William Bruce enrolled as a private in the Belfast Merchant Infantry, 'the Black Cockades', on the day after the Battle of Antrim. For his earlier career as a Volunteer and Presbyterian liberal, and his change in political outlook, see A.T.Q. Stewart, *A Deeper Silence*, pp. 124–5 and 188.

54   Nugent–Lake, 13 June 1798 (Charles Dickson, pp. 225–6)

55   [James Thomson] 'An Eye-Witness by "Iota" ', *Belfast Magazine*. Extracts are given in Charles Dickson, pp. 227–231 and in McComb, pp. 126–7.

56   Nugent–Lake, 13 June 1798 (Charles Dickson, pp. 225–6); McComb, p. 134

57   McComb, p. 122. Tone was a regular guest at Moira's town house in Dublin, and Moira was godfather to Tone's third child (Elliott, *Wolfe Tone*, pp. 166–7, 229–30).

58   McComb, p. 115; Ellison, p. 95

59   McComb, p. 128

60   Charles Dickson, p. 151; McComb, pp. 127–8

61   Edgar's Narrative (McComb, p. 138)

62   Accounts of the Battle of Ballynahinch: Nugent's Report to Lake, 13 June 1798 (Charles Dickson, pp. 148–55, 225–7); Lyttle, reprint, Appendix, pp. 153–8, with photographs including an aerial photograph of the battle site; Thomson's Narrative (Charles Dickson, pp. 229–30); Musgrave, pp. 556–7; Teeling, pp. 250–8; McCreery, pp. 163–5

63   McComb, pp. 128–9

64   Lyttle, reprint, Appendix, p. 154

65   *Ibid.*

66   Nugent's Report to Lake, 13 June 1798 (Charles Dickson, pp. 225–7)

67   Charles Dickson, p. 155; Lyttle, reprint, Appendix, pp. 154–5

68   McComb, p. 137

69 *Ibid.*, pp. 139–41
70 *Ibid.*, p. 30; Teeling, pp. 258–60
71 All the facts and legends about Betsy Gray's origins and part in the Battle of Ballynahinch are critically examined in McCoy's *Ulster's Joan of Arc*. For an earlier resumé see Lyttle, reprint, Appendix, pp. 159–63, 185–91. The miniature by Newell, possessed by C.J. Robb, is unlikely to be of Betsy Gray (p. 159).
72 The last verse of 'Bessie Gray'. The lines are apparently written by McComb, and are printed in his *Guide to Belfast*, pp. 130–1.
73 Lyttle was connected by his second marriage to the family of the executed Ballynahinch rebel, Henry Byers, and gained much of his information from this source (see p. 248). K. Robinson, 'W.G. Lyttle, Populariser of the Betsy Gray Legend', in McCoy, pp. 1–3; A. McClelland, Preface, in Lyttle, reprint, pp. vii–viii
74 McCoy, p. 19; McComb, pp. 160–1 (photographs of the monument). Newspaper accounts of the disturbances are reproduced in McCoy, pp. 18–30.
75 Lyttle, reprint, Appendix, p. 163
76 *Ibid.*, pp. 185–91; McCoy, pp. 36–58
77 James McKey–Lord Downshire, 11 June 1798 (Downshire MSS, PRONI, D 607/F/224)
78 *Formation of the Orange Order*, p. 90. In Belfast, and elsewhere, the recently formed Orangemen were being mustered to assist the regular forces, militia and yeomanry, but this is a rare example of their inclusion in military orders as Orangemen.
79 Humphrey Galbraith–Lord Downshire, 13 June 1798 (Downshire MSS, PRONI, D 607/F/235)
80 Martha McTier–William Drennan, postmarked 20 June 1798 (Drennan MSS, PRONI, D 591/718)
81 Charles Dickson, p. 156
82 J.J. Atherton–Nugent, 20 June 1798 (W.J. Fitzpatrick, pp. 347–8)
83 William Newall–Patrick Heron, 28 June 1798 and 23 June 1798 (Heron of

Kirroughtree MSS, SRO, GD 307/16/7 and GD 307/16/6)
84 For Willie Nelson see Young, *Ulster in '98*, pp. 25–7; Dowlin, pp. 49–52. For Archibald Warwick: Charles Dickson, pp. 202–4; Reid, p. 396 n. 45

V   THE HANGING DAY

1 *BNL*, 8 June 1798
2 The account which follows is largely based on the letters of Mary Ann McCracken as published in Madden's *United Irishmen*, vol. 2, pp. 485–94, and her correspondence with her brother and other members of the family after 7 June 1798.
3 Thomas Paine, *The American Crisis* (1776). The opening words, and see Keane, *Paine*, pp. 144–5
4 Henry Joy McCracken–Mary Ann McCracken, 18 June 1798 (McCracken MSS, PRONI, T 1210/42)
5 Mary Ann McCracken–Frances McCracken, 8 July 1798 (McCracken MSS, PRONI, T 1210/44); Thomas Richardson was one of McCracken's fellow prisoners in Kilmainham. Henry Joy McCracken–Captain and Mrs McCracken, 9 December 1797 (McCracken MSS, PRONI, T 1210/25)
6 Mary Ann McCracken–Frances McCracken, 8 July 1798 (McCracken MSS, PRONI, T 1210/44)
7 McNeill, pp. 14–15, 185
8 Madden, *United Irishmen*, p. 494
9 McNeill, p. 186
10 For the career of Dr MacDonnell see P. Froggatt, 'MacDonnell', *The Glynns*, vol. 9 (1981), pp. 17–31
11 McNeill, p. 186
12 Charles Dickson, p. 139; W.E.H. Lecky, vol. 4, p. 419; Musgrave, p. 217; [Joy], p. xi; Durham, MS Autobiography (Dundas MSS, SRO, TD 80/70/Box 24/9)
13 Statement by the Reverend Thomas Ledlie Birch (McClelland transcription) in Charles Dickson, pp. 250–1
14 Caldwell MSS (PRONI, D 1518/1/1); John Caldwell, Richard's father, was introduced to the lord lieutenant (Lord Cornwallis) by Lord Belmore, Lord

Enniskillen and Henry Alexander,
chairman of the Ways and Means
Committee (T.H. Mullin, *Coleraine in
Georgian Times*, p. 167)

15 T.H. Mullin, *Coleraine in Georgian
Times*, p. 168

16 Charles Dickson, p. 200

17 McClelland, 'Birch', *PBNHPS*, 2nd series,
vol. 7, pp. 31–3

18 This account of Porter's trial is based on
the narrative of his son, James Porter,
and other documents preserved by his
descendants (Porter MSS, PRONI,
D 3579)

19 Other accounts of Porter's trial and
execution: Charles Dickson, p. 191;
Latimer, *History of the Irish Presbyterians*,
pp. 180–1. The execution was
reported, without comment, in BNL,
3 July 1798.

EPILOGUE

1 Lady Nugent, *Journal*, p. 1
2 *DNB*
3 Young, *Ulster in '98*, pp. 28–31, 34–49
4 Smyth, p. 82
5 *DNB*; *Army List*
6 *OSM*, vol. 8, p. 47
7 McNeill, p. 258

8 Merrick and Clarke, *Old Belfast Families*,
pp. 179–80; McNeill, pp. 193–308. The
Charitable Institution and its burying
ground are now separated by the
Westlink dual carriageway.

9 McNeill, pp. 194, 195, 230, 300
(photograph on p. 288; the original is in
the Ulster Museum, Belfast)

10 McKerlie, pp. 64–106 (photograph
facing title page)

11 The well known title of popular verses
about Russell by Florence M. Wilson of
Bangor, expressing in local dialect the
sentiments of the men of Down who
took part in the Rising. The words are
given by Charles Dickson, pp. 248–50.

12 Charles Dickson, pp. 195–6. Dickson
gives the full inscription on tombstone.

13 William Steel Dickson, pp. 125–86;
Bailie, pp. 262–7; Merrick and Clarke,
Old Belfast Families, p. 63

14 *DAB*, vol. 19, pp. 443–4; *UJA*, 2nd series,
vol. 13 (1907), pp. 29–33

15 *DNB*; Reid, vol. 3, p. 402

16 *DNB*

17 Barker, p. 836 n. 16

18 de Latocnaye, p. 287

19 Young, *Ulster in '98*, p. 68; *UJA*, 2nd
series, vol. 2, p. 213

SELECT BIBLIOGRAPHY

In attempting to reconstruct the events of June 1798 in the north of Ireland, I have made use of a wide range of sources, from original papers to parish histories, and I have visited the scene of every incident described in the text.

Among the more useful of the documentary sources were the following:

UNPUBLISHED

PUBLIC RECORD OFFICE OF NORTHERN IRELAND

Caldwell MSS (D 1518); Castlereagh MSS (D 3030); Cleland MSS (D 714); Drennan MSS (D 591); John Galt's Diary (D 561); McCance MSS (D 272), including copies of the Nugent Papers in the National Army Museum, Chelsea; McCracken MSS (T 1210 – copies from the Madden Papers, in the Library of Trinity College Dublin); Massereene/Foster MSS (D 562); Pelham MSS (T 765/5 – copies from the Pelham correspondence in the British Library); Porter MSS (D 3579)

LINEN HALL LIBRARY, BELFAST

Joy MSS (TD 2777)

NATIONAL ARCHIVES (IRELAND)

The 620 Rebellion Papers

LIBRARY OF TRINITY COLLEGE DUBLIN

Sirr MSS (868/1 and 868/2)

SCOTTISH RECORD OFFICE, EDINBURGH

Breadalbane MSS (GD 112/152/52/Box 4)
Dundas MSS (the MS Autobiography of General Durham of Largo: TD 80/70/Box 24)
Heron of Kirroughtree MSS (GD 307/16)

EDINBURGH UNIVERSITY LIBRARY

Black MSS (874/v)

PUBLISHED

BERESFORD CORRESPONDENCE: *Letters of John Beresford*, 2 vols, ed.
W. Beresford, London, 1854

CASTLEREAGH CORRESPONDENCE: *Memoirs and Correspondence of Viscount Castlereagh*, ed. C. Stewart, 2nd Marquis of Londonderry, London, 1849

CHARLEMONT CORRESPONDENCE: *Historical Manuscripts Commission, XIIth Report, Appendix, pt. 10, and XIIIth Report, Appendix, pt. 8*, London, 1891 and 1894

Drennan Letters, 1776–1819, ed. D.A. Chart, Belfast, 1931

Fortescue MSS, *Historical Manuscripts Commission, XIIIth Report, Appendix, pt. 3*, London, 1892

Records of the General Synod of Ulster, 3 vols, Belfast, 1890–8

Report from the Committee of Secrecy of the House of Commons of Ireland, Dublin, 1798

Report from the Committee of Secrecy of the House of Lords of Ireland, Dublin, 1798

DICTIONARIES, INDEXES AND WORKS OF REFERENCE

The Army List, 1788–1803

Dictionary of American Biography

Dictionary of National Biography

Fasti of the Irish Presbyterian Church, compiled by J. McConnell and revised by S.G. McConnell, Belfast, 1951

Gravestone Inscriptions, ed. R.S.J. Clarke, Belfast, 1968–

A List of the Counties of Ireland and the Respective Yeomanry Corps in Each County according to their precedence established by lot on 1 June 1798, Dublin, 1798

A List of the Officers of the Several Regiments and Battalions of Militia and of the Several Regiments of Fencible Cavalry and Infantry upon the Establishment of Ireland, Dublin, 1799

An Index to Co. Down and Lisburn Items in the Northern Star, Ballynahinch, 1992

Annals of the American Pulpit, 3 vols, W.B. Sprague, New York, 1868

ARTICLES

Batt, Narcissus. 'Belfast sixty years ago – recollections of a septuagenarian', *Ulster Journal of Archaeology*, 2nd series, vol. 2 (1896), pp. 92–5

Bailie, W.D. 'William Steel Dickson, D.D. (1744–1824)', *Irish Booklore*, vol. 2, no. 2 (1976), pp. 239–67

Bigger, Francis Joseph. 'The *Northern Star*', *Ulster Journal of Archaeology*, 2nd series, vol. 1 (1894), pp. 33–5

Black, Eileen. 'John Tennent, 1777–1813, United Irishman and Chevalier de la Légion d'honneur', *Irish Sword*, vol. 13, no. 51 (Winter 1977), pp. 157–9

'Volunteer portraits in the Ulster Museum, Belfast', *Irish Sword*, vol. 13, no. 52 (1978 and Summer 1979), pp. 181–4

Elliott, Marianne, 'The origin and transformation of early Irish republicanism', *International Review of Social History*, vol. 23 (1978), pp. 405–28

Froggatt, Peter. 'Dr James MacDonnell, M.D. (1763–1845)', *The Glynns*, vol. 8 (1950), pp. 17–31

Hayes-McCoy, G.A. 'The government forces which opposed the Irish insurgents of 1798', *Irish Sword*, vol. 4, no. 14 (Summer 1959), pp. 16–28

'Insurgent efforts towards military organization, 1798', *Irish Sword*, vol. 3, no. 12 (Summer 1958), pp. 153–8

Kenny, James G. 'O'Hara of Craigbilly' and '"Oaklands" and its builder', *The Glynns*, vol. 22 (1994), pp. 34–43

Larkin, Patrick. 'United Irishmen in Magherafelt', *Journal of the South Derry Historical Society*, vol. 1, no. 3 (1982–3), pp. 218–20

McClelland, Aiken. 'Thomas Ledlie Birch, United Irishman', *Proceedings of the Belfast Natural History and Philosophical Society*, 2nd series, vol. 7 (1963), pp. 24–35

'Marriage and obituary notices of literary and bibliographic interest in the Belfast press, 1801–1814', *Irish Booklore*, vol. 3, no. 1 (1976), pp. 14–27

Miller, David W. 'Presbyterianism and "Modernization" in Ulster', *Past and Present*, no. 80 (1978), pp. 66–90

Morrow, Andrew. 'The Rev. Samuel Barber, A.M., and the Rathfriland Volunteers', *Ulster Journal of Archaeology*, 2nd series, vol. 14 (1908), pp. 105–19

Morton, R.G. 'The Royal Manx Fencibles in Ulster, 1796–1798', *Irish Sword*, vol. 2, no. 6 (Summer 1955), pp. 150–1

'The rise of the yeomanry', *Irish Sword*, vol. 8, no. 30 (Summer 1967), pp. 58–64

Paterson, T.G.F. 'The Volunteer companies of Ulster, 1778–1793', *Irish Sword*, vol. 7, no. 27 (Winter 1965), pp. 90–116, no. 28 (Summer 1966), pp. 204–30, no. 29 (Winter 1966), pp. 308–12; vol. 8, no. 30 (Summer 1967), pp. 23–32, no. 31 (Winter 1967), pp. 92–7, no. 32 (Summer 1968), pp. 210–17

'Sketch of the road from Belfast to Antrim', *Belfast Monthly Magazine* (October 1809)

Smith, W.S. 'Memories of '98', *Ulster Journal of Archaeology*, 2nd series, vol. 1 (1895), pp. 133–41, 210–17, 284–9; vol. 2 (1896), pp. 86–91

Stewart, A.T.Q. '"A stable unseen power": Dr William Drennan and the origins of the United Irishmen', in John Bossy and Peter Jupp (eds), *Essays Presented to Michael Roberts* (Belfast, 1976), pp. 80–92

[Thomson, James]. 'An eye-witness by "Iota"', *Belfast Magazine*, vol. 1, no. 1 (1825)

BOOKS AND PAMPHLETS

Adams, J.R.R. and P.S. Robinson (eds). *The Country Rhymes of Samuel Thomson, the Bard of Carngranny, 1766–1816*, Belfast, 1992

Akenson, Donald Harman. *Between Two Revolutions: Islandmagee, Co. Antrim, 1798–1920*, Port Credit, Ontario, 1979

Akenson, Donald Harman and W.H. Crawford. *James Orr, Bard of Ballycarry*, Belfast, 1977

Allen, W.E.D. *David Allens: The History of a Family Firm, 1857–1957*, privately published, London, 1957

Anderson, John. *History of the Belfast Library and Society for Promoting Knowledge, Commonly Known as the Linen Hall Library*, Belfast, 1888

Atkinson, E.D. *Dromore, an Ulster Diocese*, Dundalk, 1925

Bailie, W.D., *et al* (eds). *A History of Congregations in the Presbyterian Church in Ireland, 1610–1982*, Belfast, 1982

Bardon, Jonathan. *Belfast: An Illustrated History*, Belfast, 1982
A History of Ulster, Belfast, 1992

Barker, Juliet. *The Brontës*, London, 1994

Barkley, John M. *A Short History of the Presbyterian Church in Ireland*, Belfast, 1959

Beckett, J.C. *The Making of Modern Ireland, 1603–1923*, London, 1966

Beckett, J.C. and R.E. Glasscock. *Belfast: The Origin and Growth of an Industrial City*, London, 1967

Belfast Literary Society, 1801–1901, Belfast, 1902

Benn, George. *A History of the Town of Belfast from the Earliest Times to the Close of the Eighteenth Century*, London, 1877

Blair, S. Alexander. *County Antrim Characters*, Mid-Antrim Historical Group, no. 19, Ballymena, 1993

Bolton, Charles Knowles. *Scotch-Irish Pioneers in Ulster and America*, Boston, 1910

Brooke, Peter. *Ulster Presbyterianism: The Historical Perspective, 1610–1970*, Dublin, 1987

Bruce, Major W.B.A. *The Bruces of Airth and their Cadets*, privately published, Edinburgh, 1892

Campbell, Flann. *The Dissenting Voice: Protestant Democracy in Ulster from Plantation to Partition*, Belfast, 1991

Challenge and Conflict: Essays in Presbyterian History and Doctrine, Belfast, 1981

Chetwynd-Stapylton, H.E. *The Chetwynds of Ingestre*, London, 1892

Crawford, W.H. and B. Trainor (eds). *Aspects of Irish Social History, 1750–1800*, Belfast, 1969

Curran, W.H. *The Life and Times of the Rt Hon. John Philpot Curran*, 2 vols, London, 1819

Curtin, Nancy J. *United Irishmen: Popular Politics in Dublin and Belfast, 1791–98*, Oxford, 1994

Day, Angélique and Patrick McWilliams. *Ordnance Survey Memoirs of Ireland*, vols 2, 7, 8, 10, 12, 19, 23, 26, Belfast, 1990–5

de Latocnaye, Le Chevalier. *A Frenchman's Walk Through Ireland, 1796–7*, translated from the French by John Stevenson, 1917; reprinted, with an Introduction by John A. Gamble, Belfast, 1984

Dickson, Charles. *Revolt in the North: Antrim and Down in 1798*, Dublin and London, 1960

Dickson, David, Dáire Keogh and Kevin Whelan (eds). *The United Irishmen: Republicanism, Radicalism and Rebellion*, Dublin, 1993

Dickson, William Steel. *A Narrative of the Confinement and Exile of William Steel D.D.*, Belfast, 1812

Donaldson, Dixon. *Historical, Traditional and Descriptive Account of Islandmagee*, Whitehead, 1927

Dowlin, Avy (ed). *Ballycarry in Olden Days*, Belfast, 1963

Doyle, David N. *Ireland, Irishmen and Revolutionary America, 1760–1820*, Dublin and Cork, 1991

Drennan, William. *Fugitive Pieces in Verse and Prose*, Belfast, 1815

Dubourdieu, J. *Statistical Survey of the County of Down*, Dublin, 1802
Statistical Survey of the County of Antrim, Dublin, 1812

Dunfermline, Lord. *Lieutenant-General Sir Ralph Abercromby. A Memoir by his Son*, Edinburgh, 1861

Elliott, Marianne. *Partners in Revolution: The United Irishmen and France*, London and New Haven, 1982
Wolfe Tone: Prophet of Irish Independence, London and New Haven, 1989

Ellison, C.C. *The Hopeful Traveller: The Life and Times of Augustus Beaufort, LLD, 1739–1821*, Kilkenny, 1987

Ferguson, Lady. *Sir Samuel Ferguson in the Ireland of his Day*, Edinburgh and London, 1896

Ferguson, Reverend Samuel. *Brief Biographical Sketches of some Irish Convenanting Ministers*, Belfast, 1897

Fitzhenry, Edna C. *Henry Joy McCracken*, Dublin, 1936

Fitzpatrick, Rory. *God's Frontiersmen: The Scotch-Irish Epic*, London, 1989

Fitzpatrick, W.J. *The Sham Squire, and the Informers of 1798; with Jottings about Ireland a Century Ago*, Dublin, 1855
The Secret Service Under Pitt, London, 1892

Formation of the Orange Order, 1795–1798: The Edited Papers of Colonel William Blacker and Colonel Robert H. Wallace, Belfast, 1994

Foster, Roy. *Modern Ireland, 1600–1972*, London, 1988

[Frey, J.] (ed.). *Lecale: A Study of Local History*, Belfast, 1970

Goodwin, A. *The Friends of Liberty: The English Democratic Movement in the Age of the French Revolution*, London, 1979

[Gordon, A.] *Historic Memorials of the First Presbyterian Church of Belfast*, Belfast, 1887

Gordon, J.B. *History of the Rebellion in Ireland in the Year 1798*, Dublin, 1801

Hayter, Alethea. *The Backbone: Diaries of a Military Family in the Napoleonic Wars*, Edinburgh, 1993

Hill, Reverend George. *An Historical Account of the Macdonnells of Antrim*, Belfast, 1873

Holmes, R.F.G. *Our Presbyterian Heritage*, Belfast, 1985

Hutchison, W.R. *Tyrone Precinct*, Belfast, 1951

Hyde, H.M. *The Rise of Castlereagh*, London, 1933

Inglis, Brian. *Freedom of the Press in Ireland, 1784–1841*, London, 1954

Jacob, Rosamund. *The Rise of the United Irishmen, 1791–4*, London, 1937

Johnston, Edith Mary. *Great Britain and Ireland, 1760–1800*, Edinburgh, 1963

Jones, E.H. Stuart. *An Invasion that Failed: The French Expedition to Ireland, 1796*, Oxford, 1950

[Joy, H.] *Historical Collections Relative to the Town of Belfast from the Earliest Period to the Union with Great Britain*, Belfast, 1817

Keane, John. *Tom Paine: A Political Life*, London, 1995

Kernohan, J.W. *Rosemary Street Presbyterian Church*, Belfast, 1923

Killen, John. *A History of the Linen Hall Library*, Belfast, 1990

Killen, W.D. *A History of Congregations of the Presbyterian Church in Ireland*, Belfast and Edinburgh, 1886

Latimer, W.T. *A History of the Irish Presbyterians*, Belfast and Edinburgh, 1893

Ulster Biographies Relating to the Rebellion of 1798, Belfast, 1897

Lecky, W.E.H. *A History of Ireland in the Eighteenth Century*, 5 vols, London, 1892–6

Lennox-Conyngham, Mina. *An Old Ulster House*, Dundalk, 1946

Lyttle, W.G. *Betsy Gray, or Hearts of Down*, Bangor, 1888; reprinted by the *Mourne Observer*, with forty pages of notes and information contributed by readers, Newcastle, 1968

McAnally, Sir Henry. *The Irish Militia, 1793–1816*, Dublin and London, 1949

McCavery, Trevor. *Newtown: A History of Newtownards*, Dundonald, 1994

McClelland, Aiken. *History of Saintfield and District*, Saintfield, 1971

McComb, W. *McComb's Guide to Belfast*, Belfast, 1861

McCoy, Jack. *Ulster's Joan of Arc: An Examination of the Betsy Gray Story*, Bangor, 1989

McCreery, Alexander. *The Presbyterian Ministers of Killyleagh: A Notice of their Lives and Times*, Belfast, 1875

MacDonagh, T. *The Viceroy's Post Bag*, London, 1904

MacDermot, Frank. *Theobald Wolfe Tone: A Biographical Study*, London, 1939

McDowell, R.B. *Irish Public Opinion, 1750–1800*, London, 1944
    Ireland in the Age of Imperialism and Revolution, 1760–1801, Oxford, 1979
McKerlie, E. Marianne H. *Two Sons of Galloway*, Dumfries, 1928
McKinney, C.W. *Killinchy*, privately published, Killinchy [1968]
McNeill, Mary. *The Life and Times of Mary Ann McCracken, 1760–1866. A Belfast Panorama*, Dublin, 1960; reprinted Belfast, 1988
McNeven, W.J. *Pieces of Irish History*, New York, 1807
McSkimmin, Samuel. *Annals of Ulster, or Ireland Fifty Years Ago*, Belfast, 1850
Madden, R.R. *The United Irishmen*, 4 vols, London, 1857–60
    Antrim and Down in 1798, Glasgow, n.d.
Maguire, W.A. *Belfast*, Keele, 1993
Malcomson, A.P.W. (ed.). *The Extraordinary Career of the 2nd Earl of Massereene 1743–1805*, Belfast, 1972
Maxwell, W.H. *History of the Irish Rebellion in 1798*, London, 1887
Merrick, A.C.W. and R.S.J. Clarke. *Old Belfast Families and the New Burying Ground from Gravestone Inscriptions with Wills and Biographical Notes*, Belfast, 1991
Miller, D.W. *Peep o' Day Boys and Defenders: Selected Documents on the County Armagh Disturbances, 1784–96*, Belfast, 1990
Millins, S. Shannon. *History of the Second Congregation of Protestant Dissenters in Belfast*, Belfast, 1900
    Sidelights on Belfast History, Belfast and London, 1932
    Additional Sidelights on Belfast History, Belfast and London, 1938
Moore, T. *A History of the First Presbyterian Church, Belfast*, Belfast, 1983
Mullin, Julia E. *The Causeway Coast*, Belfast, 1974
    The Presbytery of Coleraine, Belfast, 1979
Mullin, T.H. *Coleraine in Georgian Times*, Belfast, 1977
Musgrave, Sir Richard. *Memoirs of the Different Rebellions in Ireland*, Dublin, 1801
Nicolson, Harold. *The Desire To Please: A Study of Hamilton Rowan and the United Irishmen*, London, 1943
Nugent, Lady. *Journal*, ed. F. Cundall, London, 1939
O'Byrne, Cathal. *As I Roved Out*, Belfast, 1946; reprinted Belfast, 1982
Old Ballymena: A History of Ballymena During the 1798 Rebellion, Ballymena, n.d.
Orr, James. *Poems on Various Subjects*, new edition, Belfast, 1935
Owen, D.J. *History of Belfast*, Belfast, 1921
Pakenham, Thomas. *The Year Of Liberty*, London, 1969
Palmer, R.R. *The Age of Democratic Revolution*, 2 vols, London, 1959 and 1964
Porter, Reverend Classon, *Congregational Memoirs of the Old Congregation of Larne and Kilwaughter*, eds R.H. McIlrath and J.W. Nelson, Belfast, 1976

Purdon, H.G. *Memoirs of Service in the 64th Regiment, Second Staffordshire*, London [1882]

Reid, James Seaton. *History of the Presbyterian Church in Ireland*, 3 vols (vol. 3 by W.D. Killen), Belfast, 1867

Roden, Lady. *The Diary of Anne, Countess Dowager of Roden*, Dublin, 1870

Rowan, A.H. *Autobiography*, Dublin, 1840

Saintfield Heritage, Newcastle, 1982

Scobie, Major I.H.M. *An Old Highland Fencible Corps*, Edinburgh, 1914

Senior, Hereward. *Orangeism in Ireland and Britain, 1795–1836*, London, 1966

Sergeaunt, B.E. *The Royal Manx Fencibles, 1779–1811*, Aldershot, 1947

Shields, Hugh. *Narrative Singing in Ireland*, Dublin, 1993

Sibbett, R.M. *On the Shining Bann: Records of an Ulster Manor*, Belfast, 1928

Smith, Jim. *The Men of No Property: Irish Radicals and Popular Politics in the Late Eighteenth Century*, London, 1992

Smith, W.S. *Historical Gleanings in Antrim and Neighbourhood*, Belfast, 1888

Smyth, Alistair. *The Story of Antrim*, Antrim, 1984

William Stavely, Mid-Antrim Historical Group, no. 18, Ballymena, 1993

Stevenson, John. *Two Centuries of Life in Down, 1600–1800*, Belfast, 1920

Stewart, A.T.Q. *The Narrow Ground: Aspects of Ulster, 1609–1969*, London, 1977

    A Deeper Silence: The Hidden Origins of the United Irishmen, London, 1993

Stewart, David. *The Seceders in Ireland with Annals of their Congregations*, Belfast, 1950

Strain, R.W.M. *Belfast and its Charitable Society*, London, 1961

Teeling, Charles Hamilton. *Personal Narrative of the Irish Rebellion of 1798*, London, 1828

Tone, Theobald Wolfe, *The Autobiography of Theobald Wolfe Tone, 1763–1798*, ed. R. Barry O'Brien, 2 vols, London, 1893

Walker, Brian M. *Sentry Hill: An Ulster Farm and Family*, Belfast, 1981

Weir, W.D. and H. Campbell. *Presbyterianism in Killead, 1630–1980*, Belfast [1993]

Wilson, Ian. *Shipwrecks of the Ulster Coast*, Coleraine, 1979

Witherow, Thomas. *Historical and Literary Memorials of Presbyterianism in Ireland*, 2 vols, London and Belfast, 1879

Woodburn, J.B. *The Ulster Scot: His History and Religion*, London, n.d.

Young, Robert M. *Historical Notices of Old Belfast and its Vicinity*, Belfast, 1896

    Ulster in '98, Belfast, n.d.

Zimmermann, Georges-Denis. *Songs of Irish Rebellion: Political Street Ballads and Rebel Songs, 1780–1900*, Dublin, 1967

INDEX

Garvaghy, Co. Down, 229
Gault, James, 74
George IV, King, 263
Giant's Causeway, Co. Antrim, 71, 144
Gibbison (Bangor), 233
Gifford, John, 37
Gill, Jack, 227
Gillan, Daniel, 40
Glastry, Co. Down, 172
Glenarm, Co. Antrim, 96–101, 133, 137–8, 165
Glenarm Castle, 96, 97, 98
Glenarm Yeomanry, 98, 137
Glencloy, Co. Antrim, 97
Glengormley, Co. Antrim, 72
Glens of Antrim, 96–7, 127, 245
Glenwherry, Co. Antrim, 160–1
Glynn, Co. Antrim, 87, 91, 95–6
Goldie, General Tom, 82, 84, 153, 176, 213, 233, 251
Gordon, John, 73
Gordon, Peggy, 110–11, 264
Gowdy, Rev. Robert, 191
Gracehill, Co. Antrim, 133–4, 155, 162, 163
Graham, Sir James and Lady, 196
Grange, Co. Antrim, 103
Gransha, Co. Down, 229
Grattan, Henry, 10, 36
Gray, Elizabeth, 227–9
Gray, George, 227
Gray, Hans, 229
Greencastle, Co. Antrim, 85, 239
Greene, Colonel, 159, 160
Greg, Cunningham, 40
Greyabbey, Co. Down, 13, 179, 190, 191, 209; Porter execution, 252, 254
Grimes, Hugh, 247
Groggan Island, Randalstown, 154, 164
Groomsport, Co. Down, 233
Gunning, Catherine and Flora, 141
Gunning, John, 141, 149, 249

Haliday, Dr Alexander, 48
Hall, Thomas, 86
Hall (yeoman), 104
Halliday (rebel), 103, 113
Hamilton, Dr A., 141
Hamilton, Gawen, 23
Hamilton, James, 140
Harmony Hill, 146–7
Harper, Joseph, 182
Harvey, William, 191–2
Haslett, Henry, 12, 24, 39
Haslett, John, 12
Hastings, Francis Rawdon, Earl of Moira, 209
Hay (rebel), 75, 264
Henderson (rebel), 75, 154–5
Heron, Lady Elizabeth, 84
Heron, Patrick, 84–5
Hertford, Marquess of, 16
Heyland, Captain Langford, 104
Hill, Rev. Adam, 49

Hill, Sir George, 28–9
Hill, Mr, 88
Hill family, 180–1
Hillis, Lieutenant, 222
Hillsborough, Co. Down, 23, 208, 220
Hillsborough Yeoman Cavalry, 227
Hobart, Emily, 17
Hoche, General Lazare, 8, 30
Holmes, Eleanor, 241, 243
Holmes, Rev. William, 161
Holmes, William, 250
Holywood, Co. Down, 179, 219
Hood (Mason), 206
Hope, James, 206, 219, 242, 260–1; activities of, 60–8; Antrim attack, 108, 110, 113, 115; at Slemish, 160; in hiding, 238
Hopkins, Captain, 190
Hudson, Mr, 92
Hudson, Rev. Edward, 132–3, 153–5
Huey, Mrs, 48
Hughes, John, 64, 67–8, 171, 177–8, 200, 202
Hull, Edward, 196–7
Humbert, General Jean, 257–8
Hunter, James, 147, 165
Hunter, John, 99
Hunter, Robert, 57–8, 176, 202
Hutcheson, Francis, 11
Hutcheson, Rev., 233
Hutchinson, George, 158
Hutchinson, Margaret, 193
Hutchinson, Prudence, 193

informers, 38–9, 58, 63–4, 89, 104, 113–14, 171, 200–1
Innishargie, Co. Down, 191–2, 204
Insurrection Act (1796), 21, 46
Irish Brotherhood, 10–12
Islandmagee, Co. Antrim, 92, 93–6, 138, 166
Isle of Man, 192

Jackson, Lieutenant-Colonel, 111, 116
James I, King, 96
Jamison (rebel), 134
Jefferson, President, 262
Johnson, Rev. Philip, 23, 29
Johnston (Bangor), 233
Johnstone (Bangor), 233
Jones, Lieutenant, 103
Jones, Valentine, 99
Joy, Henry, 57

Keady, Co. Armagh, 261
Kean, William, 250
Kearney, Co. Down, 170
Keen, Alexander, 119–20
Keen, James, 118–20
Kelburn, Rev. Sinclair, 13, 56, 244, 248
Kells, Co. Antrim, 106, 107, 148, 150, 151, 159
Kelly, William, 109–10
Kelso (rebel), 68
Kelvin, Lord, 263
Kempenfelt, Rear Admiral Richard, 82